Case Studies in American Industry

LEONARD W. WEISS

SECOND EDITION

John Wiley & Sons, Inc.
New York · *London* · *Sydney* · *Toronto*

Library of Congress Catalogue Card Number: 75-149775

ISBN 0-471-92702-3 (cloth)
ISBN 0-471-92703-1 (paper)

Printed in the United States of America

10 9 8 7 6 5 4 3 2

Introduction to Economics Series

Teachers of introductory economics seem to agree on the impracticality of presenting a comprehensive survey of economics to freshmen or sophomores. Many of them believe there is a need for some alternative which provides a solid core of principles while permitting an instructor to introduce a select set of problems and applied ideas. This series attempts to fill that need and also to give the interested layman a set of self-contained books that he can absorb with interest and profit, without assistance.

By offering greater flexibility in the choice of topics for study, these books represent a more realistic and reasonable approach to teaching economics than most of the large, catchall textbooks. With separate volumes and different authors for each topic, the instructor is not as tied to a single track as in the omnibus introductory economics text.

Underlying the series is the pedagogical premise that students should be introduced to economics by learning how economists think about economic problems. Thus the concepts and relationships of elementary economics are presented to the student in conjunction with a few economic problems. An approach of this kind offers a good beginning to the student who intends to move on to advanced work and furnishes a clearer understanding for those whose study of economics is limited to an introductory exposure. Teachers and students alike should find the books helpful and stimulating.

Kenyon A. Knopf, Editor

Preface

This revision preserves the purpose, level, and organization of the original book and brings it up to date. Revising the text turned out to be a much bigger job than I had imagined. The relevant changes in economic thought could be accounted for quite easily, but four years' experience in these seemingly rather stable industries involved remarkably widespread changes. Virtually all of the statistical series and policy narratives required some revision, and many new implications were noted in each chapter as a result. The most substantial changes occurred in Chapter 3, where the rapidly expanding and still little-noticed elements of competition in the regulated industries, including electric power, are discussed; and in Chapter 4, where new sections on conglomerate mergers and import quotas are inserted. To make room for the new sections, I greatly abbreviated the discussion of the basing-point system. After completing this revision, I am now more convinced than ever that some systematic study of industrial experience plays an important role in the teaching of economics.

LEONARD W. WEISS

December 1970
Madison, Wisconsin

Preface to the First Edition

This book is a selection of revised and updated cases from my *Economics and American Industry* (Wiley, 1961). They are meant to supplement the micro portions of a principles course. I have long felt that the microtheory in the typical elementary textbook does not get across to the student as well as other parts of economics. Many students reject the theory of the firm and market as too remote from the real business world, while others swallow it uncritically. One reason is that most students have very limited knowledge of individual product and factor markets. The cases in this book are meant to remedy the situation (1) by illustrating analytical concepts as they apply to realistic markets, (2) by introducing qualifications to theory where the empirical evidence seems to warrant it, and (3) by presenting and analyzing major elements of public policy on product and labor markets. *Economics and American Industry* had similar goals but, although its acceptance was gratifying, it turned out to be a more extensive set of materials than many teachers wanted to cover in an elementary course. I hope that this case book will permit the use of the market-study approach more widely in principles courses.

The book was prepared on the assumption that the student is simultaneously studying the microtheory portion of an elementary text. The development of concepts such as marginal cost and elasticity has been left to that text, although empirical examples of these concepts are developed, and they are used repeatedly to describe markets and to analyze policies.

The most important consideration in selecting the cases for this book has been that there should be an illustration of each of the market types ordinarily covered in the elementary course.

I have discussed a purely competitive industry, a monopoly, an oligopoly, a series of cases often characterized as monopolistically. competitive, and a number of instances of cartels with free or restricted entry as well as an important labor market.

The book is distinctly policy-oriented. A primary consideration in selecting cases was the relative importance of public policy in the various industries. Taking the book as a whole, agricultural policy, regulation, antitrust, cartels, and trade union policy are all covered.

Obviously no set of five cases can properly represent the diverse product and factor markets in the economy, but I feel that a fairly intensive study of a few cases is more valuable than a brief introduction to a dozen. The omissions are partially covered by the first chapter, which contains a brief overview of the structure of the economy and of public policy toward business, and by the last chapter where the main conclusions from the industrial organization literature on market performance are summarized.

LEONARD W. WEISS

December 1966

Contents

Case Studies in American Industry

1

Introduction—Market Structure and Performance

What makes the price of beef fall? Why do steel prices go up? What determines the number of auto workers or the rate of return on capital invested in a shoe factory? What is the effect of a rise in steel wages or of a merger between two big railroads? Economic analysis provides a useful apparatus for dealing with such questions, but it does not, by itself, provide the answers. It can offer some predictions about the price and output of beef— given conditions on the market for beef—but it is up to any user to find what those conditions are, an enterprise that may entail a good deal of digging through Department of Agriculture statistics, trade literature, and federal legislation. Moreover, the predictions it makes, like those of any other theory about the real world, are hypotheses to be tested rather than unquestioned truths. To apply economic theory and to test its predictions, economists must examine real-life markets.

This book contains several studies illustrating a number of important types of markets. In each case, we will try to cover the underlying conditions, what economic analysis would predict, and what really happens. In the process, we will have to spend some time on the major types of public policy affecting individual markets.

I. MARKETS AND INDUSTRIES

A. *The Meaning of Markets*

A *market* in economics consists of all the buyers and sellers of a particular good or service who deal with one another or could easily deal with one another. Some markets are easily defined—we can realistically speak of a United States wheat market where a half million growers in almost every state sell, and where several thousand millers, feed producers, brewers, and exporters buy. Prices at various points in this market never differ for long by more than the transportation charges. If, by chance, the price in Chicago should exceed the Kansas City price plus freight, the grain dealers can be counted on to buy enough grain in Kansas City and sell enough grain in Chicago to bring the two prices into line within a matter of minutes. Moreover, buyers neither know nor care whose wheat they are buying. They insist only that it be of the required grade and sell at the prevailing price. As a result, all United States growers of number two red winter wheat compete for the same business.

Most markets are far less easy to define than this. Do Hershey Bars and Milky Ways sell on the same market? If you think so, what else should be included? Gum drops? Packaged chocolates? Chewing gum? Ice cream? Or, for that matter, why not cigarettes or motion pictures? Is there any logical place where you can say that the Hershey Company's market ends?

If we define the market to include everything with which Hershey Bars compete in any way, then it could contain practically everything for sale in the United States. Hershey Bars are even distant substitutes for gasoline—the two compete for the consumer's dollar. It we insist that no two commodities be included in a market unless they are perfect substitutes, then the Hershey Company would be a "monopolist." Indeed, by this standard, most markets would have only one seller. The only exceptions would be standardized products like wheat or steel. Most people would probably agree that markets should be defined by some in-between standard. Perhaps we could agree that commodities that are substitutes as close as the various 5¢ and 10¢ candy bar should be counted as selling on the same market, but that products as distinct as Hershey Bars and packaged chocolates should not—but this, or any other boundary we are likely to select, would clearly be somewhat arbitrary.

B. *Industries and Markets*

The term *industry* may cause some confusion. In theoretical discussions, it usually means all the firms selling on the same market, but in empirical studies it often refers to all the firms using a technically similar process, whether or not they compete. We are apt to hear about the rental housing industry or the American dairy industry, even though penthouses and tenements, or California and Wisconsin milk producers have few customers in common. Often there is no problem, of course. Firms in the aluminum, cotton textile, wheat, and cigarette industries really do compete among themselves.

The Federal Government has developed a Standard Industrial Classification (SIC) system that covers all the goods and services sold in the United States economy. A good place to get an idea of this system is in any recent Census of Manufactures. Only a brief look at Volume I will reveal that, in spite of careful study by many experts, the SIC industries differ greatly in their correspondence to markets. Some industries, such as cigarettes, do produce a group of close substitutes. Many others have obviously non-competing subproducts such as the pharmaceutical preparations industry which includes plants making antibiotics, vitamins, cough drops, and horse medicine. Sometimes, the realistic market contains more than one SIC industry—for instance, cane and beet sugar. And every once in a while, you will come upon a mysterious industry with a name such as "Food Products, Not Elsewhere Classified." This does not mean that the formulators of the SIC system were unnecessarily arbitrary. We just have a complex economy that does not fit easily into the neat patterns used in economic theory.

II. THE STRUCTURE OF THE AMERICAN ECONOMY

A. *The Physical Structure*

Table 1-1 gives an overview of the United States economy in 1968. The *product markets*, where wheat, steel, shirts, shoes, and the services of dentists, druggists, and the telephone company are sold, are represented on the left. The groupings on the right are composed of *factor markets*, where the services of land, labor, and capital of various sorts are exchanged. All of the groupings in Table 1-1 are much too broad to constitute markets themselves, of course. In the SIC system, there are often called *sectors* and are further subdivided into hundreds and even thousands of markets.

The two sets of markets really represent two sides of the same transactions. When a firm produces a load of coal, it employs a certain amount of land, labor, and capital in the process, and the earnings of the factors correspond to the value of the net output. It is, therefore, appropriate to state the relative importance of each product market and each factor market in terms of the share of the Gross National Product (GNP) accruing in each market.

About 5% of the output of the country arises in the raw material producing sectors, such as agriculture and mining. About a third comes from the processing and fabricating industries included in construction and manufacturing. Transportation and the utilities are somewhat related to these. That leaves roughly one half of economic activity that is devoted to various services —distribution, finance, the professions, and government.

Labor accounts for by far the most important set of factor markets. The right side of Table 1-1 divides the 1968 GNP into the payments for the various factors of production (the national income) plus depreciation and indirect taxes. In 1968 some 72% of the national income (59% of the GNP) took the form of wages, salaries, and supplements. Much of the income of self-employed farmers, physicians, and shopkeepers should be assigned to labor as well. If we say that two thirds of their earnings are rewards for their effort, then about 78% of the 1968 national income (64% of the GNP) went to labor. This left 22% of the national income for owners of various sorts of property. Allowing for depreciation, which is part of the cost of employing capital, property accounts for about 27% of the GNP and labor for 64%.[1]

---

[1] The remaining 9% is indirect taxes (sales and excise taxes) which are included in the value of output but which no one counts as income.

Table 1-1. Gross National Product Originating in Specified Groups of Product and Factor Markets, 1968

Product Markets	GNP (Billions)	Percent of GNP	Factor Markets	GNP (Billions)	Percent of: National Income	Percent of: GNP
Agriculture, forestry, and fishing	$ 27	3.1	Wages, salaries, and supplements	$513	71.8	59.2
Mining	14	1.6	Income of the self-employed	64	8.9	7.4
Construction	39	4.6	Rental incomes of persons	21	3.0	2.4
Manufacturing	246	28.6	Net interest income of persons	29	4.0	3.4
Transport, communications, and public utilities	73	8.5	Corporate profits	88	12.3	10.2
Wholesale and retail trade	142	16.4	National income	$715	100.0	82.6
Finance, insurance, and real estate	117	13.5	Depreciation	73		8.4
Services	95	11.0	Indirect taxes (sales and excise tax)			
Government	108	12.4	Total GNP	78		9.0
Rest of the world	5	0.5		$866		100.0
Total GNP	$866	100.0				

Source. Survey of Current Business, July, 1969.

B. *Competitive Structure*

Those product and factor markets differ among themselves in a variety of respects, but the characteristic that has received the greatest emphasis in economic analysis is the extent of competition. There are many aspects of competitiveness, but certainly one of the most important and easiest to observe is the degree of *concentration*—that is, the number and relative size of sellers. The most obvious difference between the almost pure competition of the beef producers and the almost pure monopoly of the power company is that there are millions of sellers of cattle and only one electric utility in town.

These two examples are extreme cases, however. Realistically, competition and monopoly shade into each other. Table 1-2 shows *concentration ratios* for some leading manufacturing industries. That is, they show the percentages of total market sales accounted for by the four largest sellers. Where a SIC industry seems to contain more than one market, concentration ratios for the most important submarkets are substituted for the industry-wide concentration ratios.

There are not many monopolies such as that of the power company, but Table 1-2 contains a number of cases where a big three, or a big four, or a big five account for half the industry. Such industries as automobiles, aluminum, cigarettes, and steel are often described as *oligopolies*—they have *few* sellers instead of *just one*. The major sellers on such markets are bound to take each other's reactions into account. Ford can hardly cut prices and hope that General Motors won't notice. Such markets are expected to have some, though not all, of the features of pure monopolies.

At the other end of the scale are the apparel, sawmill, textile, and furniture industries where the largest sellers are so small that each can act independently of the other. These are often described as *atomistic* industries because their performance is the result of the independent decisions of many units, each of which is individually so small that it *can* reasonably assume that whatever it does will not cause any noticeable reaction among its rivals. It may be perfectly clear that a general reduction in price will make the industry poorer, but any one firm will

Table 1.2. Concentration Ratios in Selected Manufacturing Product Markets, 1963

Automobiles (passenger cars, knocked down and assembled)	99
Primary aluminum	93
Cigarettes	80
Tires and tubes	72
Soap and detergents	68
Complete military aircraft	68
Miscellaneous acyclic (organic) chemicals	51
Steel	
Hot rolled bars, shapes, plates, and structural shapes	63
Hot rolled sheets and strip	55
Steel pipe	40
Steel wire	37
Drugs (1958)	
Antibiotics	59
Tranquilizers	55
Veterinary	45
Vitamins	27
Petroleum refining	
Pacific	65
East North Central (Great Lakes)	46
West South Central (mainly Texas and Louisiana)	42
Wheat flour	40
Paper	
Course (for bags, etc.)	38
Container board	32
Book paper	29
Meat packing	30
Cotton broad woven fabrics	30
Footwear	25
Paints and varnishes	24
Canned fruits and vegetables	24
Men's and boys' suits and coats	13
Wood household furniture	10
Saws mills	
Pacific	16
South Atlantic	5
Dresses	8

Source. Senate Judiciary, Subcommittee on Antitrust and Monopoly, *Concentration Ratios in Manufacturing Industry, 1963*, Part I, Table 4 and 4*a*, and ————, *1958*, Part I, Table 4 and Part II, Tables 25 and 26. Table 2 shipments figures were used where no figure was given in Table 4.

still shade price if it expects to gain by so doing. Individual sellers in such markets would be foolish to keep their prices up against their own best interests because they cannot possibly have much effect on industry prices generally.

No simple straightforward boundary exists between oligopoly and atomistic markets, but most of the cases where four firms make half or more of the sales—where concentration ratios are 50 or higher—count as oligopolistic in almost anybody's book, and when the concentration ratio is no more than 25, the firms that make up a market usually compete quite freely. Some of the markets that fall between these limits are similar to the atomistic group, some are quite oligopolistic, and some display features of both. Altogether, something on the order of half of all manufacturing might be classfied as oligopolistic.

Some of the other sectors in Table 1-1 are typified by large numbers of small firms. This is true of agriculture, forestry, fishing, and large parts of construction, retail and wholesale trade, and most of the service industries. Mining and finance are mixed cases. Bituminous coal, crude petroleum, and real estate are fields with large numbers of sellers but metal mining and banking generally sell on concentrated markets. Transportation, communication, and public utilities are also concentrated as a rule, but they are mostly subject to government regulations.

In many of the atomistic fields there are some government or trade union limitations on competition. Crop restrictions and price supports in agriculture are famous. Most of the oil-producing states enforce output quotas that determine the output and, therefore, the price of petroleum. Resale price maintenance laws ("Fair Trade" codes) prevent price competition among retailers in certain lines. Government regulation suppresses competition almost completely in liquor and milk distribution in some parts of the country. Stock brokers, real estate agents, and insurance companies have been permitted to collude in determining their fees. In such fields as construction and medicine, trade unions and professional associations have been able to control entry.

Altogether, America has a mixed economy. Something like a quarter of economic activity is either carried on by federal, state, and local governments or is directly regulated by them. This includes the whole governmental sector—the armed services and the schools, as well as the post office and power projects. It also includes the regulated fields—transportation, communication, the public utilities—and those with government price and entry controls—petroleum production and about half of agriculture. Another quarter, more or less, is accounted for by oligopolies or industries where legal collusion, union activities, or professional associations prevent competitive results. This quarter includes approximately half of manufacturing and mining, plus much banking, finance, construction, and medicine. The remaining half of the GNP comes from the unregulated and nearly atomistic parts of agriculture and manufacturing plus most distribution, services, and real estate.

These estimates are clearly very rough. Another economist might easily judge the unregulated atomistic share of the national income 5 or 10% higher or lower. However, almost anyone who is honest with himself will wind up with a substantial oligopolistic sector *and* a substantial competitive sector.

The labor markets are broadly similar in competitive structure to the product markets. Almost a fifth of the workers in the United States are employed by the federal, state, and local governments, including the armed forces. Another 2 or 3% might be listed as in occupations where licensing laws and sometimes government wage and price regulations dominate the labor market. This might include the doctors, pharmacists, and real estate agents. About a fifth of all workers are union members, although in some cases the union is too weak to have much effect. At the same time, in a substantial number of communities, a few employers are very large in local markets for important types of labor. In many cases, though far from all, the large employer fields and the strongly unionized fields coincide. This leaves a little over half of all workers who are employed on nearly atomistic labor markets (a fifth of these—or a tenth of all workers—are self-employed).

III. MARKET PERFORMANCE

The question that naturally arises after an examination of the competitive structure of markets is: "What difference does it

make?" Most observers are convinced that the differences between a very concentrated market where new entry is difficult
(for example, automobiles) and unconcentrated markets with
easy entry (for example, textiles) are of real importance, but
it is not always easy to measure the differences satisfactorily.
We shall attempt the job for each of the several industries examined.

A. *Efficiency and Income Distribution*

The element of market performance that has traditionally received the greatest emphasis has been efficiency. Competition is
supposed to force producers to use minimum cost methods of
production. Moreover, if labor and capital are free to move
away from unprofitable employments and into those that offer
high earnings, they will tend to produce those goods that the
public values most highly. By contrast, barriers to movement
into good businesses or out of bad jobs leave many resources
producing less than they might in alternative employments. High
prices that restrict the number of sales or high wages that limit
the numbers employed in a field can prevent entry just as direct
restrictions on new firms or new workers do.

Ideally, we should examine the relative efficiency of resources
in the various industries we investigate, but this is a prohibitively
difficult task. Our main evidence on the subject will have to be
indirect. In a competitive economy where labor and capital may
move freely between employments, there should be no permanent differences in earnings of similar resources. Capital should
leave low profit lines and enter high profit fields until the difference in profit prospects disappears. Similarly, any substantial differences in earnings for labor of particular skills should lead
workers, and especially young people just entering the labor
force, away from the overcrowded fields and into the lines where
labor is scarce until wages are about equalized once more.
Where barriers to movement are serious, however, profit and
wage differences may persist for generations. When we find
persistently high or persistently low profits or wages, we can
infer that markets are operating inefficiently.

Persistent differences in wages and profits may be looked upon
as faults in and of themselves by many observers. A lot of people

feel that there is something unfair when one man's investment dollars or one man's skills are worth more than another's just because he occupies a strategic position in the marketplace.

B. *Price Rigidity and Inflation*

Whether or not monopolists are able to reap exceptional returns for their capital and labor, they do have a degree of control over prices and wages that sellers in competitive markets do not possess. Farmers with beef cattle to sell or manufacturers of cotton grey goods (unbleached cotton cloth) have to accept a price that is set by an impersonal market in which they individually play insignificant parts. But sellers in highly concentrated industries, such as automobiles and steel, have a good deal of leeway within which they can specify the terms on which they will sell.

This ability has suggested various problems for monopolistic and oligopolistic markets depending on the current national economic worry. In the Great Depression, it was claimed that monopolistic industries kept their prices up when demand dropped so that output fell farther and unemployment was greater than it had to be. In the 1950's and again in 1970, it was claimed that monopolistic industries were raising prices even in the face of excess capacity. Neither charge has ever been settled to everyone's satisfaction.

We will examine the pattern of prices over time in the industries studied. It is not likely that we will be able to say that prices are too high or too low in many cases, but we should be able to say something about how stable they have been in response to market changes.

C. *Progressiveness*

A third feature of market performance that has attracted increasing attention in recent years has been the rate at which new techniques and products are developed and adopted. Traditionally, competition has been thought of as a spur to progress. Even if most of us prefer to let well enough alone, a few ambitious beavers in a competitive market can assure that we will all adopt better techniques and products—or get out of business. Students with only the mildest inclination to scholarship have been known to study very hard in response to a similar phenomenon in an academic setting. The big rewards in a competitive market go to those who hit upon something new and worthwhile, and those who cling to the old ways in the face of change are usually in for punishment.

Some economists have argued, on the other hand, that a certain amount of monopoly will encourage economic progressiveness. Innovation[2] is risky. The firm cannot tell in advance whether a new location or method of merchandising will work or when a new machine will be obsolete. In view of the risks involved, the profit prospects must ordinarily be good to make such new investments worthwhile. It is a basic feature of competition, however, that profits are only temporary. Anyone in a competitive industry who finds a way to make high profits by building supermarkets or moving his business to California will soon find his exceptional returns disappearing because of a host of imitators. He is in a situation of heads he loses and tails he does not win very much. Firms in concentrated industries may be able to retain more of their winnings.

Monopolists and oligopolists may have other advantages as well. They can finance new projects easily because their assured positions make them good credit risks and provide profits that can be used in self-financing. In addition, large firms (which, in our enormous economy, is not necessarily the same thing as monopolistic firms) can often minimize their risks by undertaking a great number of projects at once instead of putting all their eggs in one or two innovational baskets.

Monopolists and oligopolists are not inevitably good innovators, however. They have sometimes been known to drag their feet in order to protect their plants from obsolescence. They may choose to relax and leave well enough alone.

It is certainly true that if profits disappear instantaneously in competition, there would be no incentive to try anything that involved risk, but in practice there is a certain amount of friction in the economic system. Even competitive innovators can expect

---

[2] The word *innovation* means the application of new ideas. It is not the same thing as invention. The first firm to install a machine is innovating even if the machine was invented ten years ago. So is one that tries a new line of products or a new location regardless of where the idea originated.

to retain their advantage for some time. Economists differ about how substantial the barriers to imitators must be to induce adequate rates of progress.

IV. PUBLIC POLICY AND COMPETITION

The United States has had three distinct approaches to monopoly and competition. For the unregulated three quarters of our economy, the government has attempted to enforce competition, but in the transportation, communication, and utility fields the government has permitted and even enforced monopoly and then attempted to control it. At the same time, government has intervened in some markets to limit rather than to promote competition.

A. *Antitrust*

The basic antimonopoly legislation in the United States is the Sherman Antitrust Act passed in 1890. It provides for criminal and civil remedies against contracts or combinations "in restraint of trade" and against persons who "monopolize or attempt to monopolize" any part of interstate commerce.

The law was written in very broad terms so its meaning was really left for the courts to decide. They soon established that formal agreements to fix prices, limit output, or allocate markets among competing firms were definitely illegal. However, they were much more equivocal in their treatment of large firms. The government was successful in dissolving some of the best known combinations in the years before World War I, notably the American Tobacco Company and Standard Oil. It was the behavior of these firms that the courts condemned, not their mere size in relation to the market. In later cases it appeared that very large firms, even when formed by merger after the new act was passed, were within the law if their actions seemed "reasonable."

In 1914 the Sherman Act was supplemented by the Clayton Antitrust Act and the Federal Trade Commission Act. The first spelled out and prohibited certain specific actions likely to enhance monopoly. These included interlocking directorates (where individuals served on the boards of directors of competing firms), intercorporate stock acquisitions, tying sales (where customers were required to buy a whole line of products if they wanted one of them), and price discrimination. The second act established the Federal Trade Commission (FTC), which was to investigate competitive practices and issue orders against those deemed unfair. Neither act produced any great changes in the 1920's and 1930's. The prohibitions of the Clayton Act turned out to contain loopholes and applied only "where the effect may be substantially to lessen competition or tend to create monopoly," so it left many decisions to the judges. In the case of the FTC, the courts limited the commission's investigating powers and retained the right to review its decisions before enforcing its orders. At the same time Congress weakened the antitrust laws in various ways. It provided exemptions for combinations among firms in the export markets (Webb Pomerene Act, 1920) and for agreements between manufacturers and retailers fixing retail prices where these were legal under state law (Miller-Tydings Act, 1937). In the Robinson-Patman Act (1936), it prohibited price discrimination in such a way that it often prevented price competition. At one point Congress virtually discarded the anticollusion rule when it established the National Recovery Administration (NRA), which had power to approve and enforce industry "codes" controlling competition in any industry whose members chose to formulate them. The NRA lasted only two years (1933-1935) before it was declared unconstitutional, but many of the practices established under the NRA codes continued thereafter. Antitrust reached a nadir in the mid-1930's.

In the 1940's the enforcement of the antitrust laws became much more vigorous, and the courts revised some of their earlier interpretations. In the Alcoa case, a corporation was convicted of "monopolizing" aluminum production mainly because it was the only domestic producer of the metal. The decision did not depend primarily on the firm's behavior. In addition, various closely parallel output or price policies in oil, tobacco, motion pictures, cement, and steel were prohibited although formal agreement was not definitely established. The significance of the FTC was greatly enhanced, and the prohibitions of the Clayton Act began to carry more weight. In 1950 Congress amended the Clayton Act to prohibit mergers of all sorts if they were likely to "substantially lessen competition." As interpreted, the new law comes close to prohibiting any merger among substantial and viable competing firms in even moderately concentrated markets.

There have been few dissolutions, however. We have been prepared to tighten up on trade practices and to limit the creation of new monopolies and oligopolies by merger, but we have seldom been prepared to dissolve existing firms, even when they were unquestionably in a position to control their markets.

B. *Regulated Industries*

In the public utility fields, the government regulates monopoly rather than attempting to prevent it. Regulatory commissions were established by state and federal governments to deal with the railroads in the 1880's, and state commissions to regulate utilities of all sorts became common in the early 1900's.

The regulatory approach to monopoly has a record which is about as spotty as that of the antitrust laws. The Supreme Court retained the power to review the decisions of the state and federal commissions. Commission decisions were often overruled, and the commissions' authority was closely limited in the 1920's. During the 1930's the powers of the commissions were increased by new legislation, and by the early 1940's the courts had largely withdrawn from the details of regulation. Today the regulators generally have powers adequate to their jobs and can usually expect their rate orders to be upheld by the courts if they followed fair procedures.

The extent of regulation was greatly increased in the 1930's. Federal agencies were given power to regulate highway freight, buses, inland waterways, ocean shipping, airlines, natural gas pipelines, and important aspects of banking, broadcasting, and security exchanges and brokerage. In addition, their powers in the traditionally regulated fields—electric power, telecommunications, railroads, and petroleum pipelines—were greatly enhanced. Once begun, regulation has proven difficult to end. All of these industries are still regulated today.

C. *Restrictions on Competition*

In many cases government has intervened to prevent competition or create monopoly rather than the reverse. The tariff and the patent laws have long been important sources of monopoly, though neither puts as serious limits on competition today as in the 1920's. During the Great Depression Congress and the states attempted to limit the effects of competition in many industries. We were saved by the Supreme Court in 1935 from the plan to cartelize all of American industry under the NRA, but government controls over price and/or output were continued under other legislation in oil, agriculture, and, for a while, coal. The federal and state laws restricting price competition in retailing date from the same period. Many state and local governments put controls on prices or entry or both in such local industries as taxicabs, real estate agencies, and dairy-product sales. The growth of trade unionism in the 1930's with government support introduced new monopolistic restraints on many labor markets.

Some of the new areas of regulation such as highway, ocean, and inland waterway freight are inherently competitive, but have become cartels as a result of regulation. In other areas such as railroads, airlines, banking, and broadcasting, regulation serves to limit or prevent competition while doing little or nothing to put upper limits on prices charged. Much of the new regulation over the last forty years has therefore had the primary effect of creating or reenforcing monopoly.

The traditional utilities where regulation seems almost inevitable—electric power, gas, communications, and pipelines—account for about 6% of the GNP today. Transport, oil, basic agriculture, banking, and brokerage, where government intervention prevents competition or creates monopoly, accounts for about 9% of it. Altogether, the government-sponsored or regulated monopoly sector is about 15% of the GNP, not a great deal smaller than the area of unregulated monopoly. Far more of the government's resources are devoted to suppressing competition and creating and maintaining monopoly in this sector than to preserving or creating competition in the unregulated three quarters of our economy under the antitrust laws.

The government's actions to limit or enforce competition are only a small part of its dealings with business today. Public policy and private enterprise come in contact at a thousand different points. The government collects taxes from business; procures supplies from business; provides such services as the roads, water-ways, post offices, research, and education for business; regulates the amounts of credit available to business; controls the level of business activity; regulates the wages, hours, and employment practices of business; regulates security issues and corporate organization; maintains minimum standards for business in such lines as food and drugs; and the list could go on.

These government policies are far too numerous to be discussed in a single book. This book attempts to examine fairly carefully the public policies that limit or extend monopoly in the product or labor markets studied. Other public policies toward business are mentioned only incidentally if at all.

V. THE REST OF THE BOOK

A. *The Markets to Be Studied*

The American economy is made up of thousands of markets, each with its own unique characteristics. We have space for only a few. The cases to be studied have been selected because they are individually important and because they illustrate, along broad lines, many important features of other markets.

Most of the major product sectors will be represented. Chapter 2 deals with agriculture, the leading raw material producing industry. Chapter 3 covers electric power, an important and fairly representative utility. Chapter 4 on steel studies one of the most important manufacturing industries. Retailing, the subject of Chapter 5, is the leading service industry. Altogether, the product markets covered in this book account for about one sixth of the GNP. Labor, the most important set of factor markets, is represented by Chapter 6 on the steelworkers. Not only do they sell their services to one of the industries that we discuss, but they are also a substantial center of controversy in their own right.

The competitive structure of the markets examined is just as diverse as their physcial structure. Agriculture and large portions of retail trade are commonly described as atomistic, although public policy introduces monopolistic elements in both fields. They differ in that agricultural products are largely standardized while the services of retailers are *differentiated*—that is, consumers draw distinctions among stores and often display considerable loyalty to particular retailers. At the other extreme is electric power, which is close to pure a monopoly in the supply of local service. Steel is a clear-cut case of oligopoly. And the steelworkers have sold their services on a labor market, the organization of which has changed several times over its history. Today, they have one of the strongest unions in the country, but at one time steel labor was the field of an exclusive union controlled by skilled workers, and at another time the steel labor market was dominated by a few employers with no union at all.

Some of the main lines of public policy toward competition are illustrated in these industries. The steel industry and the antitrust laws have developed together in this century. A study of one would be incomplete without the other. The character of the electric power industry is even more closely tied up with the policies of public utility regulation. Agriculture and retailing are two of the most important fields in which the government has intervened to limit competition. And the steelworkers have at one time or another experienced an amazingly wide variety of government policies toward unions.

B. *A Warning*

The reader should be warned, however, that while the markets covered in this book are important and varied, they cannot possibly represent the whole of the economy. Atomistic markets have many characteristics in common, but competition in textiles and apparel sometimes has results quite different from competition in agriculture and retailing. The box labeled "oligopoly" contains an even more diverse set of markets. What is true of steel often is not true of automobiles, cigarettes, aircraft, and flour mills. Some oligopolies act almost as if they were pure monopolies. Some are very close to pure competition in performance. And labor markets are as diverse as product markets. What holds for the steelworkers need not hold for the textile workers or plumbers and is usually much farther out for migrant agricultural labor or corporate executives.

A study of the limited set of cases that can be included in a book of this nature is still worthwhile for several reasons.

1. They can serve to illustrate what the predictions of economic theory mean. The full implications of the theory of the

marketplace are often well hidden when it is presented in its tightly reasoned, abstract form and only come home to the student when applied to concrete cases.

2. They can also serve to point up some of the predictions of economic analysis that need to be qualified. We will seldom find that these predictions are downright wrong, but we will often find that they are incomplete, typically because of structural features of real world markets that are assumed away in theory.

3. The case studies can be equally useful in finding some of the places where the purpose and practice of public policy diverge. The goals of public policy are not always as easy to accomplish as they may seem to Congress and the public in advance, and the particular actions taken by the government often have unexpected side effects. Economic analysis can add much to our understanding of the effects of public policy, but its interpretations are not always complete either.

4. Finally, we hope that by looking carefully at a few markets the reader can develop sufficient understanding to go on to examine other markets for himself. Certainly, the future of economics as a science lies along the road of more systematic empiricism.

VI. FURTHER READINGS

For a good discussion of the empirical application of the market concept, see P. O. Steiner, "Markets and Industries," *International Encyclopedia of the Social Sciences,* Macmillan and the Free Press, 1968, pp. 575-581. Bain, *Industrial Organization,* Second Edition (New York: John Wiley and Sons, 1968) pp. 112-154, covers the measurement and extent of concentration. Some other attempts to estimate the extent of monopoly in the country appear in G. W. Nutter, *The Extent of Enterprise Monopoly in the United States* (Chicago: University of Chicago Press, 1951) and C. Kaysen and D. F. Turner, *Antitrust Policy* (Harvard University Press: Cambridge, 1959), Chapter 2. C. Wilcox, *Public Policies Toward Business,* Third Edition (Homewood, Illinois: Irwin, 1966) is a good encyclopedic source on the various American policies toward competition.

2

Pure Competition and Agriculture

Most Americans were farmers when the country began. A third were still farmers just before World War I, a fifth just before World War II, and a tenth as late as 1958. Yet by 1970 less than one worker in twenty was a farmer. Agriculture is no longer our predominant industry, but it is still an important one.

I. THE STRUCTURE AND PROBLEMS OF AGRICULTURE

A. *Pure Competition*

In structure, agriculture comes closer to *pure competition* than any other major industry. There are a million producers of hogs and of wheat, and even 5000 of avocados, and in each case there are more ready to start production if the situation becomes sufficiently favorable. In such a setting, no one farmer can hope to do anything about the price at which he sells. The biggest feed lot in the country might market as many as 100,000 head of cattle in a peak year, possibly 2% of the nation's beef supply. If it held off the market completely, it would not force the price of beef up by even 3%. It is true that actions of all the farmers, taken together, can make the price of beef or wheat or avocados rise or fall, but for any individual the price at which he sells is like the weather. He may grumble about it, but he must adjust to it.

Farmers have been able to do quite a lot about their prices

by complaining to their congressmen. Later in the chapter there is an extensive discussion of farm policy but, to get a clearer picture of the issues, the effect of government action on agricultural markets is disregarded at this point.

Most farm products are sold to processors or distributors who draw no distinction between the products of two farmers as long as they come up to uniform standards. Number 2 red winter wheat is number 2 red winter wheat regardless of the grower. The leading crops are priced on great, impersonal, national exchanges like the Chicago Board of Trade. Quotations based on the latest transactions of these exchanges are announced throughout the country, and anyone with the means and the inclination can buy or sell almost any conceivable amount at the going price.

Individual farmers cannot take their corn or hogs all the way to Chicago, of course. There may be only a few practicable outlets available to them. The local grain or livestock dealers have a mild sort of monopoly but this is not a very serious imperfection. Farmers can usually go to the next town if they have to, and there is always the possibility of a new dealer or a cooperative. On any one day a local dealer might be able to pay a price far out of line with Chicago and get away with it, but if he follows such a policy for long he will lose most of his business.

B. *Farm Problems*

In the standard textbook analysis, pure competition seems to lead to the most efficient use of resources. In equilibrium, just the right things are produced in just the right amounts, and all resources are used where they are most productive. When they learn that agriculture is our best approximation to pure competition, students often express some doubts. Agriculture seems to be one of the eternal problems of our economy, and it seldom receives much acclamation for efficient organization. This chapter attempts to reconcile our seemingly rosy theory with the less rosy facts of farming.

The famous farm problem that has generated so much federal concern has had two main elements—instability and low incomes. Both are illustrated in Figure 2-1, which compares disposable

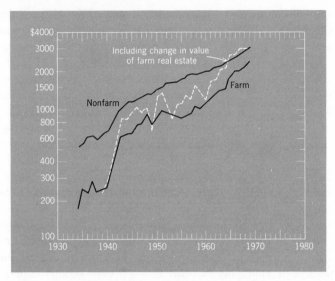

Figure 2-1. Disposable income per capita (ratio scale). *Source.* Agricultural Statistics, 1969, Tables 626, 640, and 680; *Agricultural Statistics,* 1967, Tables 635, 649, and 693; and *The Farm Income Situation,* Feb. 1970.

income per person (roughly "take home pay") for farmers and nonfarmers.

C. Ratio Scales

They are plotted against a *ratio scale*.[1] Such scales are convenient for comparing price, output, and productivity changes and will be so used throughout the book. They may not be familiar to all readers.

Ratio scales are so constructed that equal distances represent equal percentage changes. The distance from 100 to 200 in Figure 2-1 is the same as from 300 to 600 or 1500 to 3000 or any other doubling in income. As a result, a given slope represents the same percentage change in income any place on the chart.

---

[1] Technically Figure 2-1 is a semilogarithmic chart: "semi" because the income scale is in ratio form but the time scale is not; and "logarithmic" because distances on ratio scales are proportional to the logarithms of the values measured. Happily, semilogarithmic charts can be plotted and read by people quite innocent of logarithms.

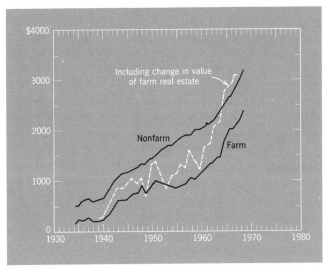

Figure 2-2. Disposable income per capita (arithmetic scale). *Source. Agricultural Statistics, 1969,* Tables 626, 640, and 680; *Agricultural Statistics, 1967,* Table 635, 649, and 693; and *The Farm Income Situation,* Feb. 1970.

It is helpful to compare Figure 2-1 with the same series plotted against an ordinary arithmetic scale in Figure 2-2 across from it. The two charts represent exactly the same numbers but you would hardly know it by looking at them. For instance, nonfarm incomes (the upper curve in both charts) seem to rise at an increasing rate in Figure 2-2, but when they are plotted against the ratio scale in Figure 2-1, they appear as an almost straight line since the end of the Great Depression. In other words, nonfarm incomes have grown at a roughly constant percentage rate for the last 30 years. They rise with an increasingly steep slope in Figure 2-2 because it takes larger absolute increases to maintain a constant percentage increase as incomes rise. Again, farm incomes have risen at a faster rate than nonfarm incomes over most of the period covered, but you wouldn't know it by looking at Figure 2-2. The difference does show up in Figure 2-1, where the slopes of the two series are comparable. It is hard to see in Figure 2-2 because a given increase in income involves a larger percentage increase for the lower in-

come series. A $100 raise is relatively bigger for a farmer earning
$1000 than for a nonfarmer earning $2000.

Ratio scales also facilitate comparisons among fluctuations.
The $130 increase in nonfarm incomes in 1940 was a tremendous
raise because it started from $671 per person. The same increase
in 1965 was no great shakes because we were already earning
$2340 apiece. The two look the same on the conventional chart
on the right, but their differing relative importance shows up
well in the ratio chart.

D. *Instability*

Though it has been growing, income per capita has been consistently lower on the farm than in the city, and it has been much
less steady than nonfarm income. A ten-percent decline in nonfarm income has not occurred since the worst of the Great
Depression, and in the years since World War II any decline at
all has been rare. By contrast, farm incomes fell substantially in
a dozen years since 1933—by more than 10% in two of them.

The instability of farm income is due mainly to unstable farm
prices. Figure 2-3 compares farm and industrial prices since
1930, using another ratio scale. Farm prices changed much more

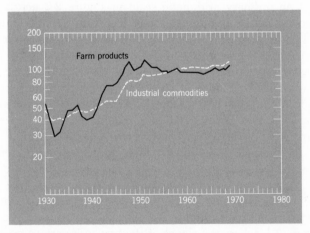

Figure 2-3. Wholesale price indexes (1957-9 = 100). *Source. Economic
Report of the President,* 1970, Table C-48.

drastically during the heroic fluctuations of the 1930's and 1940's. Both series have been more stable since the Korean War, but in spite of government controls, farm prices still fluctuated more than nonfarm prices.

E. Farm Income Levels

Per capita farm income was about half of average urban income over most of this century until the late 1960's.[2] It was less than a third of nonfarm income at the worst of the depression, and even in 1948, their best year until recently, farmers earned only two thirds as much as nonfarmers.

Farm products consumed on the farm do not account for much of the difference. They are included in farm income, though at farm rather than retail prices. Such consumption came to only $67 per person in 1969 and has been less than $100 per person since 1948.[3] Farmers, like nonfarmers, buy most of what they consume today.

The growing value of farm property is more important. Since the opening of the frontier, farmers have regularly benefited from the appreciation of their land. Of course city people own assets that increase in value also, but they are less important. Residential real estate and common stock are about three times nonfarm disposable income, but farm land is almost ten times farm disposable income. The broken lines in Figures 2-1 and 2-2 show the sum of farm disposable income per capita plus the annual increase in the value of farm real estate per capita. While adjustment for these capital gains brings farm earnings closer to nonfarm incomes, there was still a large gap in the 1940's and 1950's when present farm policies were solidifying.

The generations-old disparity between farm and city incomes narrowed in the late 1960's, and may well have disappeared. By 1969 farm income was 75% of nonfarm income, and farm earnings were close to nonfarm incomes once increasing land values were allowed for.

---

[2] D. Paarlberg, *American Farm Policy,* Wiley, New York, 1964, p. 60.
[3] *Agricultural Statistics,* 1969, Table 677; ———, 1967, Table 690; and *The Farm Income Situation,* Feb., 1970.

F. *Poverty on the Farm*

An important reason for this improvement has been the rapid disappearance of many very low income farms. Share croppers, who accounted for one farm in eight in 1950, had virtually disappeared by 1970. In 1959, 16% of all poor families with working-age heads were on farms. By 1967 this had fallen to 8%. Some 40% of all farm families (86% of Negro farm families) were classed as "poor" in 1959. By 1967 only 18% of farm families (53% of Negro farm families) were "poor."[4] Some of the gain was the general improvement in farm incomes, but much of it was simply the movement of poor farmers off of the land. The Negro farm population fell from 1.5 million to 1 million in the eight years between 1960 and 1968.[5] Often the poverty was simply relocated rather than eliminated.

There is still a good deal of poverty on the farm, however. The 18% of farm families that are "poor" compares with 12% of nonfarm families. Both are matters of great concern. We still have a half million full-time "commercial" farms that net less than $2500 per year. They are heavily concentrated in the South, the Appalachians, the Ozarks, and the cutover parts of the Great Lakes states.

From time to time one hears about the rich farmer with his Cadillac or his own plane or about the corporate farm with thousands of acres. Both exist, but neither is important. In 1968, only one farmer in 125 earned as much as $25,000, compared with one nonfarmer in 37.[6] Corporations accounted for only 5.2% of all farm land in 22 states studied in 1968. In the 12 Midwestern states that produce half of all farm output, corporations held only 1.7% of farm land, and more than half of

---

[4] *Statistical Abstract, 1969,* p. 329. The poverty standard used by the government involves higher income levels in the city than on the farm. In 1967 a nonfarm family of four was counted as "poor" if it had an income of $3335 or less, but a farm family was "poor" only if its income were as low as $2345.

[5] *Statistical Abstract,* 1969, p. 26.

[6] Bureau of the Census, *Current Population Reports,* Series P-60, No. 66, Dec. 23, 1969, p. 25.

those corporations were family enterprises.[7] Most farm output still comes from middle-class family farmers.

G. Short-Run and Long-Run Problems

Instability is a *short-run* problem. The year-to-year adjustments in output as demand or crop conditions change are accomplished by existing farms and farmers. Very few move to the city or back to the farm in response to temporary fluctuations in market conditions.

Farm poverty is a *long-run* problem. The difficulty here is the wrong number and types of farms. Its solution requires that resources leave agriculture or that the size and type of farm change. Such adjustments occur only in the long run.

The short-run problem of instability and the patterns of short-run cost and demand that contribute to it are discussed in the first half of this chapter. The long-run problem of low farm incomes and the related questions of long-run cost and mobility are covered in the last half.

II. SHORT-RUN COST AND SUPPLY

The pattern of costs varies with the line of business, inside of agriculture as well as outside, but there are enough important similarities to warrant a careful examination of a particular case. Different patterns of cost in other industries will be pointed out when we reach them.

A. Agricultural Costs—Dairying

In some types of agriculture, experimental studies have been made that show short-run cost patterns quite precisely. One of the most extensive of these was in dairying. Several hundred cows at 10 experimental stations in a number of states were fed at various levels for three years and their milk production compared.

The feed "inputs" that went with the various milk outputs are

---

[7] Economic Research Service, Department of Agriculture, *Corporations Having Agricultural Operations*, August, 1968.

Table 2-1. Feed Input and Milk Output per Cow per Year for 392 Cows Fed at Six Levels

Number of Cows in Each Group	Average Total Digestible Nutrients Consumed (Pounds per Year)	Average 4% Fat Corrected Milk Produced (Pounds per Year)
65	5654	7626
60	6117	8184
66	6575	8824
55	7132	9400
52	7531	9780
94	7899	9965

Note: "Total digestible nutrients" includes all types of feed (grain, hay, etc.) expressed as pounds of carbohydrate feed (dry weight) according to feed value. A correction was applied to express all milk production as of a uniform butterfat content.

Source. Einar Jensen, John W. Klein, Emil Rauchenstein, T. E. Woodward, and Ray Smith, *Input-Output Relationships in Milk Production*, U.S. Department of Agriculture Technical Bulletin No. 815, May 1942.

shown in Table 2-1 and Figure 2-4. A cow requires a certain amount of feed simply to maintain herself. Beyond that, more feed leads to more milk, but at a decreasing rate. The cows fed at high levels produced more than less generously treated cows but,

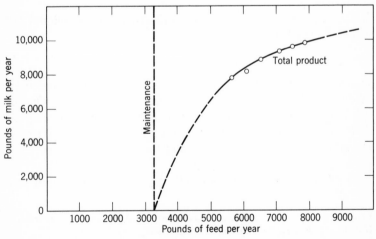

Figure 2-4. *Source.* Jensen et al., *op. cit.*, p. 39.

as we would expect, milk output did not increase as fast as feed consumption. These production figures can be used to estimate the costs of a hypothetical dairy farm. Imagine a 25-cow farm near one of the large cities on the eastern seaboard. Let it produce enough hay, silage, and pasture to provide 3000 pounds of feed per cow per year. It must buy any feed above that level. For simplicity, assume that purchased feed is the only *variable cost*. The farm might have the following *fixed costs* per year.[8]

Depreciation and maintenance of buildings and equipment	$ 800
Property taxes	400
Miscellaneous (seed, fertilizer, gasoline, veterinarian, marketing costs, etc.)	1300
Labor (3300 hours at $1.00)	3300
Interest (5% on $24,000)	1200
	$7000

Labor is treated as a fixed cost because the operator and his family do all the work. In many nonfarm businesses labor is the leading variable cost, but in American agriculture three quarters of the labor is supplied by the farmers and their families. This sort of labor will be employed no matter what the farm produces. A farmer can hardly fire his wife if he has had a bad year.

The only way to put a value on this family labor is by looking at its *opportunity cost*, that is, what it can earn in its best alternative employment. In 1964, hired farm labor was paid about $1.00 an hour on the average. The farmer could undoubtedly earn more than this in the city, but for most American farmers a dollar on the farm is worth more than one in the city.

Interest has been treated in the same way as labor costs in this example. If the farmer had borrowed the $24,000, the interest charge would obviously be part of his fixed costs; but even if he put it up himself, the farmer's capital costs something. If he were to sell his farm and put the proceeds into securities, he could earn $1200 or so per year on his money. Farming would be profitable only if it paid enough to give him a normal return on his investment as well as the going wage for his labor. At any

---

[8] This farm is similar to, but a little smaller than a typical "Central Northeast Dairy Farm" as reported in *Farm Costs and Returns* (Agriculture In-

Table 2-2.   Total Costs at Various Levels of Output

A Total Output (Thousands of Pounds of Milk per Year)	B Total Fixed Costs (Dollars per Year)	C Total Varable Costs (Dollars per Year)	D Total Costs (Dollars per Year) B + C
0	7000	—	7,000
200	7000	3000	10,000
210	7000	3250	10,250
220	7000	3550	10,550
230	7000	3900	10,900
240	7000	4350	11,350
250	7000	5000	12,000
260	7000	6000	13,000

lower level, the farmer would be taking losses and would do well to quit if he has the opportunity.

The total costs of this farm at various levels of output are shown in Table 2-2. Column B of Table 2-2 shows the $7000 fixed costs that apply whether the farmer sells a little, or a lot, or nothing at all. Column C shows the total variable costs—purchased feed in this case—assuming that he pays 4¢ a pound for concentrates. The figures in column C are approximately in line with the experimental data given in Table 2-2, but they have been rounded to make arithmetic easier.[9] Total costs are just the

---

formation Bulletin No. 230, Revised, August 1965, p. 14). The farms in that sample had 33 milk cows and total farm capital, including the residence, of $45,000. They employed 4610 man-hours of labor in 1964, of which 3800 was family labor. In the early 1970's even such a farm will seem small.

In this example, some $10,000 of the capital and corresponding amounts of depreciation, taxes, and interest have been assigned to the residence rather than to the dairy business. This farm buys about 30% more feed than the typical farm. Livestock costs and receipts have been left out for simplicity. They would partially offset each other, but the typical farmer might net $500 to $800 on the sale of cattle and calves in addition to the income we will consider. Obviously, some of the miscellaneous items are really variable costs, although such items as seed, fertilizer, and veterinary costs cannot be avoided so long as the farmer maintains his herd.

[9] The exact derivation of the figures in Table 2-2 is of decidedly secondary importance, but is given here for those who wish to know how it was worked out. The quantities correspond roughly to those in Table 2-1 multiplied by 25 (we are assuming a 25-cow herd). The feed per cow at each output was estimated on the basis of Table 2-1. The total variable cost is just the num-

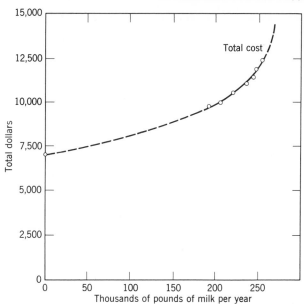

Figure 2-5

total variable and total fixed costs added together. Total costs at various outputs appear as the upward sloping total cost curve in Figure 2-5.

B. *Cost and Revenue*

Just which of the outputs in Table 2-2 is most profitable depends on the receipts that the farmer can expect. Table 2-3 compares his total costs with the prospective receipts at a price of 5¢ a pound for milk, and again at 4¢ a pound.

Since this is a case of pure competition, milk sells for 5¢ a pound whether Farmer Brown produces 260,000 pounds per year or 200,000 per year or quits dairying completely. The difference between the total costs and the total receipts of the farm is its total profits. In this case, the farmer would just break even at 200,000 pounds and at 260,000 pounds, but could make consider-

---

ber of pounds of feed per cow times $1 (4¢ a pound for 25 cows). The dots in Figure 2-4 show the costs that result if the exact inputs and outputs in Table 2-1 are used without any rounding.

Table 2-3.   Total Costs, Total Receipts, and Total Profits at Various Levels of Output

A Output (Thousands of Pounds of Milk per Year)	B Total Costs (Dollars per Year)	C Total Receipts at 5¢ per Pound (Dollars per Year) A × 5¢	D Total Profits at 5¢ per Pound (Dollars per Year) C — B	E Total Receipts at 4¢ per Pound (Dollars per Year) A × 4¢	F Total Profits at 4¢ per Pound (Dollars per Year) E — B
0	7,000	0	—7000	0	—7000
200	10,000	10,000	0	8,000	—2000
210	10,250	10,500	250	8,400	—1850
220	10,550	11,000	450	8,800	—1750
230	10,900	11,500	600	9,200	—1700
240	11,350	12,000	650	9,600	—1750
250	12,000	12,500	500	10,000	—2000
260	13,000	13,000	0	10,400	—2600

able profits at intermediate outputs. His most profitable level of operation according to column D is at 240,000 pounds per year.

Total costs, total receipts, and total profits at a price of 5¢ a pound are all reproduced as curves in Figure 2-6. Since total receipts rise in proportion to output, the total receipts curve is a straight line. At outputs of less than 200,000 pounds or more than 260,000 pounds of milk per year, the total receipts curve of this farm is below the total cost curve and profits are negative—in other words, the farmer is taking a loss. The distance between the cost and revenue curves is greatest at 240,000 pounds of milk, the level of production that a profit-maximizing farmer would select.

Columns E and F of Table 2-3 show what would happen at a price of 4¢ a pound. They are plotted in Figure 2-7. This time there is *no* output where the farmer can make a profit or even avoid a loss. Dairying has turned out to be a big mistake, but the farmer will still find it worthwhile to keep producing in the short run. He can cut his losses to $1700 per year by keeping output at the 230,000-pound level. At any lower output he would lose more. If he tried to avoid all of his variable costs by just maintaining his herd, he could lose as much as $7000 a year. So long as he sticks to dairying, a loss of $1700 is the best he can manage. Remember that a "loss" here means he gets $2800 for his cap-

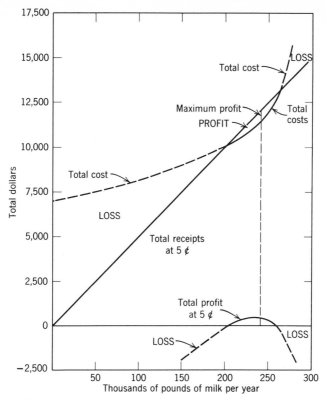

Figure 2-6

ital, time and effort, while he could be earning $4500 for the same resources somewhere else.

C. Average and Marginal Costs

The *average costs* for this hypothetical farm are derived in Table 2-4. The *averaged fixed costs* in Column B are just the $7000 per year of overhead divided by the successive quantities. The average variable costs in Column D are the feed costs divided by the numbers of pounds of milk. Average cost is the sum of these two.

Marginal costs are also worked out in Table 2-4. When milk production expands from 200,000 to 210,000 pounds per year, total costs rise by $250 from $10,000 to $10,250. If milk came in 10,000 pound tanks, this $250 would be the marginal cost of a

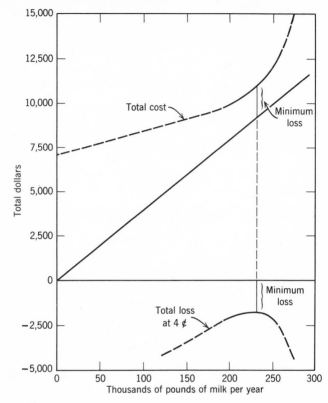

Figure 2-7

tank of milk. On a per-pound basis, the marginal cost within the
200,000 to 210,000 pound range is about $250/10,000 lbs or 2.5¢
per pound.

These average and marginal costs are plotted in Figure 2-8.
Because of the substantial fixed costs, average costs decline
sharply at first, and because of the marked diminishing returns
to additional feeding, the marginal cost, the average variable
cost and the average cost all ultimately rise.

D. *The Supply of Milk*

A farmer trying to make the most of his opportunities should
keep increasing the cow's ration so long as another pound of
feed increases the value of milk produced by more than it in-

Table 2-4. Average and Marginal Costs of a Hypothetical Northeastern Dairy Farm

A Quantity Produced per Year (Thousands of Pounds of Milk)	B Average Fixed Cost (Dollars per Year) $7000 ÷ A	C Total Variable Costs (Dollars per Year)	D Average Variable Cost (Cents per Pound) C ÷ A	E Average Cost (Cents per Pound) B + D or F ÷ A	F Total Cost (Dollars per Year)	G Change in Total Costs with Each 10,000 Pounds Change in Output (Dollars per Year)	H Marginal Cost (Cents per Pound) G ÷ 10,000
200	3.50	3000	1.50	5.00	10,000		
						250	2.5
210	3.33	3250	1.55	4.88	10,250		
						300	3.0
220	3.18	3550	1.62	4.80	10,550		
						350	3.5
230	3.04	3900	1.69	4.73	10,900		
						450	4.5
240	2.91	4350	1.81	4.72	11,350		
						650	6.5
250	2.80	5000	2.00	4.80	12,000		
						1000	10.0
260	2.70	6000	2.30	5.00	13,000		

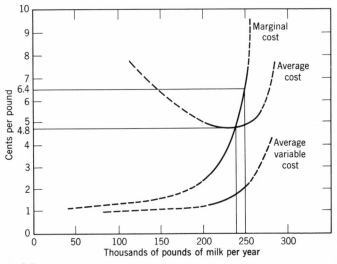

Figure 2-8

creases feed costs. He should stop when the last addition to feed
is worth just as much as the last addition to milk receipts—in
other words, when the marginal cost just equals the price. The
marginal cost curve in Figure 2-8 will, therefore, trace out the
farm's supply of milk. At a price of 4¢ it will sell 230,000 pounds,
at 5¢ it will sell 240,000 pounds, at 7¢ it will sell 250,000 pounds,
and so forth.

While the farm in this example is hypothetical, its marginal
cost curve was derived from empirical data, so its supply curve
might be expected to correspond to real life supply curves. There
is some evidence that it does. Figure 2-9 compares the milk-
grain price ratio with the output of milk per cow in 16 northern
dairy states in 1963.[10] The milk-grain price ratio is the price of

10 While dairying occurs in all states, these states embrace the major dairy

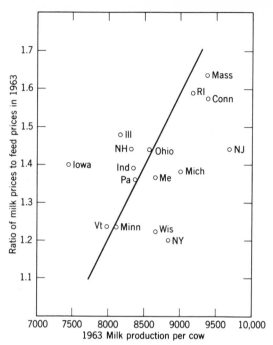

Figure 2-9. Response of milk production to milk-feed price ratios, 1963. *Sources. Agricultural Statistics,* 1964. Milk price is average receipts for whole milk sold plus milk skimmed for cream (page 386). Feed price is the average value of the concentrates fed (page 376). Milk production per cow is from Table 557.

milk divided by the price of grain. For instance, on our hypothetical farm the price of grain was assumed to be 4¢ per pound. The price of milk would have to be 4.8¢ for the milk-feed price ratio to be 1.2 (=4.8/4), as it was in Minnesota. It would have to sell for 6.4¢ per pound for the ratio to be 1.6 (=6.4/4) as in Massachusetts.

The "supply curves" in Figures 2-8 and 2-9 are quite similar.

region of the country. In 1964 they accounted for 63% of milk and cream marketings (*Agricultural Statistics—1965*, p. 386). There are other dairy centers in the West and the South, but differences in climate, quality of stock, and availability of year-round pasture make these areas difficult to compare with the North.

The 25-cow farm would produce about 20,000 pounds more milk at 6.4¢ than at 4.8¢ or about 600 more pounds per cow. In Figure 2-9 those states with milk-grain price ratios of 1.6 produce about 1000 more pounds per cow than those where the ratio is 1.2. In southern New England, where nearness to the large cities makes milk prices high, cows are fed more intensively than in the corn belt states where the price of milk is low. Only part of the interstate difference in the rate at which cows produce milk is accounted for by the milk-grain price ratio. Some of the remaining variability in milk per cow is due to the differences in hay prices, in climate, and in type of stock.

E. Fixed Costs in Farming

Each type of business has its own cost patterns, although they generally resemble dairy farms in having some fixed and some variable costs. An important consideration is the proportion of total costs that is fixed. This proportion is high for most farms. Table 2-5 shows the main expenses of the average American farm in 1968. Incomes of farm operators have been listed with the fixed costs in addition to such obvious items as depreciation, property tax, interest, and rent. The business part of the average

Table 2-5. Production Expenses and Receipts per Farm, All United States Farms, 1968

Operating Expenses	Dollars	Fixed Expenses	Dollars
Feed purchased	2122	Depreciation of buildings	
Livestock purchased	1189	and equipment	2028
Seed purchased	219	Property taxes	798
Fertilizer purchased	687	Interest on farm mortgages	485
Hired labor	998	Rents paid to nonfarm	
Repairs and operation of		landlords	425
buildings and equipment		Net farm income of	
(includes gas and oil)	1512	operators from farming	4805
Miscellaneous	1453		8541
	8180		

Total fixed plus operating expense (equals gross
farm income per farm) 16,721

Note: The cost listed are derived from *The Farm Income Situation*, July 1969. The totals have been divided by 3,054,000 (the number of farms in 1968) to find the cost per farm for each item. Number of farms from *Agricultural Statistics*, 1969, p. 477.

American farm represents an investment of about $60,000 and employs 1.4 man-years of family labor. In 1968 it yielded an average net income of $4805, in addition to which, its land appreciated by about $3100 for a total earnings per farm of a little less than $8000.[11] Even with a generous allowance for rural-urban differences in the cost or quality of living, this does not seem like an excessive estimate of the opportunity cost of such a substantial investment plus substantially more than a year's labor.

About half of all costs were clearly fixed in 1968, and some of the operating expenses were really overhead costs. This is true of feed used for maintenance and of building and machinery repairs. The other variable costs that remain are not nearly so variable as those of urban businesses. A steel mill or an auto plant can change the rate at which it uses labor and materials in a matter of days or—at most—weeks, but once the crop is in, the farmer has committed almost all of his inputs for that year.

With so many of their costs fixed, farmers can be expected to keep producing even if farm prices fall by half or more.[12] This has certainly been American experience. Figure 2-10 compares the index of industrial production with an index of farm output. Industrial and farm production in each year appear as percentages of the 1957-1959 levels. These indexes measure physical volume of output only. They show what would have happened to the value of output if prices had not changed. Industrial output grew faster than farm production, but farm output changed much less from year to year. The main ripples in farm output

---

[11] *The Balance Sheet of the Farm Sector* (Agricultural Information Bulletin No. 340) shows total farm equity (assets minus liabilities) of $233.0 billion or $76,400 per farm in 1968. About a fifth of this was assignable to nonbusiness assets such as residences, furnishings and appliances, and securities. The value of farm real estate is reported in the same source to have increased by $9.5 billion or $3100 per farm between January 1, 1968 and January 1, 1969.

[12] Output can still fluctuate with price changes, depending on how flat the marginal cost curves are, but few farmers will move in and out of production because of changing prices in the short run. If, in addition, the marginal cost curves on most farms rise steeply, as they did in the dairy farm discussed a few pages back, the output would show little response to price changes.

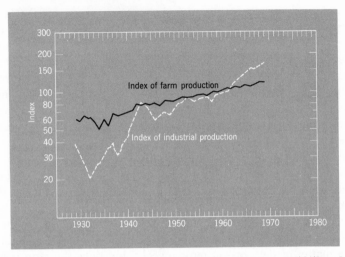

Figure 2-10. Indexes of farm and industrial production, 1957-59 = 100. *Source. Economic Report of the President,* 1970, Tables C-35 and C-80.

that did occur were due to the weather. During the Depression years, when farm prices were falling disastrously, farmers continued to produce. In some deep Depression years, 1931 and 1932, they actually produced more than in 1929. In other years, 1933 and 1935, they produced only slightly below the 1929 level, and even in the drought years of 1934 and 1936 farm production never fell more than 20% below the 1929 level. By contrast, industrial production was 47% below 1929 in 1932. Farmers did not stop producing when prices fell because they still had the mortgage to pay and the family to feed.

F. *Diversified Farming and Year-to-Year Adjustments*

Even if he is committed to agriculture, the farmer often may choose between several possible crops. While some farmers are specialists in dairying or cotton or wheat, a substantial proportion of American farmers has more than one product. If the price of farm products in general declines, a diversified corn belt farm will go right on producing, but if just the price of hogs falls off, the operator can feed more of his grain to beef cattle or he can plant soy beans.

As a result of the farmers' ability to shift between products in the short run, there can be substantial fluctuations in the output of individual farm products from year to year in response to price changes. While total farm output almost never changes as much as 20% from one year to the next, wheat or cotton marketings often do. This is partly due to regional weather conditions, which can change much more in one year than the weather of the whole country, but it is also farmers' adjustments to price changes. Figures 2-11 and 2-12 show some cases of this.

Figure 2-11 shows the total cattle population of the country since the end of the Civil War. There is a surprisingly regular cycle. Every decade or so, cattlemen respond to good prices by increasing their herds 20 to 40%. The large numbers of marketings that result make the price unfavorable for the last part of the cycle, and ranchers cut their herds back once more.

Hog producers have a similar cycle. Figure 2-12 compares hog marketings and the hog-corn price ratio since 1920. Here the fluctuations are shorter. Hogs mature in a year and have litters of a half dozen pigs, while cattle take two years or more to mature

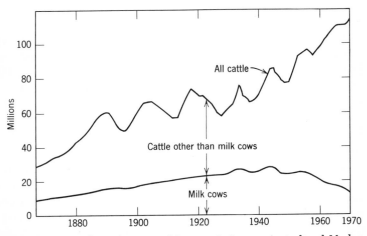

Figure 2-11. Cattle on farms as of January 1. *Source. Agricultural Marketing Service,* Neg. 430A-57(2) and *Livestock and Meat Situation,* March 1970, pp. 5-6.

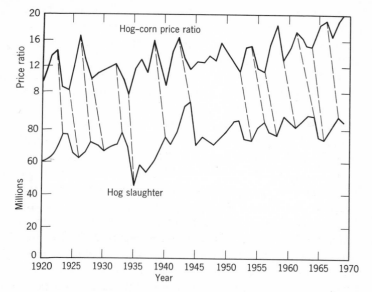

Figure 2-12. *Source. Agriculture Outlook Charts,* 1955 and 1960, and *The Livestock and Meat Situation,* March 1970.

and have one calf at a time. In Figure 2-12, a high price for hogs compared with corn is typically followed a year or two later by large marketings. All these hogs mean low prices, and these in turn are followed a year or two later by low production. It looks very much as if farmers are growing feed and hogs with an eye to prices at planting and farrowing time. Of course, it is their estimates of price at harvest that determine their output, but these estimates are often very uncertain and are strongly influenced by prices in previous years.

It has been suggested that unstable hog production can be explained by supply and demand curves like Figure 2-13. Suppose that in year 1 the output of hogs is low (at Q_1) so that the price is temporarily very high (P_1). Expecting this price to continue, farmers grow a large number of hogs next year (Q_2) and when they come to sell them find a price of only P_2. This leads to low output and high prices in year 3, heavy feeding and low prices in year 4, and so forth. This idea has come to be known as

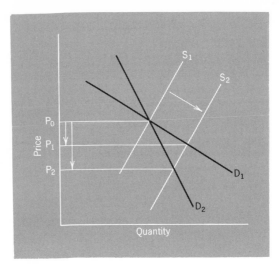

Figure 2-14

not fall very much to clear the market. On the other hand, if the demand is unresponsive to price changes (D_2 in Figure 2-14), it will take a large drop in price to sell any additional output when there is a bumper crop. D_2 might represent a product like wheat. If strawberry and wheat production show similar fluctuations from year to year, strawberry prices should be more stable than wheat prices. Figure 2-15 shows this. In both the strawberry and wheat cases, output is 40% higher in odd-numbered years than in even. Prices fluctuate within a 20% range for strawberries, but by 50% for wheat.

We would have had similar results if instability had been caused by shifts in demand instead of supply. In Figure 2-16, both the demand for strawberries and the demand for wheat are reduced by the same quantity at each price. It takes only a small reduction in price to bring consumers back to strawberries, but it takes a large price reduction to get them to take all the extra wheat.

B. *Estimating Elasticity*

It is clear that an understanding of farm instability requires a knowledge of the elasticity of demand for farm products, but

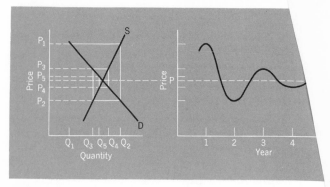

Figure 2-13

the cobweb theorem because of the way the supply and d
diagram looks after several go-arounds.[13]

Various writers have thought they have seen cobwebs c
sort in cattle, chickens, strawberries, coffee, and tree-grown
In this illustration, output was assumed to shift annuall
simplicity, but it could just as well have taken a decade to
from year 1 to year 2. Of course, weather, crop restrictions,
prices of other goods, and changes in demand all affect the le
of price so that actual price fluctuations cannot be expected
be as regular as those in Figure 2-13. If they ever were th
regular, farmers could probably figure out what was happenir
to them. Then the cycle would be stopped, or at least changed

III. ELASTICITY

A. *Demand and Instability*

The effect of shifts in supply or demand on price and income depends on the character of demand in part. If consumption is
very responsive to changes in price (D_1 in Figure 2-14), a given
shift in supply will produce little change in price. Consumers will
take up additional strawberries so readily that the price need

---

[13] The price fluctuations do not necessarily become less severe as time passes.
By flattening the supply curve or steepening the demand, you can make the
price go off the page.

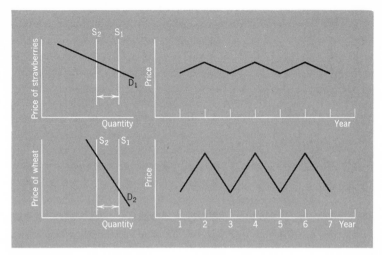

Figure 2-15

where is such knowledge to come from? Most economics texts
define elasticity. Realistic estimates of elasticity are harder to
come by, but they are far from impossible.

Figure 2-17 illustrates some of the problems in estimating the
elasticity of demand. It shows the average retail price of chuck

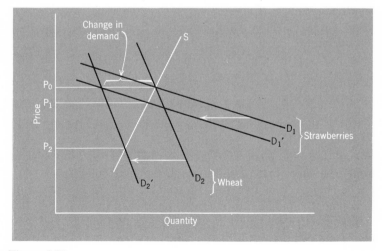

Figure 2-16

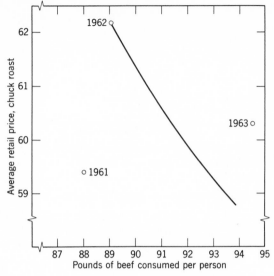

Figure 2-17

roast in 45 cities, and per capita beef consumption in the United States in 3 years. In 1961 with a fairly low price for beef, Americans bought 88 pounds apiece. In 1962, with the price averaging about 5% higher, they actually bought a bit more. If these two points are on the same demand curve, it must have a very unorthodox shape. The problem is that the usual textbook demand curve (including the curves in this book) is drawn on the assumption that everything except price is constant but in practice, everything else is continually changing. Between 1961 and 1962 consumers' incomes went up by about 3%. In addition, a long-term shift in preferences toward beef has been evident for a generation. These factors tended to increase the quantity consumed at the same time that rising prices were decreasing it. In other words, the conventional textbook demand curve passing through the 1962 point is different from (higher and to the right from) the curve that passed through the 1961 point.

The change from 1962 to 1963 seems a little more reassuring. This time, the public did buy more beef when the price fell. But actually, we have no more right to connect up the 1962 and 1963 points and call the result the demand curve for beef than we did for 1961 and 1962. Income rose again in this year, and, to complicate things further, the price of pork fell.

It is possible that the *decrease* in demand due to the fall in pork prices and the *increase* in demand due to the rise in incomes and the long-term upward trend toward beef just offset each other and that we really would get a textbook demand for beef by connecting the second pair of points, but it is much more likely that they were less nicely balanced.

In spite of the complexity of this tale, it is possible to make a fairly solid estimate of the rate at which consumption changes in response to changes in the price of beef. By using a statistical technique known as multiple regression analysis, economists have been able to combine the evidence from many years and arrive at estimates of how beef sales changed with beef price, holding such other variables as income and the price of pork constant. The elasticity of demand for beef at the consumer level has been estimated at 0.75, 0.77, 0.79, 0.9, 0.96 and 1.11,[14] using somewhat different techniques or periods and controlling for different variables. In general, it appears that a 10% fall in beef prices results in approximately an 8 or 9% increase in beef consumption. The line through the 1962 point in Figure 2-16 shows a demand of this nature.

C. The Determinants of Elasticity

Elasticity estimates have been made for a large group of commodities, many of them agricultural. Table 2-6 lists a few of these. Different scholars often find quite different elasticities, depending on the period they study and the statistical method they use. Many of the methods used have been subject to considerable criticism. Nevertheless, these figures do show the rough patterns of demand elasticities. For one thing, the demand for beef, or pork, or mutton, each taken separately, all seem to be more elastic than the demand for all meat, and this in turn is more elastic than the demand for all food. This is to be expected. Buyers with good alternatives will drop out of a market rapidly as the price rises, but where there is no good substitute, higher prices

---

[14] See notes to Table 2-6.

Table 2-6.

Commodity	Elasticity	Source	Commodity	Elasticity	Source
Automobiles (retail)	0.8–1.5	(A,B,C)	Beef (retail)	0.8–1.1	(G,H,I,M)
Electric power for residential use	0.2–1.0	(D)	Pork (retail)	0.7–1.0	(G,H,I,M)
Steel (at factory)	0.2–0.4	(E)	Lamb (retail)	1.8–2.3	(G,H,M)
Aluminum (at factory)	0.4–1.2	(F)	All meat products (retail)	0.4–0.6	(H,I,M)
Cotton (at farm)	0.1	(G)	Chicken (retail)	1.1–1.2	(H,M)
Wheat (at farm)	0.02–0.2	(G,M)	Eggs (retail)	0.3–0.4	(H,M)
Corn (at farm)	0.03–0.5	(G,M)	Milk (retail)	0.2–0.5	(J,M)
Apples (retail)	1.3	(H)	Butter (retail, prewar)	0.3–0.4	(J)
Peaches (retail)	1.5	(H)	Butter (retail, postwar)	0.8–1.4	(J,M)
Citrus fruit (retail)	0.8	(H)	Margarine (retail, postwar)	0.3–0.8	(J,M)
All fruit (retail)	0.6–1.1	(H,M)	All food (retail)	0.2–0.5	(H,K,L,M)

Sources:

(A) C. F. Roos and V. VonSzeliski, "Factors Governing Changes in Domestic Automobile Demand," in *The Dynamics of Automobile Demand*, General Motors, 1939, pp. 90–91.

(B) G. C. Chow, *The Demand for Automobiles in the United States*, North Holland Publishing Company, 1957, p. 34.

(C) D. B. Suits, "The Demand for New Automobiles in the United States, 1929–1956," *Review of Economics and Statistics*, 1958, p. 273.

(D) F. M. Fisher and C. Kaysen, *The Demand for Electricity in the United States*, North Holland Publishing Company, 1962, pp. 42, 50.

(E) U. S. Steel, TNEC Papers, Vol. 1, *Economic and Related Studies*, U. S. Steel, 1940, pp. 169–170.

(F) Meston J. Peck, *Competition in the Aluminum Industry, 1945–1958*, Harvard University Press, 1961, pp. 30–31.

(G) Henry Schultz, *The Theory and Measurement of Demand*, University of Chicago Press, 1938, passim.

(H) Karl A. Fox, *The Analysis of Demand for Farm Products*, U. S. Department of Agriculture Technical Bulletin No. 1081, Sept., 1953.

(I) Elmer Working, *The Demand for Meat*, University of Chicago Press, 1951.

(J) A. S. Rojko, *The Demand and Price Structure for Dairy Products*, U. S. Department of Agriculture Technical Bulletin No. 1168, 1957 and various sources quoted by Rojko, pp. 109–110.

(K) James Tobin, "A Statistical Demand Function for Food in the U. S. A.," *Journal of the Royal Statistical Society*, Series A, Part II, 1950, p. 134.

(L) M. A. Girshick and T. Haavelmo, "Statistical Analysis of the Demand for Food," *Econometrica*, April, 1947.

(M) G. E. Brandow, *Interrelations among Demands for Farm Products and Implications for Control of Market Supply*, Penn. State Agricultural Experimental Station Bulletin 680, August, 1961.

will do little to discourage consumption. In many cases, individual farm products are quite adequate substitutes for each other. It does not take an exorbitant drop in price to eliminate a surplus of beef *or* pork *or* lamb individually. But the substitutes for broad categories of goods like "meat" and especially "food" are much poorer in the eyes of consumers, so that a larger drop in price is necessary to sell a surplus of all meats or all foods.

Most of the farm products in Table 2-7 have elasticities of less than 1.0. Since the substitutes for food in general, in the eyes of most consumers, are very few and very inadequate, the elasticity of demand for farm products as a whole must be very low indeed.

This is especially likely on the farm because of the processors' markups between the consumer and the farmer. The canning of peaches, the butchering of pork, or the milling of flour involve costs that do not necessarily go up and down with farm prices. For many foods, processing and distribution account for half or more of the consumer's dollar. Suppose that this has been true of chuck roast, and that it has been selling for $1 a pound in the stores. If the price of beef now falls by 25¢ *at the farm,* and if the meat packers and distributors still require 50¢ a pound for their services, the retail price will fall to 75¢. The response to a 50% drop in price at the farm is likely to be disappointing because it involves only a 25% drop in price from the consumer's point of view.

Since prices fluctuate less with a more elastic demand, the problem of instability should be less severe for a single commodity with good substitutes than for farm products in general. For instance, the decline in the demand for butter that occurred as margarine became more popular in the early 1950's need not have caused surpluses of butter for long. Obviously, many consumers considered margarine a good substitute for butter. A cut in price would have won many consumers back to the dairy product. The loss of foreign demand for American food products in general as the world food shortage ended at about the same time was a much more serious problem. A substantial drop in all food prices seemed unlikely to make Americans eat much more.

D. *The Elasticity of Supply*

A few empirical studies of the elasticity of supply have been made. In one of these, the output of milk in the years 1940 through 1957 was related to milk prices in previous years holding the long-term trend in milk production and the prices of hay and concentrates constant. The short-run elasticity of demand was estimated at 0.29. This is similar to the results derived earlier in this chapter. In Table 2-5 when the price is in the neighborhood of 4¢ per pound, a 25% increase in price seems to lead to a 4.3% increase in output, so that the elasticity of supply would be about $\dfrac{0.043}{0.25}$ or 0.17. At the center of Figure 2-9 a 7% increase in the price of milk relative to the price of feed leads to a 3% increase in output for an elasticity of $\dfrac{.03}{.07}$ or 0.43. These are all *short-run* elasticities. They show the effects of changes in rates of feeding and, therefore, changes in output per cow, but they do not allow for changes in the number or size of herds. In the long run, when herds can be built up or reduced and when new herds can be formed or old dairy farms can be diverted to other products, the elasticity of supply would be greater. The study of milk supply mentioned above estimated the long-run elasticity of supply of milk to be above 0.52.[15]

The stability of farm prices depends on the elasticity of supply as well as of demand. We concluded earlier that total farm output would change very little with price changes. In effect, we were concluding that supply of farm products, like demand, is inelastic. The supply of individual products may be more elastic because farmers, like consumers, can shift from one product to another when the price changes, even though they cannot stop producing much more easily than consumers can stop eating.

---

[15] Harlow Halverson, "Response of Milk Production to Price," *Journal of Farm Economics*, December 1958, pp. 1101-1113. The short-run elasticity was based on the response of milk production in each year to the price in the immediately previous year. The long-run elasticity took earlier prices into account as well.

An inelastic supply will intensify the instability of farm prices. It would not have taken an impossible fall in price to remove a surplus of butter, because Iowa farmers who previously found it worthwhile to feed corn to dairy cows will now feed it to pigs. It would have taken an intolerable fall in farm prices in general to adjust for the loss of the European market in the short run. Not only will consumers eat very little more; but farmers will keep right on producing in spite of the low prices.

E. *Elasticity and Farm Incomes*

The instability of farm incomes as well as farm prices can be traced in part to the inelastic demand for farm products. If the elasticity of demand for some farm product is equal to one, the gross receipts of its producers would be the same regardless of their output, and if elasticity is more than one, farmers will actually receive more for their crops when the price is low than when it is high. Most of the elasticities estimated in Table 2-7 are less than one, however. This implies that changes in output will make gross farm receipts rise and fall with farm prices.

F. *Depressions and Farm Incomes*

Not all fluctuations in farm prices and incomes are attributable to the weather or output decisions by farmers. Shifts in demand can do drastic things to farm prices and incomes. Figure 2-3 showed that the really extreme changes in farm prices were associated with the reduced demand during depressions and with increased demand during the world-wide post-World War II food shortage.

If the demand for a product falls, total receipts of sellers are almost bound to decline regardless of the elasticity, since both the price and the quantity of sales are likely to be reduced. However, the amount of the decline will be more, or less, depending on the elasticity.

Figure 2-18 shows the effect of a decline in an inelastic demand. To isolate and dramatize the effect, assume that farmers have an elasticity of supply of 0; in other words, their supply curve is S_a. Contrast with this a situation that often occurs in manufacturing, where the price of goods sold does not fall in a

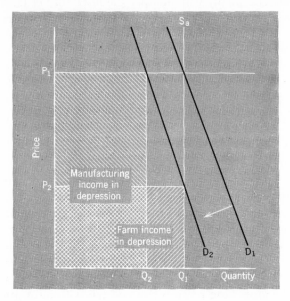

Figure 2-18

recession. The manufacturers would supply any amount at P_1 out to the capacity of the plants. A decline in demand will hurt both industries. In manufacturing, it will show up as a decline in output and employment from Q_1 to Q_2, in agriculture as a decline in price from P_1 to P_2. However, with an inelastic demand, the fall in price must be very great, but the reduction in output is relatively small. The loss in farm incomes will be much greater than the loss in manufacturing incomes. If the demand had been elastic, then a policy of maintaining the old price would have caused an enormous drop in employment and incomes in the city, but a policy of maintaining the old output would have caused only a slight drop in price and income on the farm. At least the more monopolistic manufacturers could pick prices that minimize their losses in view of their demands, but the farmers, acting individually, cannot keep the price from falling when demand is inelastic. Farmers, who produce almost the same amount regardless of the price, and who face a very inelastic demand, do very badly in depressions.

IV. GOVERNMENT POLICY AND FARM INSTABILITY

The general public gains very little from only temporarily low farm prices followed by temporarily high ones. A fairly plausible case can be made for some government controls to level out farm prices and incomes from year to year.

The short-term fluctuations in farm prices are due to shifts in supply or demand. The main reasons for these shifts have been: (1) changes in supply as farmers overestimated or underestimated future prices; (2) changes in supply because of weather, insects, or disease; and (3) changes in demand because of depressions or booms in the country as a whole. A somewhat different government policy is indicated for each of these problems.

A. *Forward Prices for Agriculture and the Hog Cycle*

When swings in output result because farmers consistently miscalculate future markets, as in the case of the hog cycle, the argument for government intervention is particularly strong. In Figure 2-19, the price of an unregulated market would swing up to $15 and back to $10 indefinitely, but if government would guarantee a price of $12.50, it could avoid awkward surpluses or shortages and still stabilize the price. Farmers would be able to estimate the market correctly and would no longer overproduce and underproduce.

Of course, the trick is to determine what price will clear the

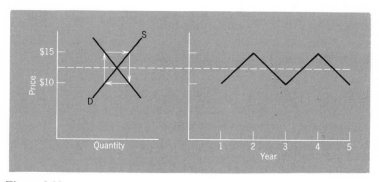

Figure 2-19

market. In practice, supply and demand do not stay put year after year. The government would have to announce new guaranteed prices before each planting on the basis of its best estimate of demand and supply at harvest time. These prices would not necessarily guarantee farmers profitable prices at all times, nor even perfectly stable ones, but they would avoid price instability of the farmers' own making.

Some economists who have rejected most other proposals for agricultural price supports have continued to urge "forward prices" of the sort described here. Prices in a free market are expected to act as guides to production, but they perform that function very imperfectly if producers consistently judge future markets inaccurately. Others have disapproved of even guaranteed forward prices, however. They feel that the Department of Agriculture statisticians would not be allowed to make objective estimates of the future demand and supply of pork or chickens because of the farm senators looking over their shoulders.

B. *Nature, Speculators, and the Ever-Normal Granary*

Government intervention to offset the effect of the weather is only a short step beyond the "forward price" proposal. The idea that government should maintain an "ever-normal granary," buying up part of bumper crops and storing them until poor years, has been suggested again and again. By following such a policy, the government would automatically reduce price fluctuations, and for commodities with inelastic demands this would even out farm incomes as well. Figure 2-20 shows the supply of wheat in year 1, when it rained in Kansas, and in year 2, when it did not. The government might buy up quantity *a* in the good year and sell it during the drought. As a result, the price fluctuation would be reduced as in the right-hand diagram.

Private speculators might do the same sort of thing. By buying during periods of surplus when prices are low, and by selling during shortages when prices are high, not only do the speculators make profits, but prices and supplies tend to be evened out, as in Figure 2-20. Speculators sometimes upset rather than stabilize the market, however. When they make up a large part of the supply and demand of a product, speculators are as likely to buy with an eye to other speculators as to the weather. When

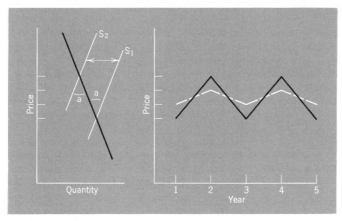

Figure 2-20

Smith buys because he is sure Jones will buy, and Jones is buying because he is sure Adams will buy, and Adams is betting on Smith, prices may sometimes rise farther and at other times fall farther than if there were no speculators at all. For speculation to have a stabilizing effect, speculators must be a small enough part of the market that they can generally be disregarded by each other. The government can operate an ever-normal granary even when its intervention represents a large part of total output.

The big problem of the government in an ever-normal granary program is to know when to buy and when to sell. What constitutes an unusual crop? If the large crop is due to good weather in Kansas, government purchases may be desirable, but if the bumper crop is because more farmers planted wheat this year, the government will just perpetuate the large supply by buying up part of it. By keeping the price high, the government encourages the same farmers to keep planting wheat in future years. Similarly, if the large crop is because of improved seed, the government will find itself buying wheat every year from now on. The ever-normal granary is in danger of becoming a permanent price support program unless the government limits itself to clearly temporary surpluses and shortages. It is often difficult for the Department of Agriculture to determine in advance what sort of changes are temporary, especially if it is under constant pressure from a powerful group of legislators and lobbyists.

C. *Depression and "Disaster Insurance"*

The problem during a depression is a little different. If the government were to buy up some of the surplus in such years, it would be keeping farm prices and incomes high by withholding goods from the urban public which is suffering from the same depression. A better solution would be to attack the depression itself. The farmer has a strong interest in full employment in the city.

If we are unable to prevent depressions, however, there are good arguments for guaranteeing farmers some minimum income. Urban workers are guaranteed against impossible losses by unemployment insurance or, as a last resort, by welfare. Many feel that if we hold up a net for everyone else, a guarantee against complete disaster for farmers is only equitable. Since farmers are not unemployed during a depression, their protection must take the form of some sort of price or income program rather than the insurance and welfare programs of nonfarmers.

D. *Storage Programs Versus Direct Income Payments*

A minimum price support which would apply in any period of general depression sufficient to assure the farmer, for example, 75% of his predepression income is one possibility. An alternative would be to allow farm prices to fall and to make direct payments to farmers sufficient to guarantee them the same minimum income. With a direct subsidy program there would be no large surpluses carried over to burden markets in subsequent years. The lower prices would benefit city people who suffer from the same depression, while the direct payments would give farmers the same incomes they would have with price supports.

The two approaches to maintaining farm incomes can be seen in Figure 2-21. In both cases, the total income of wheat farmers is to be kept at $1 billion dollars (500 million bushels at $2 a bushel). If the price is to be maintained, the government must buy up 100 million bushels, the entire output in excess of consumption at $2. If the government makes direct payments to farmers instead, consumers will take all 500 billion bushels of

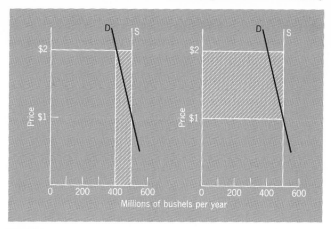

Figure 2-21

wheat at a price of $1. Farmers will receive $1 per bushel from the grain dealer and $1 from the government. The public will have all of the wheat and at a lower price, and the farmer will be receiving the same billion dollars that they had with the price support program.

If the demand is inelastic, as is shown here, the government will have to pay more in the case of the subsidy program than in the storage program, but the total payment by *consumers plus government* will be the same in both cases.

E. *Parity*

The Department of Agriculture's price programs have gone far beyond forward prices, storage against crop failure, and disaster insurance in time of depression. The government has maintained prices for many commodities so high that there have been inadequate markets through normal channels even in prosperous years. It was clearly not just evening off the peaks and the valleys, but trying to bring all prices up to the peaks. The congressman or Secretary of Agriculture was more apt to seek "fair" prices than prices that would clear the market over a period of years.

The popular standard of "fair" prices for farmers is *parity*. This had its origin in the 1920's. The first two decades of the century had been prosperous for farmers. During World War I and its immediate aftermath, farm prices had risen particularly rapidly. From 1920 on, however, farm prices were much less favorable, and farmers struggled under the heavy debts incurred during the earlier boom. Farm leaders tended to look back to the pre-World War I years as a time when farmers had received prices "in line" with nonfarm prices. In the 1920's, they felt, the farmer had fallen behind, and in the 1930's his position was even worse. As the interwar years progressed, the prices of the years just before World War I became established as the "fair" or "parity" prices. Their restoration became a main concern of farm pressure groups. In the Agricultural Adjustment Act of 1933, passed during the early days of the New Deal, Congress expressed its goal of restoring the relative prices of farm products to their levels of 1910-14.

Of course, the actual dollar price of wheat or cotton in 1910 to 1914 was irrelevant because of changes in the general price level. The parity price of a bushel of wheat was to be one that gave its seller the same purchasing power as he would have had in the base period. In 1948, Congress redefined parity so that the changes in diets, in exports, and in costs since 1914 could have some effect on the relative prices of different crops. The parity level of farm prices generally is still set to give a composite unit of farm output the same purchasing power it had in 1910-14, but the parity prices for individual commodities can now drift up or down depending on their prices during the previous ten years.

There is still room for criticism of parity, however. Its overall level is still pegged to 1910-14. These were some of the best peacetime years that the farmers had from the end of the Civil War until the present. Even in the 1920's and 1930's, a nonfarmer might reasonably wonder whether a less advantageous period would not be closer to "normal" for farmers. By now, a "normal" period more than half a century ago seems almost preposterous to many.[16]

---

[16] The Nixon administration, in its proposals for legislative revision of the agriculture program in 1969-1970, made a valiant effort to eliminate parity as a determinant of price support levels, but when the Agriculture Act of

F. *Price Policies—Crop Restrictions*

The prices of farm products would not obediently slide up to parity levels just because Congress said that is where they were to be. Congress had to take some action to bring about the relative prices that it set as its goal in 1933. In the main, these actions have consisted of (1) output restrictions and (2) price supports. Both programs began in 1933,[17] but the main reliance was on crop restriction in the early years.

Crop restriction, if effective, would certainly raise prices. Whether it would raise incomes or not would depend on the elasticity of demand. If the demand were inelastic (case A in Figure 2-22) the price would increase enough to more than offset the reduction in quantity sold, but if the demand were elastic (case B in Figure 2-22) the price increase would reduce farm receipts, not raise them. Crop restriction makes sense because most farm products have inelastic demands. The restriction programs have been most consistently applied to a group of commodities described as "basic" in the law: cotton, wheat, corn, rice, tobacco, and peanuts. The estimates available show extremely low elasticities for these commodities.

Crop restriction has been subject to much criticism. The waste involved has seemed obvious to many. In the depression years, when living standards were already low, a further reduction in the nation's output was highly vulnerable. There were many tears shed in Congress and in the press for the cotton ploughed

1970 emerged from Congress, parity was fully enshrined for at least another three years.

[17] There had been attempts to improve farm prices before 1933. In the last part of the nineteenth century, farmers had sought inflationary policies and government regulation of monopolies to improve their price positions. Farmers who competed in an important way with imports received tariff protection. In the 1920's a program to restrict domestic supplies and export the surpluses at low foreign prices passed Congress twice but was vetoed both times. From 1929 on there was a Federal Farm Board with authority to buy and sell farm products. Its funds were insufficient to deal with the disastrous price decline of the depression, however. The Agricultural Adjustment Act of 1933 was certainly a far more drastic step than any that preceded it. Most of the present federal farm price programs are direct descendants of the 1933 legislation.

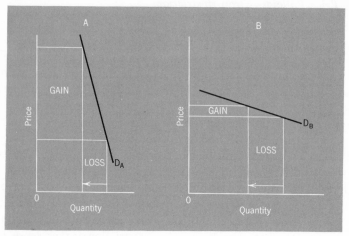

Figure 2-22

under and for the little pigs slaughtered during the early New Deal programs.

Individual farmers often resented the "regimentation" involved in crop restrictions. Some were simply objecting to the paper work or outside interference with their personal affairs, but for many the difficulty was economic. Suppose that the government set the price of wheat at $2, as in Figure 2-23. Then Farmer Brown, whose cost curves appear at the left, would make the greatest profit at an output of 2000 bushels this year. To keep the price at $2, however, the government had to impose production quotas. Brown could not be allowed to produce more than 1400 bushels. From his point of view, there was a fine opportunity for profit right under his nose if only he could reach out and take it, but then the bureaucrats stepped in. Of course, if every farmer did take advantage of these opportunities, the price would fall and they would all be in worse condition, not better.

Crop restriction programs have not always accomplished their objectives. The farmers generally retire their least promising land and then apply their efforts and equipment more intensively to what is left. As a result, output is not reduced in proportion to acreage.

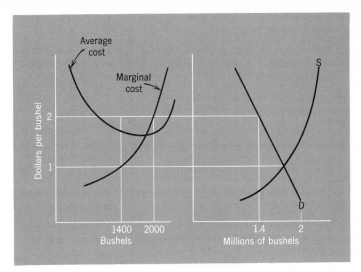

Figure 2-23

G. *Direct Price Supports*

In addition to restricting output in many years, the government has provided a floor for at least some farm prices in every year since 1933. At harvest time, farmers who have complied with their acreage allotments are permitted to borrow a certain amount per bushel of their crops while storing them. The loans are "non-recourse," meaning that if the farmers choose to just keep the money the government must be satisfied with the crop in full settlement. During the marketing period, the farmer may always pay off the loan and sell the crop. If the price rises above the loan level any time during the year, he almost certainly will do so. If it stays near the support level, the Commodity Credit Corporation (CCC) will probably wind up with the crop at the end of the season. Since many farmers are guaranteed at least the loan rate, the open market price cannot fall much below that level.

The price levels at which loans have been made and the particular commodities supported have been the subject of regular debate. Support prices rose to a peak of 90% of parity at the end of World War II and fell thereafter amid cries of anguish from the farm states. In spite of the lower prices, the outpouring of crops continued, and the CCC was left holding a large part of each year's output. At the end of the 1960 marketing year, it still held an amount of wheat equal to the whole 1960 crop or about two years' consumption. Its corn and wheat stocks were five and eight times what they had been in 1952. A similar pile-up of cotton had been stopped by a drastic and expensive export program.

H. *Direct Subsidies and Two Price Systems*

Since then, the Department of Agriculture has induced substantial restrictions of acreage planted in the basic crops by reducing market prices and by making large direct payments to farmers who participated in its programs.

By 1971, such programs were in operation in feed grains, wheat, and cotton. Figure 2-24 illustrates the 1971 feed grain program for a corn producer with a 100 acre feed grain base.[18] If the government had supported corn prices at $1.35 and left him to his own devices, he would have planted 110 acres and embarrassed the CCC. Even if it set a price of $1.05, he would have planted 100 acres and caused some embarrassment—and his congressman might have had a hard time explaining the low farm incomes at the next election. Instead, the government offered him a subsidy of 30¢/bushel on the estimated yield of his first 50 acres plus a support price of $1.05 on all the corn grown, on condition that he plant only 80 acres altogether. Alternatively, he can plant all the corn he wants (apparently 100 acres) and feed it or sell it at an open market price near the support level. If he participates, he receives a subsidy represented by the area marked "A" in Figure 2-24. If not, he will receive the proceeds from another 20 acres of corn, but that will not all be profit. Subtracting the marginal cost of working the extra 20 acres, he

---

[18] His feed grain base was set by a county committee. It is generally equal to the acreage devoted to corn, oats, barley, or sorghum in 1959 and 1960. It is less than the total usable acreage on the farm, since some land was already diverted in 1959 and 1960. The non-base acreage could be planted in uncontrolled crops such as hay or soybeans in the 1960's, and since 1970 it has been available for any crop provided other rules are met.

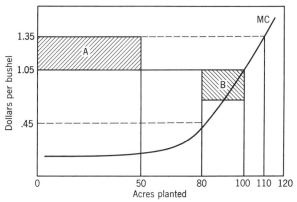

Figure 2-24

might have additional net income of "B" from raising the extra corn. If the subsidy "A" is greater than the profit "B," he will gain by signing up. The government can change the subsidy rate until enough farmers participate.

Since 1970 a farmer has been free to shift among crops provided that a specified percentage of his base is put in "set aside" (left unplanted). The farmer in Figure 2-24, after idling 20 acres, can plant the rest of his farm in feed grains, wheat, soybeans, or hay, and the Department of Agriculture will still pay him 30¢ per bushel on the estimated corn yield on his 50 acres. This way the supply of individual crops can adjust to changing market conditions, but the supply of all crops on participating farms is still controlled.

In addition to making acreage controls effective—even though expensive—this approach makes the disposal of accumulated surpluses easier. The market prices of export crops, such as wheat and cotton, have been brought down to levels within shouting distance of international prices. At the same time, the low price of wheat has made it profitable to feed about a fifth of our wheat to livestock, instead of shipping it all to market. In 1965, Congress finally even saw fit to reduce the price of cotton that is sold to domestic textile mills to about what foreign mills pay for it. This put the United States cotton textile industry in a better position to compete with foreign mills and with synthetic fibers. The one price adjustment at which Congress has boggled, however, is a reduction in the price that American consumers pay for bread. Wheat sold for domestic use still has a minimum price of $2 (compared with $1.25 export price) because the millers must buy a 75¢ certificate before they can market the flour from a bushel of wheat domestically. This way Congress "saved the taxpayers money."

I. Other Programs

The feed grains, cotton, and wheat programs are just the largest of a bewildering variety of agricultural price programs. Rice, tobacco, and peanuts are also "basics" and as such have had acreage allotments and loan programs since the 1930's. Wool and sugar prices are maintained partly by tariffs, partly by direct subsidies that bring them up to prescribed levels regardless of world prices, and, in the case of sugar, by both import and production quotas. The Agriculture Department may support the price of almost any farm product and has supported those of most nonperishables, including almonds, beans, turpentine, and tung oil.

In most areas fluid milk for human consumption sells under Department of Agriculture marketing orders that specify high prices. Output in excess of fluid milk sales goes to manufacturers at lower prices supported by government purchases of butter, cheese, and powdered milk. Farmers receive a single "blend" price that depends on the average mix of fluid and manufacturers' milk sold in their localities. The high prices set under the marketing orders induce high milk production near the cities and in the South, where most output is sold as fluid milk. This reduces fluid-milk sales in more distant dairy areas. As a result, blend prices are low, and milk production is discouraged in the natural dairy regions such as Minnesota, Wisconsin, and upstate New York. Marketing orders exist for many fruits, nuts, and vegetables as well as for milk.

There are no direct price supports for meat, poultry, eggs and much perishable produce—items accounting for about half of farm sales. The government has spent some funds in diverting such products from their usual customers. They have been exported, contributed to welfare and school lunch programs, and diverted to new manufacturing uses. The essential point was to keep the goods away from anyone willing to buy them. It would not improve prices to reduce demand and supply equally.

Until the mid-1960's, these diversion programs were very small compared with the price-support programs, but in recent years they have grown in response to foreign-aid needs and as part of our efforts to assure adequate diets for low-income children. By 1968 some $1.6 billion a year was going in various farm export programs to low-income countries and another billion was distributed in food stamps, school lunches, and the like. It seems doubtful whether these programs would be abandoned even if the possibility of farm surpluses were fully removed. They are no longer primarily farm-price programs.

J. Price Programs and Instability

A case was made earlier for control of prices to deal with instability. Forward price guarantees to improve farmers' planning, an ever-normal granary to offset crop fluctuations, and disaster insurance against a major depression all makes sense to many people. How has American farm policy performed in regard to these proposals?

The support prices have amounted to forward prices. The Secretary of Agriculture must announce support prices in advance of each crop year and keep that price throughout the season. However, the price support program has not eliminated the hog and cattle cycles because price supports do not apply to livestock. For years, the loan rates were far above any plausible estimate of equilibrium price but, under the new wheat, cotton, and feed grains program, there is an attempt to set them near equilibrium levels. These loan rates, which apply to the marginal output of the covered products, may now be used to guide farmers as to how much of particular crops to grow. In view of the subsidies in addition to the supports, however, farmers will still receive doubtful guidance about whether to stay in farming or not.

The CCC stocks have certainly provided buffers against bad years. They were largely used up twice—during World War II and the Korean War. Our surpluses in the 1950's and early 1960's went far beyond any foreseeable need, however. At their peaks in 1961, CCC stocks of corn and wheat exceeded their pre-World

War II or pre-Korean War peaks by three and four times. Stocks are smaller now. We have shifted to a greater reliance on output controls. These, of course, provide little protection against unexpected shortages.

The acreage control and price support programs began as depression relief measures, although they helped farmers at the expense of urban consumers. The programs were continued into good times, however. Indeed, the support levels of the 1940's and 1950's were much higher than those of the depressed 1930's. We finally introduced direct subsidies under the feed grains and cotton programs of the 1960's, but the incomes of wheat and dairy farmers are still being enhanced at the expense of urban bread and milk consumers. And the acreage controls in all these programs mean "market prices" well above what would prevail without government intervention.

V.   EXCESS CAPACITY

Over most of the four decades of our price-support program, farm incomes remained far below urban incomes. By the late 1960's average farm and nonfarm incomes were finally almost in line, but this was only accomplished under a program in which the government controlled the prices of half our farm output and paid direct and indirect subsidies exceeding a quarter of all farm income.[19]

A. *Productivity Growth*

The main reason for the persistent problem has been the rapid increase in the supply of farm products in the face of only slowly growing demand. Figure 2-25 compares output per man-hour, total farm output, and number of man-hours used in agriculture, all as percentages of the 1947-49 levels. Output per man-hour

---

[19] Subsidies rose from 20% of net income from farming in 1960 to 27% in 1968 (*Statistical Abstract, 1969,* pp. 383-4 and *Agricultural Statistics, 1969,* p. 477). The subsidies did not account for all the farm gain, however. Income from farming per person including subsidies rose by 81% between 1960 and 1968. Excluding subsidies, it rose by 69%. Non-farm disposable income per person rose 48% in the same period.

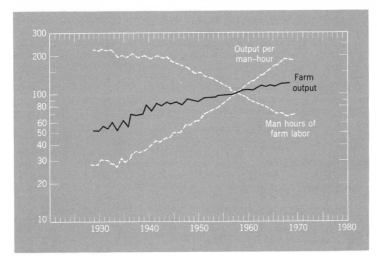

Figure 2-25. Indexes of farm labor, output, and output per man-hour (1957-1959 = 100). *Source. Economic Report of the President, 1970.*

in agriculture now doubles in about 12 years. Productivity has grown faster in farming than in manufacturing in the years since World War II. The total supply of farm products has grown more slowly than this only because so many farmers have left the land in the same years.

The rapid growth in output per man-hour was partly due to such famous changes in farm techniques as hybrid corn and milking machines, but much of the growth could be attributed to conditions in the markets for farm inputs and, in some respects, it goes back to our agricultural price policies.

Farm wage rates in 1968 were 7 times what they had been in 1940, largely as a result of greatly improved nonfarm employment opportunities. The cost of farm real estate was 5 times as high, prices of trucks and tractors had tripled and the price of fertilizer was a little more than 1⅓ times as high in 1968 as in 1940. In other words, the cost of mechanized agriculture has increased much less than the cost of hand agriculture in the past generation. Farmers have responded by changing the combinations of inputs they use. In 1968, agriculture employed a third as much labor as in 1940, approximately the same amount of land

and improvements, more than three times as much machinery, and eight times as much fertilizer.[20]

Capital has entered agriculture as fast as labor has left. The high and assured price and income supports of the last third of a century have surely played a major role in facilitating this change. A good part of the increased farm earnings went into mechanization directly, while the assured markets made it easier for farmers to borrow. The result was more rapid increases in productivity than might have occurred if the old, unstable, and often depressed farm prices had continued.

B. *Growth in Supply and Demand*

The demand for farm products has not grown as fast as the supply, even with the declining number of farmers. Our demand for food increases only slowly as we get richer. On the average, a 10% increase in consumers' incomes leads to an increase in demand for farm products of only 2.5 to 4.5%.[21] There is only so much room in the average American stomach and, although we can switch to more expensive foods as we get richer, we are apt to spend more of our growing incomes on nonfoods.

If the demand for farm products rises less rapidly than total national output, while the ability of the farmers to produce rises more rapidly, the net result will be lower prices. In Figure 2-26, the demand for farm products might grow from D_1 to D_2, while the potential supply would grow in the same time from S_1 to S_2, if no one left agriculture. The result would be a fall in farm prices from P_1 to P_2. If enough farmers went to the city, the supply might wind up at S_3 and the price decline would be avoided,

---

[20] Karl A. Fox, "Commercial Agriculture: Perspectives and Prospects" in *Farming, Farmers, and Markets for Farm Goods,* Committee for Economic Development, 1962, pp. 33-36. (Updated using *Economic Report of the President,* 1969, Tables B81-83.)

[21] Karl Fox, "Factors Affecting Farm Income, Farm Prices, and Food Consumption," *Agricultural Economic Research,* Vol. III, 1951, pp. 71-79; James Tobin, "A Statistical Demand function for Food in the U.S.A." *Journal of the Royal Statistical Society,* Series A, Pt. II, 1950, p. 134; Ser. A, and M. A. Girshick and Trygve Haavelmo, "Statistical Analysis of the Demand for Food," *Econometrica,* Apr. 1947, p. 109. In technical terms, the income elasticity of demand for farm products is 0.25 to 0.45.

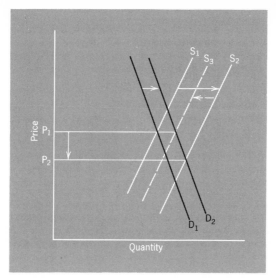

Figure 2-26

but the prospect of profits must be low enough to make large numbers leave the land each year just to keep prices from falling.

C. Foreign Trade and Agriculture

In one important respect, the demand for farm products has actually declined during the twentieth century. Before World War I (in the base period used in parity calculations), the United States was the world's leading exporter of agricultural products, but our position as world supplier of food and fiber has declined drastically since then. In 1910-14, we exported an average of 9 million bales of cotton per year (roughly 60% of the rest of the world's supply), but by the late 1960's this was reduced to 3 million bales per year (about 7% of the rest of the world's supply). Similar though less drastic declines occurred in the exports of other farm products. Figure 2-27 shows farm exports as a percentage of farm sales since 1910. The percentage reached a peak during World War I and then fell off until after World War II. After 1945, the percentage of farm products exported returned to the level of the early 1930's, but no higher. Much of

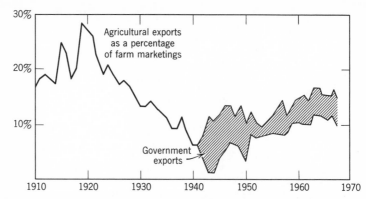

Figure 2-27. *Source.* U.S. Department of Agriculture, Statistical Bulletin No. 179, August 1956, Table 16; Murray Benedict, *Can We Solve the Farm Problem?* Appendix Table 8-3; and *Agricultural Statistics,* 1965, Table 831 and 1969, Tables 677 and 823.

this increase was in the form of government exports—foreign aid grants, sales for foreign currencies for which we had little use, or barter deals in which we received stockpile commodities, often far in excess of our needs. Moreover, a large proportion of the commercial exports that did occur were only possible as a result of export subsidies.

Public policy has played a part in this loss of foreign markets. American tariffs and quotas that restrict foreign sales in the United States reduce foreign demand for American exports in the process. The tariff may help some farmers such as those in sugar and wool production but, since American agriculture is traditionally a net export industry, trade restrictions generally hurt it.[22]

Agricultural price programs have hurt farm exports also. Price supports and crop restrictions in the 1930's raised American agricultural prices above those on world markets. As a result, Amer-

---

[22] In the 1960's, increasingly restrictive European import policies cut into our exports of feed grains, wheat, and poultry products. The European Economic Community has adopted tariffs that adjust to maintain high European prices regardless of world prices. This induces increased European production and gradually squeezes out low-cost American supplies.

ican exports declined and world prices were kept higher than would otherwise have been the case. The relatively high prices encouraged the development of new sources of supply. Much of the gain from the American cotton program went to producers in Egypt and Brazil who could take advantage of the good prices without any limitations on output. Once lost, these foreign markets have proved hard to regain.

D. *Long-Run Adjustments in Capacity and Rents*

In theory, farmers should adjust to the rapid growth in productivity, the slow growth in domestic demand, and the loss of many foreign markets by leaving the industry. All of these changes may produce short-run losses (that is, earnings for farm labor and capital below what they might receive elsewhere) but, in the long run, any exceptional profits or losses are expected to disappear.

In pure competition the price should settle at a point where it just covers the opportunity cost of the land, labor, and capital employed by marginal farms. All higher cost farms—that is, all farms where the land, labor, and capital involved could earn more somewhere else—will be closed and their resources will be diverted to more useful employments. The value of factors employed on lower cost farms should then adjust to reflect the value of what they produce in farming. If a farm is low cost because of the particular fertility or good location of the land involved, that land will be bid up in value until it yields its owner a return on its market value no higher or lower than he can earn on the same sum invested elsewhere. The resulting *rents,* the payment for the land in excess of its opportunity cost, should mean that all operating farms yield the same rate of return. Including the *rents,* in addition to the opportunity cost, a wheat farm ten miles from Kansas City should be no more profitable than one a thousand miles away, and a wool producer in the semidesert of Nevada should earn just as much as a corn-hog farmer on the best land in Iowa.

If prices fall, the farms with the highest opportunity costs should leave farming. It may no longer be profitable to raise wool on the semidesert even if the land is free, and the farm ten miles from Kansas City may thereafter be more profitable as a drive-in movie. But the farms with low opportunity costs will go right on producing. The owners of those farms may see their property decline in value. Some may even go bankrupt. But so long as the land, labor, and capital employed on these farms can still earn more there than in any other employments, the farmers, or the people who foreclose on them, or someone else who buys the farm will still find that the way to make the best of their less rosy situation is to go on producing. Only the rents will be reduced.

E. *Barriers to Long-Run Adjustment*

This idyllic long-run adjustment where there is no excess capacity, where the high cost producers have all left agriculture, and where returns are the same for all farms that remain has been a difficult state to attain in American agriculture. Historically profits have disappeared readily enough, but losses—that is, low farm incomes—lasted for decades. What prevented the expected adjustment for so long? What kept farm incomes at half of city incomes for two generations or more? Part of the answer was that farm incomes were not as low as they seemed to be. A man who likes to be his own boss and dislikes traffic and crowded apartments may get more out of life at $4000 a year on the farm than at $8000 a year in the city. In money he could better himself, but, taking nonmonetary considerations into account, he is making his maximum income on the farm. There is no more reason to raise this man's low income than to raise the rest of ours.

The exodus of people from the farm in the past 40 years shows that farm incomes are not adequate for many, however. Farmers have been adjusting, as competitive theory suggests they would, but the problem is continuously recreated. If supply increases by 5% and demand by 2% every year, people will have to leave the farms in droves just to keep the situation from getting worse.

It is not easy to leave the farm. A worker who leaves a job in the dying buggy-whip industry in the city and moves to the more sprightly spark-plug industry, must punch a new time clock and perhaps learn a new trade if skills are involved, but he goes on living in a similar environment, often even in the same house. Leaving the farm means changing your home and your whole way of life. The upheavals that go with a move from rural or small-town life to the city are a wonderful source of all kinds of social problems according to the sociologists, psychologists, and soap operas. Farmers have moved anyway. As Figure 2-27 shows, there has been some net migration from agriculture in all but four years since 1929.

Moving to the city does not make much sense if there are no jobs there. Figure 2-28 shows that the great exodus occurred in prosperous years, which were often good years for farmers too. In the depression years very few left the farm, and in the really bad years some of the unemployed left the city. Back home on the farm they could at least eat.

VI. ADJUSTMENTS IN SCALE

A. *Farm Size and Efficiency*

Not every farm has been poor during the long, painful periods of agricultural adjustment, and even prosperous years like the late 1960's were still miserable for many farmers. The great differences in income among farmers are largely due to divergences in size and technique.

The 1964 Census of Agriculture collected information about commercial farms of the following six sizes:

Class   I: Large scale—more than $40,000 sales annually.
Class II: Large family farm—$20,000 to $39,999 sales.
Class III: Upper-medium family farm—$10,000 to $19,999.
Class IV: Lower-medium family farm—$5,000 to $9,999.
Class V: Small family farm—$2500 to $4999 sales.
Class VI: Small scale—$50 to $2499 sales, provided that the operator was under 65 and did less than 100 days of work off the farm.

In all but the first class, the operator and his family generally provide the bulk of the labor. Only the commercial farms where farming is clearly a business are included. Part time and partial retirement farms are segregated in the Census.

The 1964 results for dairy farms are shown in Table 2-7. The large-scale, 130-cow farms sold more milk per cow, per man, and

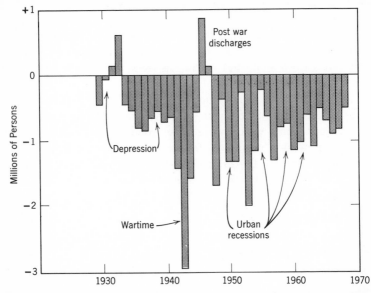

Figure 2-28. Net immigration to (+) or from (−) farms. *Sources. Economic Report of the President, 1960* and *Statistical Abstract of the United States, 1969.*

per dollar invested than the 49-cow farms, and they in turn sold more on each count that did the 31-cow farms.

Column H shows some rough estimates of the cost of $100 gross sales on various farms if family labor is valued at $3000 per man-year and capital yields 5%. The last includes depreciation as well as return on investment, but remember that in addition to the direct return, farm land also appreciated by about 6% during 1964. At these rates, the Class I and II farms made some profit over and above the opportunity cost of their investment, the Class III farms just about broke even on the average, and the smaller farms experienced losses.[23] Their operators paid themselves less than $3000 per year.

---

[23] These losses are exaggerated because of output consumed on the farm and because of the exclusion of the appreciation of farm land. The families that lived on Class IV, V, and VI farms earned more than the farming statistics suggest because many of their members did quite a lot of work off the farm as well.

Table 2-7. Productivity and Costs on 1964 Dairy Farms by Size

A Census Class of Farm	B Average Number of Milk Cows Per Farm	C Number of Farms (Thousands)	D Milk Sold per Cow (Pounds per Year)	E Gross Sales Per Man-Year (Dollars)	F Total Investment per $100 of Gross Sales (Dollars)	G Purchased Inputs per $100 of Gross Sales (Dollars)	H Estimated Cost of $100 of Gross Sales (Dollars)
I	130	15.4	10,250	20,000	345	54.5	78
II	49	53.2	9,590	14,500	407	42.9	84
III	31	117.3	8,463	10,450	450	38.9	97
IV	20	104.0	7,050	6,100	531	38.0	126
V	13	59.3	5,350	3,345	670	43.4	183
VI	7	17.7	3,778	1,402	1078	55.2	346
All	31	367.0	8,610	10,050	438	44.1	99

Source. Data derived from *Census of Agriculture, 1964,* Vol. II, Ch. 10, Table 16. Man-years estimated on basis of hours worked in previous week. Investment based on reported value of farm real estate plus 30% for equipment plus estimated value of reported livestock. Purchased inputs include feed, seed, livestock, fertilizer, machine hire, and hired labor reported in the Census. Estimated cost per $100 of sales was derived by multiplying estimated man-years of family labor (not shown) by $3000 and estimated investment by 5%, and adding the two products to the total reported expenditure on purchase inputs.

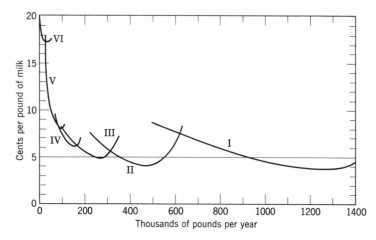

Figure 2-29. Approximate average costs of U. S. dairy farms by size, 1964.

The short-run cost curves for the average farms in each of the six classes from Table 2-7 are plotted in Figure 2-29 on the assumption that the price of milk is 5¢ a pound and that each farm is operating at its most profitable level. If these farms were all as efficient as possible, given their sizes, Figure 2-29 would trace out the long-run average cost curve for 1964 dairy farms. In fact, minimum possible costs in each size class are undoubtedly below the average computed in Table 2-7 because many obsolete or ill-run farms were included in the Census from which Table 2-7 was derived. The true long-run average cost curve probably follows the pattern shown in Figure 2-29 but is somewhat lower at each farm size.

The most efficient possible 7-cow farm has higher costs than do farms with larger herds because some equipment is too expensive to use in such small enterprises; or, if it is installed, it will stand idle for a large part of the time. The farmer himself may not have enough to keep him busy at very useful work and, at any rate, he can produce much more if he has more land and animals to work with. Larger farms show lower costs, as equipment and labor are used more fully and more complex mechanization becomes worthwhile, but costs decline more slowly as scale increases.

It is hard to believe that average cost will go on declining with greater size indefinitely. A 5000-cow herd would probably be too complex an operation to control efficiently under normal conditions. We do have a few dairy farms with herds in the thousands, mostly on the edges of cities such as Los Angeles and Miami. These farms buy their feed and most of their cows and limit themselves to the relatively simple process of putting grain into and taking milk out of mature cows. The economies of scale in the more complex business of raising feed crops, maintaining pasture, and building herds seem not to extend much beyond the 100-cow herd.

The pattern of costs in Figure 2-29 applies in most types of agriculture. The 1964 sales per man-year and per dollar invested are higher on Class I and II farms than on smaller farms in every type of farming. However, in most lines, there is probably a maximum size beyond which administrative problems made it difficult to gain any lower costs by expanding.

What was most efficient in 1964 may not be so in 1980. The best methods of agriculture are changing all the time. In the days before milking machines, a man could not milk more than 10 or 15 cows per day so that larger scale dairies required many hired hands. With mechanization and the simultaneous rise in labor cost, the smaller farms have become more expensive to operate relative to the large ones. A comparison of dairy costs from the 1954 and 1964 Censuses shows higher costs per $100 of sales for farms that would now fall into Classes V and VI, lower costs for those in Classes I, II and III, and little change for those in Class IV. Similar changes have been underway in most lines of farming.

Farm sizes have adjusted upward as a result. The number of farms that would now count as Class IV, V, and VI has dropped rapidly—from 4.2 million in 1954 to 2.2 million in 1964. At the same time, the number of Class I, II, and III farms have almost doubled—from 583,000 in 1954 to 869,000 in 1964. For all of agriculture, these larger farms' sales rose from 59% to 82% of all farm sales in the same ten years.[24] By 1964, more than half of all output in some lines came from Class I farms. This was true of cotton, sugar, fruit, vegetables, livestock ranching, and poultry. In the greater part of agriculture, however, large family farms are still the predominant source of output, but such farms now sell as much as the large-scale farms with mainly hired labor did in 1954.

B.   *Adjustments in Scale in Practice*

In spite of the rapid adjustment, a large proportion of the farms in the country are still in the smaller classes. These inefficiently organized farms have to compete with the larger ones. Prices tend to fall to a level that leave the Class I and II farms profitable, but make the owners of Class IV, V, and VI farms miserable.

Farm property values have risen in spite of relatively low farm prices partly for the same reason. An acre of land on a 400-acre Iowa farm today adds much more to production than it would as part of three or four smaller farms on the same property. With improved seed and increased capital and fertilizer, it produces much more now than it could a few years ago. As a result, the relatively large farmers and those trying to put together large farms are willing to pay an ever increasing price for farm land even when farm-product prices do not rise. The smaller, less efficient farms that continue in production find their land costs rising as well as their prices falling.

In theory, in pure competition the low-cost producers should force the high-cost firms out of production. Profit prospects would result in an increase in Class I and Class II farms until prices fell so far that they just covered the costs of such farms. The Class IV, V, and VI farms would then be forced out of business.

---

[24] Data on numbers and sales of farms by size are derived from *Census of Agriculture, 1964*, Vol. II, Ch. 6, p. 615 and total farm sales from *Agricultural Statistics, 1967*. The 1964 size class limits were used. The growth in numbers of large farms is not due to rising prices. Average prices received by farmers *fell* by about 3% from 1954 to 1964.

In practice, many inefficient, small farms persist for years. Partly, this is due to the old problems of constant change and immobility. Farms that were up to date a few years ago are obsolete today.[25] The need for larger farms means fewer farmers, and, as we have seen, it is not easy to pull up roots and move to the city.

To some extent, the problem of inefficient farms is traceable to inadequate sources of capital. An efficient farm may involve an investment of $100,000 or more, and many farmers are simply unable to raise that kind of money. They recognize that they would be better off with more land, but they do not have the funds themselves, and lenders understandably put limits on the amount of money they will lend to a small enterprise, especially in such an uncertain business as agriculture. Capital is typically rationed to borrowers in proportion to their equity and the stability of their earnings. On both grounds, millions of farmers are limited to farms that are too small and inadequately equipped.

The adjustments in farm size that have occurred have contributed to other social problems just as serious as the farm problem ever was. Many of the small farms that disappeared in the 1950's and 1960's were operated by share-cropping tenants from southern cotton areas. They had to leave the land when its owner shifted to large scale, mechanized farming, but in many cases they had no place to go. The problem of Negro unemployment, poverty, and unrest in northern cities and in many small towns throughout the South is, in part, a problem of rapid change in the techniques and scale in southern agriculture. Where small farmers own their land, the shift to the city will only occur if the farmer thinks he will be better off there. Where the farmer is a tenant, the cost of mobility will not automatically

---

[25] Improving techniques are not the only reason for rising farmland values. As the cities pushed out into the countryside in the postwar years, some farmland values went up because of the high price of urban real estate. For instance, the short-run cost example given on pages 27-36 was originally worked out (in 1959) using data for the 1940's and 1950's and was meant to represent a large family farm. By 1964 it was a small Class III farm. It will probably have been "driven out of business" by the next edition of this book.

be considered in deciding about the method and scale of agriculture.

VII. GOVERNMENT POLICY AND LONG-RUN ADJUSTMENTS

Unregulated private enterprise may theoretically lead to "low-cost" methods of production without any overcapacity or undercapacity in the long-run, but with immobility, limited alternatives in the city, and capital rationing, these "low costs" may be socially undesirable and the long run may be very long in coming. If the market place, left to its own devices, yields less than ideal results, what government policies will improve the situation?

A. *Price Supports Once More*

The price support and crop control program is certainly of limited value in dealing with low farm incomes and farm poverty. At best it is a palliative, providing higher incomes by subsidy or protection without dealing with the cause of the poverty. It is like aspirin, which reduces the unpleasant symptoms of a disease but does not cure it. Aspirin may be a good idea for an occasional headache that lasts only a short time, but it is better to clear up the basic cause of a longer term disease.

The price support program is not even a very good palliative for farm poverty. It does very little about the really low income farmers. Programs that raise farm prices help farmers in proportion to the amounts they sell. The large farms reap most of the benefits. The really poor of agriculture, who have very little to sell, do not gain much from price supports.

Price supports intensify the basic farm problem to some extent. By keeping prices and incomes from falling they reduce the pressure on farmers to leave agriculture. By attracting too much capital into agriculture, they have increased the surpluses. The subsidy program introduced in the 1960's may have made short-run farm decisions more rational, but it did not greatly change the long-run effect of farm policy. A farmer still receives more for his labor and capital than he would in an unregulated market.   .

B. *Farm Education and Research*

If the price and subsidy programs provide only temporary solutions to long-run problems, what alternative is there? One important area of action is education.

We have had publicly supported agricultural education and research since the Morrill Act of 1862 which made land grants to the states to establish agricultural colleges. The Federal Government has made annual grants to the states for agricultural experimental stations since 1887 and has done important research of its own as well. Since 1914, there has been a national extension service to get the new techniques to the farmer.

These programs have clearly done much to increase farm productivity and, thus, to lower prices. This has benefitted the consumer as well as the farmer, but has it helped on the farm income problem? The recurring surpluses are partly due to the new techniques. Moreover, the services of the land grant colleges and the county extension agents have been used primarily by the better farmers and have intensified the pressure on the poorer ones if anything. Efforts have been made to reach the small farmers, but their effect is necessarily limited. Many of the techniques of modern agriculture require more formal education and more capital than most small farmers have.

What many of the poor of agriculture need is training for *nonfarm* employment. Lack of education has long been a major impediment to mobility for farmers and farmers' sons. The low income areas, where the need for mobility is greatest, have generally had the poorest schools. The average farm boy spends less time in school than the city boy in every part of the country, but the situation is much worse for the depressed agricultural regions. The education that is available is often inappropriate. The only vocational training available is likely to be in agriculture or in local trades that are typically overcrowded with people who left agriculture a few years earlier. Students in farm high schools need more courses in shorthand or drafting and fewer in agriculture and home economics. The Elementary and Secondary Education Act of 1965, has provided federal funds for low income area schools. While some observers have expressed doubts about how much money reached the schools in poor districts of large cities, most agree that the program has resulted in a net transfer to schools in low income rural areas. This program should improve the possibilities for movement out of overcrowded and obsolete forms of agriculture in the future.

C. Farm Credit

The problem of credit for farmers has been a recurrent subject of public policy. Since the first years of the country, reformers have been going to Washington from farm districts to get easier money for farmers.[26]

Many special government farm credit institutions developed in this country. Twelve Federal Land Banks were established in 1916 and 12 Intermediate Credit Banks in 1923. These were combined with several new agencies in 1933 to form the Farm Credit Administration (FCA). One of the new agencies saved thousands of farms from foreclosure during the Depression by purchasing and refinancing farm mortgages. The FCA programs generally offered lower interest rates and longer repayment periods and introduced amortized loans. Similar terms have been widely adopted by commercial lenders since then. The FCA programs are run on a regular business basis. Loans go to good credit risks, so the programs primarily benefit the large, progressive farms.

Loans to farmers who are not eligible for conventional credit on regular terms have been made by the Farmers Home Administration (FHA)[27] since 1946. It makes operating loans to finance livestock, equipment, and crops, and farm-ownership loans to finance farm purchase or expansion by small farmers. Supervision of these loans is thorough and often involves supervision of farm methods, so the FHA supplies education as well as credit. FHA also makes or insures loans for rural (not necessarily farm)

---

[26] Much of the agitation in the nineteenth century was concerned with price levels as much as with direct credit for farmers, though both was considerations in the western opposition to the Banks of the United States in the early part of the century and to the gold standard during the greenback and silver eras. The midwestern farmer built up a strong distrust of "Wall Street" partly because it was the banker who seemed to be his main obstacle to progress and efficiency. There were wonderful opportunities almost within his grasp but for the eastern bankers.

[27] Not to be confused with the Federal Housing Administration, also FHA.

housing and for water, sewer, or recreational investments by rural groups where conventional credit is not available, and it is responsible for emergency loans to farms of all sizes. The FHA program is much smaller than the credit facilities for substantial farmers. At the end of 1968, the FCA had $9.4 billion in loans outstanding, and the commercial banks and insurance companies had another $18.7 billion of farm loans. On the same date, FHA had $2.1 billion outstanding, and part of this was in disaster or rural community loans in which large farms participated.[28]

The economic effect of these credit programs is mixed. Bringing farm credit terms closer to those of other businesses should improve the efficiency with which capital is allocated among industries. Perhaps too much capital has gone into agriculture, but, if so, it has been because the better access to credit coincided with high prices and income supports. The low interest disaster loans, while politically popular, involve more questionable economics. They sometimes subsidize farms in flood or drought areas that might better be returned to grass or forest. The relatively small scale of the FHA programs is to be expected. Only a limited number of the low income farmers should stay in farming. For a majority of them, financial help in developing non-farm sources of income is more appropriate. The FHA now makes economic opportunity loans of up to $2500 per low-income farm family which are often for such purposes. A good case can be made for credit to such families to finance education in urban high schools and vocational schools.

D. *Farm Adjustments and Economic Activity*

Farm adjustment requires, above all else, opportunities for employment in the city. Urban jobs must absorb all the net increase in rural populations plus the net outflow. Solving the problem of small and inefficient farms also requires urban prosperity. The way to have larger farms is for some farmers to buy the others out, and the others must have a place to go. The South's industrialization since World War II has provided many new employment opportunities and has been an important factor in the declining number of inefficiently small farms.

---

[28] *Agricultural Statistics, 1969,* pp. 499 and 500.

Urban prosperity will not be enough in the case of the displaced sharecropper, however. Little can be said for protecting his old job—it was one of the worst jobs in our society—but the role of unemployed urban slum dweller is not much as an alternative. His skills are those of a specialized and obsolete type of agriculture that are of little value in the city. He is often illiterate, and he faces overt or covert discrimination in many aspects of his urban life. A great deal of education and perhaps some initial favoritism will have to accompany urban full employment if he is to live a useful life off the farm in this generation.

E. *Permanent Land Retirement*

We have emphasized labor mobility, but land is even more committed to agriculture. Some people have proposed that the government buy or lease farm land in order to withdraw it from production.[29] The crop restriction schemes of the 1930's, the "soil bank" of the 1950's, and the present acreage diversion programs all paid farmers to withdraw parts of their land or to put it into "soil-conserving crops." These payments supplemented farm incomes and sometimes reduced the output of basic crops, but they left most farms intact. Farmers stayed in agriculture and let the payments and the output from the remaining land make up for the acreage retired. If the government purchased or leased whole farms instead of parts of them, it would be more likely to encourage the permanent withdrawal of labor and capital—as well as land—from farming.

Such proposals have been coolly received by farm district merchants and congressmen who seem unenthused about having their constituents leave. Some disinterested observers were also worried that the government would bid up farm land prices even faster, thus making the adjustment to efficient scales harder.

A small but controversial amount of "soil bank" money went into permanent land retirement in the late 1950's. In the mid-1960's, a "cropland adjustment program" came into existence.

---

[29] Committee for Economic Development (CED), *Toward A Realistic Farm Program*, 1957, and CED, *An Adaptive Program for Agriculture*, 1962. The latter also called for low market prices and direct subsidies. This was denounced with amazing violence by farm groups when it appeared in 1962, but by 1970 it was well along toward adoption.

The latter pays farmers 40% of estimated support payments for permanently retired acreage and helped to finance the acquisition of farm land for recreational purposes by local governments. Such long-term land-adjustment programs can help solve the basic problem, but they simply do not sell politically.

F. Something May Turn Up

American farm programs pursued to date have not really offered much in the way of a permanent solution to the farm problem, but by the late 1960's it seemed to be disappearing anyway.

The flow of labor off the farm has proceeded at a spectacular rate. If it continues at the same levels for another decade there will be hardly any farmers left. The reapportionment of state legislatures under court pressure in the 1960's seems to have eliminated much of the political power of farm groups making such concepts as parity less sacred. There is still a serious problem of farm poverty, but a portion of this was transformed, though not solved, by the migration of some of the poor to the cities. Although no substantial farm land retirement program ever got off the ground, we are diverting increasing amounts to nonfarm uses, even including some belated attempts to save recreational space for the population of growing cities. It seems altogether possible that with urban populations continuing to grow and the farm population still declining, agriculture may before too long become an industry that attracts entrants—something that has not been true since the closing of the frontier.

VIII. SUMMARY

Unstable prices and incomes are the natural result of very inelastic demand, high fixed costs, and large year-to-year changes in market conditions owing to weather, shifts between crops, and general business fluctuations. Low farm incomes and inefficient farmers are consistent with competition if mobility is difficult and credit is rationed, especially in a setting of rapidly improving techniques and slowly growing demand.

A plausible case can be made for government intervention to even out the extreme fluctuations in farm incomes and prices and to improve the farmer's adjustment to long-term changes in market conditions and techniques. However, present-day policy provides only a partial solution to instability and practically none for poverty and inefficiency. Price supports do little for perishables such as meats, and are of only minor assistance to the inefficient small farmers who sells little. Most government expenditures for farm credit and for education and research have also been on programs helpful primarily to the more substantial farmers. They have probably intensified the problems of the less efficient farmer, if anything, although the general public certainly gains from a more efficient farm economy. Farm poverty has been reduced in recent years, but more because of urban prosperity, especially in the South, than because of the government's policy.

To deal with agricultural instability, economists have proposed forward prices at realistic levels, a true ever-normal granary, and emergency payments in time of depression. The direct subsidy programs of the 1960's moved in these directions. To deal with poverty and inefficiency, some economists would propose a permanent acreage reserve involving the elimination of whole farms as well as credit and education programs that emphasize nonagricultural options. These programs taken together leave the government with a substantial role to play in farming but let market prices eliminate shortages and surpluses and direct farm output.

Many oppose some or all of these plans and advocate a more complete withdrawal of government from farm markets. Others would retain more of the present programs. Either policy may work without impossible hardship for farmers or expense for the government in view of our rapidly growing population and incomes. The most important farm policy is one of maintaining general prosperity.

IX. FURTHER READINGS

Agricultural economics is a whole discipline in itself. *The Journal of Agricultural Economics* is a regular professional journal devoted almost exclusively to the subject. New contributions to the field are likely to appear there. There are a large number of basic textbooks on the subject. Two good ones are J. P. Doll,

L. J. Rhodes, and J. G. West, *Economics of Agricultural Production, Markets, and Policy*, Irwin, 1968; and C. E. Bishop and W. D. Toussaint, *Introduction to Agricultural Economic Analysis*, Wiley, 1958. On a more advanced level, J. D. Black, M. Clawson, S. R. Sayre, and W. W. Wilcox, *Farm Management*, Macmillan, 1947, develops cost examples for various types of farms in detail, and Earl O. Heady, *Economics of Agricultural Production and Resource Use*, Prentice-Hall, 1952, is a good intermediate theory book with many applications of analysis to agriculture. The classic on empirical estimates of elasticity is Henry Schultz, *The Theory and Measurement of Demand*, University of Chicago Press, 1938. A good textbook-level discussion containing many recent examples from agriculture is to be found in Fredrick V. Waugh, *Demand and Price Analysis*, U. S. Department of Agriculture, Technical Bulletin 1316 (GPO, 1964). There is an almost limitless supply of material on the agricultural economy from the Department of Agriculture and the Bureau of the Census.

On agricultural policy: J. D. Black, *Parity, Parity, Parity*, Harvard Committee on the Social Sciences, 1943, gives an interesting history of the origin of American farm policy. D. G. Johnson, *Forward Prices for Agriculture*, University of Chicago, 1947, and *Trade and Agriculture: A Study of Inconsistent Policies*, Wiley, 1950, contain careful criticisms of American policies and many of the proposals for change discussed in Chapter 2. *Farming, Farmers and Markets for Farm Goods* (Committee for Economic Development, 1962) contains excellent and refreshing studies on the character of modern commercial agriculture by Karl Fox, on the sources and solutions for farm poverty by Vernon Ruttan, and on the prospects for domestic and foreign markets for farm products by Lawrence Witt. They constitute a background paper for *An Adaptive Program for Agriculture* (CED, 1962), the once controversial proposal for farm policy which resembles the policies adopted in the mid-1960's in so many respects. Don Paarlberg's *American Farm Policy* (Wiley, 1964) and W. Cochrane, *City Man's Guide to the Farm Problem* McGraw-Hill, 1966 are two lively discussions of farm policy.

3

Monopoly and Regulation—Electric Power

Pure monopoly, where there is only one seller in some market, is at least as rare as pure competition. Most real-life industries fall somewhere between the two. Both are worth studying, however, because they provide means of analyzing and evaluating the many industries that show elements of both monopoly and competition. Moreover, while only a small number of industries even approach pure monopoly, they have been subject to unusual amounts of government control and public debate.

There are a few unregulated monopolies or near monopolies in the United States. American Metal Climax controls most of the world's molybdenum in one mountain in Colorado. IBM makes 90% of our tabulating equipment (and about 70% of our computers). General Motors is almost that strong in the bus and locomotive fields, and Xerox holds a similar position in copying equipment. And a large percentage of American cities have only one newspaper publisher. Earlier in the century the list would have been longer. Monopoly or near monopoly once existed in aluminum, cigarettes, synthetic fibers, tin cans, and petroleum refining, but the development of substitutes, the growth of international trade, the appearance of new sellers, and direct government intervention have resulted in at least a few rivals for each of these erstwhile monopolists.

Most of the pure monopolies in the United States today are public utilities, such as the firms that supply local electric power, telephone, gas, or water services. Monopoly is commonly required by law in these cases. Instead of relying on competition or potential competition to produce private decisions in the public interest, public officials try to order businessmen in these industries to do the right thing. Since this is a completely different tack from that followed by American governments in most fields, the peculiarities of these industries and the problems involved in this approach to business warrant some special study.

Altogether, about 4% of the national product accrues in these regulated monopolies. Another 4% comes from the various transportation industries that are also regulated, although these are often not pure monopolies. To keep the discussion within bounds, this chapter deals mainly with electric power, but we point out some of the differences in other regulated industries, particularly the transport industries, as we go along.

I. UTILITY COSTS AND MONOPOLY

A. *"Natural Monopoly"*

Public utilities, such as electric power, are often described as "natural monopolies" because the long-run pattern of their costs make competition impossible, or at least intolerably inefficient. In most industries, cost per unit declines for a while as scale is increased as it did in the dairy farms illustrated in Figure 2-29, but usually producers can attain most of the economies of large scale with plants that are quite small compared with the market. There would be room in the United States for 80-100,000 dairy farms, about 300 cotton textile mills, 100 petroleum refineries, and even 15 or 20 aluminum producers each with plants that were large enough to attain minimum average costs.

In natural monopolies, on the other hand, producers attain lower average costs with larger scale out to the limits set by demand. This makes competition costly because the existence of two or more firms implies higher average costs. Competition would also be temporary, since any firm that got ahead would have lower costs than its rivals and would ultimately drive them out.

B. *Economies of Scale in Electric Power*

Electric power involves three major processes: (1) production, which accounts for about 50% of costs; (2) transmission, with about 13%; and (3) distribution and sales, with about 37%.[1] Cost patterns vary from stage to stage.

The economies of scale in distribution seem obvious to everyone. The presence of two or more sets of poles, wires, transformers, and meter readers in a neighborhood would almost always imply so much unnecessary capacity that almost all observers accept the need for monopoly in the "retailing" of electricity. This does not mean that distribution utilities need large total sales to be efficient. Actually, distribution costs can be quite low even in small communities. Within a given geographical area, however, unit costs decline continuously as sales increase. Similar economies impose monopolies on the local supply of gas, water, sewer, and telephone services, since these industries also have tentacles extending into every part of the city.

Transmission from the power plant to the consuming centers also involves very large economies of scale. When transmission capacity over a given distance is doubled, investment in transmission lines increases by only about 2/3;[2] thus, the larger the capacity, the better if there is enough power to transmit and enough customers to use it. In the more common case with many power sources and many consuming centers, what seems to be developing is a whole grid of transmission lines which the generating plants can supply and the distribution systems can tap. The optimum transmission system involves only one such grid in a region, though the various lines that make it up may be owned by different firms.

There are also economies of large scale in generation, but they do reach a limit. Some 83% of the power generated in the United States today comes from thermal plants that convert heat from coal, oil, gas, or nuclear reactors into power, and the percentage

---

[1] Derived from Federal Power Commission, *Statistics of Privately Owned Electric Utilities in the United States, 1968,* Tables 11, 17, and 20. Administration and general expense and assets were excluded as unallocable. Depreciation, taxes, interest, and return on equity came to $9.1 billion or 13% of the $70 billion of electric utility plant in use in 1968, so total costs were derived by adding 13% of electric utility plant in use to the operating and maintenance expense.

[2] Estimated on the basis of Federal Power Commission, *National Power Survey,* 1964, Figure 84, p. 15.

is rising. Both fuel used per kilowatt hour and investment per kilowatt decline sharply and continuously out to the limits set by the equipment and materials available as the size of such plants increases. Most of the boiler-generator units that went into operation in the late 1960's had capacities in excess of 300 megawatts[3]—one of them could supply a metropolitan area the size of Duluth-Superior. These were ten or fifteen times the optimal scale of a unit in the 1930's. The units installed in the early 1970's will be much larger. In 1968 the Federal Power Commission (hereafter called FPC) listed 114 units planned or under construction that had projected capacities of 500 megawatts or more—55 had a capacity of 750 megawatts or more.[4] A 750-megawatt unit would be large enough to supply the whole state of Nebraska or a metropolitan area the size of Denver. Power plants typically include more than one such unit, and utility companies that attempt to be self-sufficient must have a number of power sources, so a self-sufficient power company will need perhaps 4000 generating capacity to be efficient. This would make it larger than all but our dozen largest utility systems.

While there is sufficient demand for only a few efficient generating plants in most localities, total demand in the country exceeds the capacity of several hundred units of the largest scales now contemplated.

C. *Load Factors, Fixed Costs, and More Economies of Scale*

Large power systems enjoy other economies besides the technical gains from big boilers and generators. Perhaps their main advantage is their ability to run their plants nearer to capacity.

Utilities supply a service that cannot be stored and must be

---

[3] A megawatt (mw) is 1000 kilowatts (kw) or 1 million watts. All three are measures to capacity—the amount of power needed to operate a piece of equipment (e.g. a 100-watt bulb) or the amount of power a plant can produce (for example, Grand Coulee Dam, with a capacity of 2025 mw). The amount of power actually generated or used can only be measured over time. If a 100-watt bulb were to burn for an hour, it would use 1/10 kilowatt-hours (kwh) and if Grand Coulee were to run full blast for an hour, it would generate 2025 megawatt hours of electricity—enough to light 20,250,000 bulbs for an hour or to light one of them for 2312 years.

[4] FPC, *Steam Electric Plant Construction Cost and Annual Production Expenses, 1968,* pp. xxvi-xxx.

available instantaneously when the customer throws the switch, so they must have the capacity to supply all customers at the time of peak load. This means excess capacity most of the time, because demand is irregular. It is common for a city to use four or five times as much power at 2 p.m. on the hottest day in July as it does at 5 a.m. on April 10. To meet its peak demand, the utility must operate at 20% of capacity at some other times of the day or year.

Operating at less than capacity means high costs per unit because electric companies, like most public utilities, have high fixed costs. Much more of the cost of electricity is in interest, depreciation, and property taxes than for most industries because it requires so much plant for each dollar of sale. Table 3-1 shows

Table 3-1.   Total Assets as Percentages of Annual Sales in Various Industries

Nonutilities	Percent	Utilities	Percent
Motor vehicles and equipment	62	Class A and B electric utilities	430
Textile mill products	62	Natural gas pipelines	459
Primary iron and steel	103	Class I railroads	298
Petroleum refining	134	Telephone (AT & T and principal telephone subsidiaries)	
All manufacturing	74		322

Sources. Federal Trade Commission, *Quarterly Financial Report, United States Manufacturing Corporations*, 1969, and Moody's *Public Utilities* and *Transportation Manuals*, 1969. All figures are for 1967 or 1968.

the total assets of firms in various fields as proportions of their annual sales. While manufacturing usually requires investments of less than a year's revenue, many utilities have assets of three times their annual receipts or more. Many of the labor costs of electric utilities are also fixed. A large part of the maintenance, administration, and accounting expenses must be incurred regardless of the level of output.

Short-run average-cost curves of electric utilities and steel companies are illustrated in Figure 3-1.[5] The two curves are set up

---

[5] Figure 3-1 is drawn to roughly represent typical utility and steel companies, though the capacities, outputs, and average cost levels were arbitrarily chosen to facilitate comparisons. Transmission, distribution, and transport costs are included, as well as production. In 1967, electric utilities

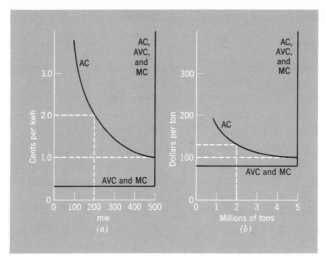

Figure 3-1. (*a*) An electric utility; (*b*) a steel company.

so that minimum average cost can be compared directly. It is assumed that variable cost per unit is the same at all levels of output up to capacity, where it rises abruptly because the firms cannot produce any more regardless of cost. This is a convenient simplification that does not seem to differ drastically from reality in much of industry. At capacity, average variable cost (mainly fuel in electric power and materials, freight and hourly labor in steel) is about a third of average cost in the power plant but almost 80% in the steel mill. Average costs are higher at lower outputs because fixed costs must be spread over less production. When the plant is operating at 40% of capacity, the power

had electric operating revenues of $15.2 billion and fuel costs of $2.5 billion (FPC, *Statistics of Privately Owned Electric Utilities in the U.S.,* 1968, Table 17). The average steam plant operated at 53% of capacity that year (FPC, *Steam Electric Plant Construction Costs and Annual Production Expenses,* 1967, p. xxii). Figure 3-1*a* was drawn so that AVC would be 20% of AC at 50% of capacity. Steel companies reported $16.7 billion in revenues in 1967, of which 7.5 billion went for purchased materials, supplies, and freight, and about 5.0 for hourly labor (6.5 billion for all labor) (American Iron and Steel Institute, *Annual Statistical Report,* 1968 p. 10 and 15). The industry appears to have operated at about 79% of capacity that year (see page 197). Figure 3-1*b* is drawn on the assumption that AVC is 75% of AC when the firm operates at 80% of capacity.

company's average costs are double their minimum level, but the steel mill's average costs are only about 30% above what they are when the mill runs at capacity. Actually, steel mills have fairly high fixed costs for manufacturing firms. The average cost curve for a textile mill would be even flatter than that in Figure 3-1*b*.

The ratio of average demand over the year to peak demand is called the *load factor*. If a utility runs at 240 mw on the average but demand gets up to 400 mw sometime during the year, is has a load factor of 240/400 or 60%. Average cost is less, the higher the load factor, so buyers who use power continuously, that is, those who have load factors approaching 100%, are very desirable customers.

One way to even out production and reduce average cost would be to diversify customers. For instance, imagine three neighboring cities, one primarily residential (city R), one industrial (city I), and one commercial (city C). They might have the demand patterns shown in Table 3-2. If each city had its own

Table 3-2.   Time of Day

City	2 P.M.	5 P.M.	7 P.M.	2 A.M.
R	30	60	100	20
I	100	60	60	40
C	60	100	70	10
Total	190	220	230	70

plant, each would have to have a capacity of 100, making a total of 300 but, since their peaks do not coincide, a single company could supply all three cities with a capacity of only 230. Load factors can often be improved even more by combining areas with different seasonal patterns. Geographically, large systems usually have more diverse demands than small ones, so they can attain higher load factors and correspondingly lower unit costs.

A power system must maintain some excess capacity even in periods of peak load, to allow for unforeseen events. Capacity should exceed peak demand by at least the capacity of the system's largest unit if service is to continue even with an unexpected outage. A large system with a smaller percentage of capacity in any one unit needs less excess capacity on these grounds than does a small system.

Most utilities at times have excess capacity beyond what is needed to cover the largest likely outage, because new capacity comes in lumps. They build plants larger than their immediate needs call for, in order to have the economies of scale later on— like parents who buy pants too long for growing sons. Large systems incur less excess capacity for this reason, because an efficient unit is smaller relative to their total demand than it is in a small system.

D. Holding Companies

Because of the economies of large-scale generation and the high rates of capacity utilization possible in large systems, the power-supply industry has long felt an urge toward consolidation. In the first years of the industry, every town had its own power company, and some cities had several. During the first thirty years of this century, there was a continuing and accelerating merger movement combining these small firms into unified city or regional utilities. This was often accomplished by *holding companies*, which acquired the stock of utilities or the stock of other holding companies that controlled utilities. There were cases in which the center of control was six steps away from the operating companies. In the late 1920's the movement became a race, with rival holding companies bidding recklessly for small utilities. Purchases were sometimes for cash, but the holding companies often simply exchanged their own securities for the stock of the acquired firms. The game was enlivened by big promoters' fees, lots of debt, razzle-dazzle accounting, and large speculative profits for those who got into the right holding companies early. The conglomerate merger wave of the late 1960's repeated many of the same experiences for those who had missed out on the event 40 years earlier, though this time the electric utilities were not involved.

When the Depression came and the incomes of operating firms dropped off, the holding companies saw their receipts (their subsidiaries' dividends) fall drastically. Then the excessive debts of some structures brought them down in collapse, and the public suddenly became aware of holding company abuses. In 1935,

Congress passed the Public Utility Holding Company Act under which holding company structures have since been drastically simplified. Holding companies more than two steps removed from operating firms have been eliminated, each company's holdings have been reduced to an "integrated" system in a contiguous area, and the accounting, service fees, dividends, security issues, and consolidations[6] of utilities and holding companies have become subject to public control. Some of the new firms that were created by the reorganizations in the 1940's have turned out to be among the lowest in cost of American utility systems.

E. *Interconnection and the Sale of Bulk Power*

The economies of large plants and of high load factors may be attained by creating large systems following the holding-company route, but this will mean that a limited number of companies must come to dominate the entire country's power supply, each operating on a largely monopolistic basis within its region. The same economies can be attained with more systems and with possibilities for competition if the utilities buy and sell power among themselves. Most systems are now sufficiently interconnected to facilitate such transactions.

In the short run, with generating capacity given, the utilities of a region can plan output jointly so that power comes from the plants with the lowest short-run marginal cost (mainly fuel cost) regardless of who owns them. This is in the interest of all concerned if the power is sold at a price above the marginal cost of the supplying utility but below the marginal cost in the lowest-cost idle unit of the buying utility. The selling utility then adds more to receipts than to costs by the sale, and the buying utility gets the extra power more cheaply than it could from any of its own plants. Groups of utilities in a number of parts of the country now continuously allocate short-run capacity on this sort of basis. The milk producers in the last chapter turned out to produce about where their estimated marginal feed costs and prices suggest they should, but few of them consciously used marginal

---

[6] The electric-power industry avoided the merger mania of 1966-69 in part because of the requirement that acquisitions be approved by the SEC (Securities and Exchange Commission).

cost to get there. The dispatchers who allocate output among a region's plants and the accountants who work out the compensation for net interutility transfer *do* use marginal concepts quite explicitly.

In the long run, firms with capital or location advantages can install new units of efficient scale and sell blocks of capacity to any other utility connected to the regional grid that may be interested. It would be cheaper to buy pieces of such capacity than to build your own if the buying price is less than your long-run marginal cost in the best plant you could build for yourself. As a result, each addition to capacity in a fully cooperating system should have the lowest costs possible in the system.

In most regions we are far short of such a fully interdependent system of utilities, but are moving in that direction. Such systems can have the advantages of large-scale units, diversity, reduced emergency reserves, and reduced excess capacity when new units go on stream, just as large systems under a single corporate control can enjoy. In the process, the bulk power industry can come much closer to pure competition than has been commonly imagined.

II. FORMS OF REGULATION

A. *Franchises*

Electricity production has had public utility status from its beginning, but regulation has taken several different forms at various times. When the first central station opened in New York City in 1882, local governments were attempting to control public utilities through their *franchises,* special charters which permitted the companies to operate under specified conditions and granted such privileges as the use of streets and the power of eminent domain. The conditions set were not usually very exacting in the first years. Advantageous franchises were offered by public-spirited governments to get power companies into their cities and further their growth.

Later, the franchise became more a matter of control and less of promotion. In franchise renewals or revisions, the city councils often attempted to include better rate and service provisions, but with limited success. The franchise was a poor method of control. Once set, the franchise provisions often could not be changed for long periods. In many cities, the awarding of franchises and the setting of their terms became a matter of wholesale graft. Much of the civic corruption at the turn of the century had to do with public utility franchises.

B. State Public Utility Commissions

One of the main reforms of the "progressive era" was the transfer of public utility regulation to expert supervisory commissions at the state level. Most of the states established public utility commissions in the decade before World War I with power to set rates and regulate service. Most public utility regulation is in the hands of such commissions today. Locally issued franchises still exist, but in most states they have little significance. The commissions have control over electric utilities in 46 of the 50 states.[7]

C. Federal Regulation

The Federal Government has played an important role in the control of electric utilities since 1935.[8] Its participation was necessary for several reasons. The Constitution gave the Federal Government jurisdiction over navigable streams and rivers, and in the eyes of the courts this meant that Congress or its appointees could determine who might develop most of the hydro-

---

[7] The exceptions in 1967 (the most recent tabulation published by the FPC) were Minnesota, Nebraska, South Dakota, and Texas. FPC, *State Commission Jurisdiction and Regulation of Electric and Gas Utilities*, 1967. All Nebraska utilities are publicly owned.

[8] Federal regulation came earlier in some fields. The Interstate Commerce Commission (ICC) was established in 1887 to regulate the railroads, though its powers were very limited until additional legislation was passed in 1906. It also controlled pipelines from 1906 and was given some power over interstate telephone, telegraph, and cable service after 1910. In the 1920's the Federal Government began licensing hydroelectric developments and radio stations, but no rate regulation was involved. After 1935, federal regulation was expanded and reorganized. The ICC was given control over trucking and, later, some inland water carriers; a Federal Communications Commission (FCC) was formed with more power over telephone and telegraph companies than ICC had, and with control over radio and television licenses; and a Civil Aeronautics Board (CAB) was established to regulate rates and services on the airlines.

electric sites. The FPC was formed in 1920 to issue licenses for such development.

With the long-distance transmission of electric power, interstate commerce became involved. The courts ruled that the commissions in neither consuming nor generating states could regulate rates in such cases. To fill this gap, a reorganized FPC was given power over rates and service in interstate commerce beginning in 1935. For similar reasons, it was also given control over the interstate transmission of natural gas beginning in 1938.

Because of the financial excesses of the 1920's and the inability of the state commissions to deal with them, the FPC was also given extensive power over accounting, security issues, and consolidations within its jurisdiction. It was at the same time that the Securities and Exchange Commission (SEC) received the job of simplifying the organization and finances of public utility holding companies.

State commissions still have the main job in regulating electric utilities, but the new federal agencies took the lead in introducing many new methods and policies. The FPC has been more aggressive than many state commissions, and its rules have been stricter on such matters as accounting. It attempts to cooperate with state commissions, though conflicts have arisen at times. For the most part, its orders supplement rather than override those of state agencies.

III. THE GOALS OF PUBLIC UTILITY REGULATION

A. *Monopoly Pricing and Rate Making*

Left to their own devices, at least the local electric companies would have a good deal of monopoly power. The threat of imports or of new competitors that limits the monopoly power of some manufacturers is negligible in the markets where the utilities sell.

In order to analyze the price policy of an unregulated power company, it is convenient to start with the *quite unrealistic* assumption that in the long run, when it can build as little or as much capacity as it wants, the company can produce any amount of power at the same cost per kw-hr. If its peak load were twice

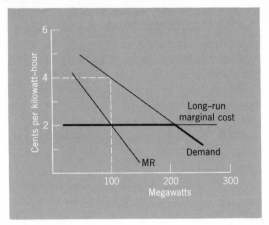

Figure 3-2

as large, it could just install twice as many identical units and produce twice as much power at the same unit costs. The *long-run marginal cost* of electric power would then be just equal to the average cost, because in the long run the extra cost of supplying a bit more power includes the cost of the extra plant as well as the extra fuel.

The position of a monopolist with such a long-run marginal cost curve is shown in Figure 3-2. To make the most profit in this situation, the power company would set a rate of 4¢ per kwh and would build only enough facilities to accommodate the average demand of 100 mw that it can expect at that price. The public would use more power at a lower rate, but left to its own devices, an unregulated power company would not find a rate reduction profitable. It would lose more by cutting price below 4¢ than it could gain from the additional business.

From the consumer's point of view a lower rate with a capacity sufficient to meet the greater demand would be better. The capital, labor, and fuel that go into another kwh cost only 2¢ meaning that they would produce 2¢ worth of turnips or toothpicks in their best alternative uses, but they will produce up to 4¢ worth of power here. We would lose only 2¢ worth of other goods and gain up to 4¢ worth of power for each additional kwh that the company can be persuaded to produce out to 200 mw, but such a transfer of productive resources from other industries to electric power would require rate reductions that would cut into the company's profits. A profit-maximizing utility would not make these reductions on its own.

To eliminate the effect of the utility's monopoly position, the regulator would have to set a price of 2¢ per kwh in this case. At that rate, there would be no monopoly profits for the firm. If it sold to all comers at 2¢, power production would be expanded until the last bit of current produced would cost just as much as someone would pay for it. Then there would be just enough electric power produced compared with other commodities.

The result of this analysis is a bit surprising. Normally one thinks of a price reduction leading to decreased output. Yet here a government-imposed price reduction resulted in new facilities and expanded production. The reason is that with a public utility commission ruling that the rate must be 2¢ no matter what, the heavy horizontal line in Figure 3-2 becomes the effective demand curve of the utility. The company would not be allowed to force the price above 2¢ by keeping the plant at the 100 mw level and, if it is to satisfy its customers' demands, it would have to expand.

Regulators usually try to set rates that will cover costs of production and yield a "fair" return on the company's capital, but in a case like Figure 3-2, where marginal costs are constant and therefore identical with average costs, the commissions' policy and the economists' recommendation could come to about the same thing. Remember that "cost," as the economist uses the word, includes a return on the owner's investment equal to what he can earn anywhere else. The earnings of the utility in Figure 3-2 would be enough to keep it in business if its rate were set at 2¢.

The usual rule of public utility regulation with regard to service is that the firm must stand ready to supply all comers within its regular market area. The company may not be required to send a line ten miles up Wildcat Gulch to the only house up there, but if new customers can be served without excessive loss, the company is bound to do so. In the simple case of Figure 3-2, the commissioners would require the power company to supply everyone who is ready to pay 2¢ per kwh and who can be served at an additional cost of no more than 2¢. Its output would have to expand to the 200 mw level.

B. *Decreasing Costs*

Things are more complicated if the costs of a regulated firm decline as capacity increases, and that is apparently the case with most electric utilities. Table 3-3 shows such a situation. If aver-

Table 3-3.

Average Output per Hour (Kilowatts)	Total Cost per Hour (Dollars)	Average Cost (Cents per Kilowatt-Hour)	Marginal Cost (Cents per Kilowatt-Hour)
100,000	2000	$\dfrac{\$2000}{100{,}000 \text{ kw}} = 2\text{¢}$	$\dfrac{\$280}{20{,}000 \text{ kw}} = 1.4\text{¢}$
120,000	2280	$\dfrac{\$2280}{120{,}000 \text{ kw}} = 1.9\text{¢}$	

age hourly production is 120,000 kw, cost per unit will be less than at 100,000 kw (assuming load factors are the same in both cases) because larger plants have lower costs. As is always the case when the cost per unit declines, the marginal cost turns out to be less than the average cost. If the commission were to set a price equal to the marginal cost in this case, it would leave the utility operating at a loss!

Public utility commissions cannot set rates that impose losses in this way. In the eyes of the law, such rates would amount to confiscation of the company's property. Under the constitutional provisions preventing the government from taking property without "due process of law," the courts have repeatedly ruled that commissions must allow public utility owners a reasonable return on their investments if market conditions permit. A public utility regulator would hardly be prudent to require operation at a loss anyway. Utility companies would be unable to raise new capital or render adequate service if such a situation continued for very long.

A decreasing average cost curve and the marginal cost curve that goes with it are shown in Figure 3-3. If the commission applied its usual standards in this case, it would have to set a rate of 2¢ per kwh, meaning an output of the 100 mw level; but at that rate consumers would be willing to pay considerably more

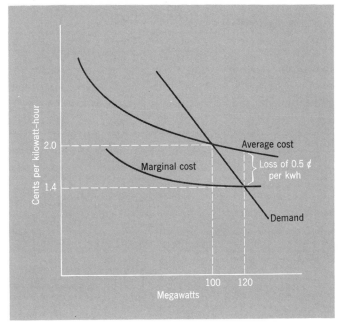

Figure 3-3

than its marginal cost for additional current. Economic theory suggests that the public interest would be better served by a rate of 1.4¢, where the last unit produced cost just as much as it was worth to its buyer, but that would involve the company in a loss of 0.5¢ on every kilowatt-hour sold. To get such a rate, the government would have to pay a subsidy equal to the loss.

By and large, we have not been willing to subsidize public utilities in this way. Indeed, it is more usual to put especially heavy taxes on them. The public utility commissions set prices that give the companies normal returns *after taxes,* so these exactions simply raise rates and discourage service. Whether or not subsidization of public utility rates is feasible, there is a good case for the elimination of special taxes on public utilities at least in situations with continuing economies of scale.[9]

---

[9] There is another criticism that applies to excise taxes in general, including public utility taxes. Such taxes have the general fault that they distort consumer choice and lead people to buy the second best. A good example is

IV. PROBLEMS OF PUBLIC UTILITY REGULATION

It is one thing to decide that utility rates should cover costs plus a reasonable return and quite another to actually set such rates. Competitive markets automatically determine what production costs and normal profits are, and the entry and exit of firms results in prices that just cover these. In the utility field, however, a government agency must somehow find out the appropriate costs, profits and prices. Public utility commissions face a bewildering list of difficulties that no one has to deal with in competitive markets.

A. *Costs*

For one thing, what costs should the rates cover? When economists construct average cost curves like the one in Figure 3-4, and conclude that, at 100 mw, it costs 2¢ per kwh to produce electric power, they are discussing only the lowest possible cost. It is perfectly feasible to produce that much power at 3¢ or 4¢ or 5¢: points A, B, and C in Figure 3-4. The writer feels confident that he personally could contrive to produce electricity at costs as high at $10 or $15 per kwh. Cost curves are drawn as they are because we normally assume that profit-seeking businessmen will use the best methods available. In situations where the public utility commission sets rates that cover costs, however, the pressure to keep costs down may not be very great.

At any rate, some costs need scrutiny. What is there to stop the managers from giving themselves fine salaries and letting the customers foot the bill? How much can the holding company legitimately charge its subsidiaries for supplies and services? Should the utility be allowed to set prices that cover its mistakes?

---

a tax that New England towns used to have on windows. As a result, New Englanders built houses with few windows, but of course they did not pay any less total taxes because the government had to raise just as much money as before. Similarly, a tax on public utilities leads the consumer to buy less electricity. As a result, he is not only out the tax, he also has a darker house just as his New England forebears did. To the extent that electricity is a decreasing cost industry, he also pays higher utility rates in addition to the tax. The tax raises the price, discourages consumption, and, as a result, keeps output at a high cost level.

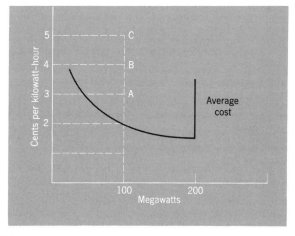

Figure 3-4

Some mistakes may have seemed wise in advance. Yet a competitive market would not bail out a businessman no matter how honest his errors. If every wage increase leads automatically to a rate increase, how can the company be made to bargain effectively with the union? May advertising expenses legitimately be included in the price of power, especially when many of them are intended primarily to improve the company's political position? To be effective, a commission must carefully scrutinize the books of the utility and rule on many such issues before it sets rates.

B. *Accounting*

This is likely to be a difficult job because accounting is a complex art. When the accountant presents a picture of the firm's incomes and property, he must make a large number of more or less arbitrary estimates and, in many cases, there are a variety of recognized ways of making these.

Depreciation is an important example. No one can say with certainty how long a piece of machinery will last or when it will become obsolete. If the company accountants conclude that their machinery has a short life or depreciates rapidly at first and slowly later on, their costs will seem high, at least in the first years, and the company's investment, low. The opposite assumptions yield low costs and large assets. Since depreciation and returns on the investment are a large part of utility costs, it makes a great deal of difference for electric rates how equipment is presumed to depreciate.

Depreciation is just one of a large number of accounting problems. Public utility commissions have found it necessary to specify accounting methods if their regulation is to be workable.

C. External Costs—Pollution Control

Some of the costs of electric-power production do not appear on the books of the utilities at all but fall on society as a whole. Important examples of such *external costs* are the contributions that fossil-fuel plants make to air pollution by their emissions of sulfur and nitrogen oxides and carbon compounds; and the "thermal pollution" from nuclear plants, which is sometimes great enough to seriously threaten local marine life if water is used for cooling. These environmental effects have caused increasing concern in recent years as the tide of smog and water pollution has risen. While most industries produce some external effects, the utilities have come under particular criticism, partly because they account for one of the largest and most rapidly increasing combustion industries, partly because they are located in the large population centers, and partly because they are regulated. The regulators provide a natural focus for complaints about environmental deterioration.

The typical solution to the problem to date has been for the regulators to try to set maximum pollution standards. A number of proposed additions to capacity have been overruled or postponed in the process. The resulting delays helped account for the power shortages that became regular events in such places as New York in 1970.

There can be no doubt that smog and thermal pollution should be taken into consideration, but our present way of dealing with them is crude. Like other regulatory ventures, the control of pollution is more difficult that it appears. Such control can be expensive. How big a cost are we willing to accept for this purpose? How bad is a ton of sulfur dioxide in the air per year compared with an increase in the temperature of the river by 2°? Some would reply that both are bad and that the real solution is to stop expanding power production. If so, who should turn off his air conditioner? And how do we get him to do it? And how do you prevent regulation of pollution from being vitiated by political pressure from the affected industries?

These problems solve themselves when costs are *internal*— for instance, the cost of fuel which the producer has to bear directly. The producer has a direct incentive to minimize fuel costs. The unavoidable part of fuel costs are ultimately included in the price, and the consumer then gets to decide whether an air conditioner is worth the extra fuel cost or not.

One way to make external costs internal is to impose a tax on pollutant emissions. If power plants had to pay $10 for every pound of sulfur oxides emitted, $1 for every pound of nitrogen oxide, possibly 1¢ for every pound of carbon monoxide, and 2¢ for every million BTU of heat diffused in the river, the utility would have an internal reason to reduce these costs and consumers could decide for themselves whether the new air conditioner is worth the extra smog. Of course we would still have to decide what tax rates to change—that is, what smog really costs us. Maybe we really do want to stop expanding the power industry. Then we would have to impose a very high emissions tax. In making such a decision, we would explicitly take into account what the cutback is costing us—something we often do not do when we simply set such stringent standards that no plant can be built and power shortages develop as a result. Emissions taxes are not a panacea, but they are quite feasible. After ignoring the idea for years, the administration finally proposed an emissions tax on sulfur compound emissions in late 1970.

D. *The Rate Base*

In addition to production costs, the commission as a rule allows the utility a "fair" return on its investment. To do so, it must decide how much the company's investment is and what rate of return is "fair."

The firm's investment, properly evaluated for purposes of rate regulation, is known as the *rate base.* There are a variety of possible ways of determining it, and the battle over which method should be used raged violently in the courts and commissions for decades.

One possibility can be ruled out immediately. It will not do to use the market value of the utility's property or of its outstanding securities. The amount that the firm or its securities will sell for depends on what it earns, so any rate could be justified on this basis. If the commission were lax, market values would go up and high rates would seem appropriate. If it were strict, the company would have a lower value to investors, so the low rates would also seem justified.

To determine a reasonable rate base, the commission must put a value on the actual plant and equipment of the company. But what value? Commissions tend to favor the original cost of installing the utility plant. At least it is fairly easy to calculate. The companies argue that their plants are undervalued at prices of 20 years earlier and that the rate base should depend on the cost of reproducing them now.

The standard used by the courts until the 1940's was something called "fair value" which required that *both* original *and* reproduction costs "be given such weight as may be just and right in each case."[10] Moreover, the courts insisted on their power to review the commission rulings in detail. Rate cases took years and, with such vague standards, the commissions were always in danger of being overruled. The net result was a ritual suitable for musical comedy in which an august body of judges, commissioners, engineers, lawyers, and accountants labored to determine a hypothetical value for a utility so that it would not be deprived of its property without due process of law, while the price of its common stock soared. The simple way to avoid all this was for the commission to be relatively lax in its regulation and keep disputes from arising. Then, of course, the stock soared even more.

The weary legal battles over rate-base valuation were largely ended by Supreme Court decisions in the early 1940's.[11] Since then the courts have generally accepted the expert findings of the regulatory commissions and have reviewed only questions that were clearly issues of law or procedure. Finally free to de-

---

[10] Smyth v. Ames, 169 US 546 (1898).
[11] Notably FPC v. Hope Natural Gas Co., 320 US 602 (1944).

cide the valuation issue themselves, most commissions opted for original cost.[12]

E. *Original Cost Versus Reproduction Cost*

The legal and administrative questions about how to evaluate the utilities' plants may be settled, but the economic question is still open. If the criteria used to judge the economic efficiency of other industries can be trusted, the original cost standard is open to criticism.

In *purely competitive* industries, the problem would be solved automatically. The long-run equilibrium price would be one that afforded a normal return to the last firms to enter the industry. The value of their plants would depend on the *current* cost of erecting them. If the original cost of an older plant in a purely competitive industry exceeded the current cost of building the same amount of capacity, the owners of the old plant would show less than normal profits on their books until their plants wore out. If the old plants cost less to build than their current replacements, the owners of the old plants in an expanding industry would show more than normal book profits as long as their plants lasted. No one could compete away their profits even with completely free entry because new firms would have higher dollar costs. In other words, purely competitive prices tend to settle at levels that cover replacement, *not* original costs.

The widespread use of original cost in public utility rate making could result in rates that are *too low* for economic efficiency after a period of rapidly rising plant construction costs. A price for electricity that covers the cost of power plants built in 1965 might be considerably below the long-run marginal cost of power in 1970. The long-run marginal cost in an expanding industry depends on the cost of new plants, not old ones. A price below the long-run marginal cost would encourage consumers to buy too much electricity. They would increase their consumption beyond the point where they are just paying the full cost of the last kilowatt-hour used.

---

[12] FPC, *State Commission Jurisdiction* . . . , op cit. Of 44 reporting commissions, 28 said that they preferred an original cost base, one (Ohio) was required to use reproduction cost by law, and 15 reported that they used "fair value" or "considered all elements."

There are good arguments against using replacement cost, however. As we have seen, decreasing costs, public utility taxes, or ineffective regulation may result in rates that are *more than* long-run marginal costs. To some extent, at least, the tendency for rates to be too high on these counts, and the tendency for them to be too low in time of inflation because of original cost valuation will cancel each other out.

The main argument for original cost is that it makes regulation much easier and, therefore, more effective. Replacement costs would require continuous changes in the accounts of the firms because of changing price levels and changing technology. They would provide much more room for argument in evaluating plant than original costs do. Moreover, replacement costs would probably be an acceptable substitute for original costs only so long as construction costs rose. If rapid improvements in technique resulted in a *reduction* in the cost of a kilowatt of capacity, the commission would probably not be able to reduce its valuation of existing plants. In a competitive market, the owner of an obsolete plant may incur losses as long as his plant lasts, but for a commission to set rates that impose money losses on the utility companies would be taking property without due process of law!

Even in the heyday of "fair value" the utility commissions did not use replacement costs in this sense. They used "reproduction cost," the cost of reproducing the *same* plant at current prices even if the plant was out of date and no one would think of actually reproducing it. There is some plausible economic justification for using replacement costs, but reproduction costs made a mockery of any logic there might have been.

The most common argument presented by the public utilities against original cost valuations had to do with questions of "fairness" rather than economic efficiency. They claimed that their stockholders were being cheated out of some of their property because of the commissions' actions. By using original cost in evaluating the plants, the commissions were maintaining the dollar return to the investors, but in time of inflation when the dollar was decreasing in value, this meant that the stockholders received less in purchasing power than they had when the plants were first built.

A constant dollar income undoubtedly means a declining real income in time of inflation, but whether the public utility commissions have an obligation to make up for inflation with higher rates is open to question. After all, the same thing happened to anyone who bought bonds or mortgages or life insurance during the same period, but few would argue that the government (or the public utilities themselves) should scale up the interest on bonds that have already been sold.[13] People who bought public utility stocks knew they were buying securities that offered stable incomes, just as the buyers of bonds did.

F. Fair Return

Having arrived at some sort of rate base, the commission must next decide what rate of return is reasonable. In view of all the uproar over valuation, the commissions worried surprisingly little about the return. They often selected some convenient figure, such as 6%, and applied it generally year after year.

In recent years, however, an increasing number of commissions have attempted to determine the interest, dividends, and retained earnings necessary to raise the company's capital on current security markets and have set rates that would cover these. In other words, they have attempted to determine the rate of return on the basis of the "cost of capital," just as they cover the cost of labor and of other factors employed. Since the "cost of capital" for utilities depends on what investors can earn on their money elsewhere, it might approximate the "normal return" of pure competition.

From time to time the utilities have predicted that with their rate bases fixed at original cost and with strict regulation of returns they would have difficulty in raising capital in the future. The "cost of capital" approach would automatically solve this problem, however. If new issues could only be sold at higher interest or dividend rates, the commissions would have to allow higher earnings. The "cost of capital" would have risen. There

---

[13] It is often necessary for the government or other borrowers to pay more interest on *new* bonds to make particular issues more attractive during an inflation, but this is a different point. The analogous argument that public utilities need higher yields to attract capital is taken up in the next section.

has been little sign of any drying up of capital supply to the utilities in any case. They have been among the most active issuers of new securities over the whole period since World War II. During the 1960's they accounted for 32% of all new corporate issues, though they had only 15% of nonfinancial corporate assets.[14] They were always able to market their new securities at yields comparable to those of unregulated companies.

G. Rates of Return, Inadequate Service, and Inflated Rate Bases

If the regulatory authorities were to set a "fair return" below the cost of capital, the first effect would probably be to discourage utilities from borrowing rather than to turn off the lenders. Something like this may be a partial explanation of the apparently inadequate investments of many utilities in the late 1960's. Long-term interest rates were rising rapidly. Throughout 1966 and 1967 they were higher than at any time since the early 1920's; in 1968 they reached levels not seen since the 1870's, and by early 1970 new high-grade corporate bonds were being issued at yields close to 9%—rates that can hardly be matched over the entire history of organized corporate bond markets in the United States. Utilities could and did borrow at these rates, but commissions were slow to adjust the "fair return" to reflect the rising cost of capital. As a result, utilities added more to capital costs than to earnings whenever they borrowed to pay for additional capacity. They tended to keep such unprofitable investments to a minimum. It is doubtful whether utility executives consciously decided to leave any demand unsatisfied, but some seem to have pared their margin for error very thin. This is another reason for

---

[14] In the years 1960-1968 the private electric, gas, and water utilities issued $31 billion in new securities for cash, the communications companies (mainly AT&T) issued $14 billion, and all corporations issued $141 billion (*Statistical Abstracts*, 1965, p. 475 and 1969, p. 458), so all utilities taken together accounted for 31.9% of the new issues. In 1965 all these utilities had $127 billion in assets against $1724 billion for all corporations and $839 for nonfinancial corporations (*Statistics of Income*, 1965, Table 2), so utilities account for 7.4% of all corporate assets and 15.2% of nonfinancial corporate assets.

the electric brownouts in 1970 and how it happened that telephone customers in downtown New York sometimes had to wait ten minutes to get a dial tone.

Public-utility-commission rate proceedings always take time, and the commissions might reasonably have been reluctant to let the return on utility investments rise to the unprecedented levels that the cost of capital had reached. It was not obvious that the "fair return" would be allowed to fall again if interest rates were to decline later.

Things can also go wrong if the "fair return" is set too high. If utilities are consistently allowed to earn more than the cost of capital, it will pay them to make investments merely to increase their rate base. Every additional dollar invested would then yield more to the company than it must pay for the additional capital, so that the earnings available to existing stockholders would be increased. Unnecessary investments or high-priced capital goods could enhance the value of the company up to the most profitable price for a monopolist. Some economists think that the utilities accepted the high prices charged by electrical-equipment suppliers during the conspiracies of the 1950's and were reluctant to sue for damages even after the conspiracies had been proven in court because the high-priced equipment had produced a larger rate base and higher returns for them.

Altogether, it is not easy to regulate rates of return so that utilities will have an incentive to give adequate services and at the same time have no incentive to waste capital resources. Neither problem arises in a competitive market or even in an unregulated monopolistic one.

H. *Utility Rates*

Finally, having determined allowable expenses, a valuation of the rate base, and a rate of return, the commission must set a price that will cover these. What prices will yield a company a profit of $15 million a year? The answer obviously depends on the elasticity of demand, something we usually have to guess about. Commissions seldom study demand very carefully. They often act as if the elasticity of demand were 0 so that a 10% decrease in rates would reduce total revenue by 10%.

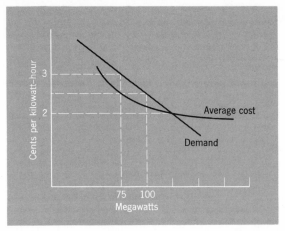

Figure 3-5

The effect of this assumption is shown in Figure 3-5. Suppose that the commission is faced with a situation where rates are 3¢ and output 75 mw. If it assumes that there will be no change in the quantity purchased when rates change (that is, that elasticity of demand is 0), it will cut rates to 2.5¢, eliminating the excess profits. At first the commission may seem to be right. It takes time for people to buy air conditioners in response to lower rates. But before long, output will be up to the 100 mw. level because elasticity really was more than 0. Then, with decreasing costs, the company will be making large profits again and another rate reduction will be in order.

Since it takes a long time for each rate decision and subsequent demand adjustment, it will be years before rates reach 2¢ in Figure 3-5. If the regulated firms could take temporary losses, rates could be reduced from 3¢ to 2¢ immediately and the public would have the advantage of lower rates and more service much sooner. Federal power projects in the Tennessee Valley and in the Pacific Northwest have priced electricity on the assumption of a fairly elastic demand and these projects have had spectacular results.[15] Per capita residential consumption in the

---

[15] Part of this was an increase in the whole demand curve rather than a movement along the old demand curve. The coming of TVA brought higher

Tennessee Valley is about triple the national average. Some cities in the area have even higher levels of consumption.

I. *Rate Differentials*

Electric utilities seldom charge the same rates to all customers. Commonly there are different rates for residential, commercial, and various types of industrial buyers, as well as quantity discounts. Power companies are in a good position to maintain price differences of this sort because it is legally and practically impossible for users who pay low rates to resell to those who pay more.

Discrimination was one of the reasons for regulation of the railroads in the late 1800's. The public rightly associated discrimination with monopoly, and there was much criticism of the advantages that large industrial buyers had over their smaller competitors as a result of rebates. Consumers who pay high rates have understandably objected, and economists have raised the further criticism that prices do not ration goods among consumers as efficiently with discrimination as when there are uniform rates.

In spite of a long-standing public distrust of price discrimination, however, public utility commissions have allowed much of it to remain. Blatant inequities may be disallowed, but an aggressive regulator is more likely to scale down all rates, leaving rate differentials intact.

There is some justification for rate differentials. For one thing, they are not always discriminatory. If electricity that is delivered to the only house at the head of Wildcat Gulch costs twice as much as that sold to a house in the middle of town, a uniform rate will really discriminate against the people who live close in. Of course, it may not pay to adjust rates for only slightly different costs, but customers can be grouped in broad categories and

---

incomes to the Tennessee Valley area in particular, and these led to a higher demand for power. Yet Tennessee Valley residential consumption in 1964 came to 13,575 kwh per person against 5706 kwh per person over the whole country. The 0.91¢ per kwh bills against 2.25¢ for most of us must account for much of this. FPC., *Statistics of Electric Utilties in the United States, 1968; Publicly Owned,* p. xxii; and ————, *Privately Owned,* p. xxxiii.

treated differently according to the costs of the different services.

A class of customers would be less costly to serve if it had a large off-peak demand requiring no additional plant, if it had a steady demand over time so that it could be served with little excess capacity, or if it offered a large demand at one point so that the company could save on distribution and office costs. Some, though not all, of the advantageous rates paid by industrial users can be defended on this basis.[16] However, the utilities have good reason to set lower rates for large industrial users than for the rest of us even when there is no cost advantage. Since the large user has the alternative of supplying his own power or locating in another part of the country, he has a much more elestic demand for electricity than other buyers. A profit-maximizing electric utility would normally discriminate in favor of such a customer.

Some price discrimination may be in the public interest in an industry with decreasing costs. Figure 3-6 shows such a case. Here a commission that must set a single rate can go no lower than 2¢ per kwh, so output cannot exceed 100 mw. If the utility is permitted to charge 2¢ for the first 100 mw and 1.4¢ for additional power, however, it can operate profitably at 120 mw, producing power to the point where consumers are just willing to pay the cost of the last bit produced. It costs 1.9¢ per kwh to produce at 120 mw, but the company does not take a loss by selling power at 1.4¢ because of the profits made on the rest which sells at 2¢. In this case, nobody pays more for power than with the single rate, some pay less, and output is expanded.[17]

---

[16] Initially, industrial demand coming at midday was clearly off-peak and required no extra capacity. In many areas today, however, industrial demand far exceeds residential demand, and it is as likely to be the reason for new plant as household use.

[17] Strictly speaking, the demand curve in Figure 3-6 is not quite the same as demand curves shown elsewhere in this book. Demand curves usually show the amounts that would be bought at various uniform prices. This one differs on two counts. (1) A general price cut would permit all consumers to expand consumption but, in discriminating, the utilities are apt to cut rates for only some customers, especially industrial users with elastic demands. The rest of us are left at the 2¢ level and buy no more than before. (2) A general price cut would leave us with a bit more money than a partial one, and we would very likely spend some of it on extra electricity.

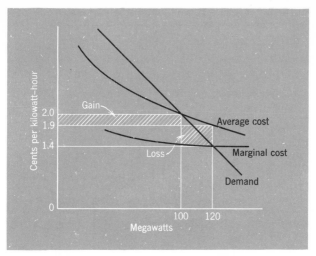

Figure 3-6

Most electric utilities charge block rates, that is, lower rates for increased consumption like the following:

First   25 kwh per month   6¢
Next   75 kwh per month   4¢
Next 100 kwh per month   3¢
Next 200 kwh per month   2¢

Instead of cutting the price on all electricity in order to sell more, they cut only the price on additional sales.[18] If their rate schedules fit buyers' demand curves, as in Figure 3-7, they can come close to the level of sale that they would have with a simple price of 2¢, but they would earn total revenues equal to the entire shaded area (A plus B) rather than just that below the 2¢ line (B).

Public utility rates are very complex. Railroads charge so many different rates for various types of freight and for different dis-

On both counts, the quantity of electricity would be somewhat greater if all the rates were cut to 1.4¢ instead of just some of them.

[18] To some extent, these block rates reflect cost differences. The distribution line, meter, and billing expenses are likely to cost the company as much in total for the 25 kwh household as for the 75 kwh household.

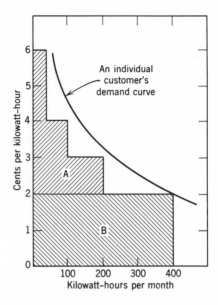

Figure 3-7

tances and regions that their rates fill volumes. Electric utility rates are simpler, but it is not uncommon to find 30 different rate classifications in a single town, not to mention quantity discounts. It is close to impossible for commissioners to determine whether these rate differences are all justified by cost. The regulators often accept the rate structures that the companies propose and try to regulate their over-all levels.

∨ **J. *The Regulators***   *No9 Bit New Pay Tou Light*

Although the details of the last few pages may seem complicated to anyone new to the subject, he should be warned that this discussion has only skimmed over the surface of rate making. Perhaps the most important conclusion he should draw is that public utility regulators have a very complex set of questions to consider. It is no simple task to duplicate the effects of competition in a monopolistic industry.

Not all public utility commissions have been equal to the tasks imposed upon them. The funds appropriated for their use are often inadequate. In many states, technical staffs are too small. Salaries are often too low to attract good men. In 1967, the average state paid its public utility commissioners $15,962, and eight states paid them $11,000 or less.[19] Utility companies often pay engineers, attorneys, and accountants higher starting salaries than this.

Commissioners are appointed in some states and elected in others. If elected, they are fairly far down a long ballot and are unknown names to most voters. It is really the nominating machinery that determines who gets the job. It often goes to a loyal party worker. The best commissions are appointed, but some appointed commissions are far from the ideal. The governor may find that the public utility commission is an excellent place to reward his political supporters.

Most states have legal provisions protecting the commissioners' independence by such devices as long tenure and staggered terms, but legislative and administrative officials sometimes do influence their decisions, and outright graft has occurred.

Some observers have felt that even scrupulously honest and clearly competent commissions tend to see things from the point of view of the regulated industry. It takes only a short step for commissioners to conclude that their job is not only to prevent excessive profits but also to assure normal ones, at least so long as the management is reasonably careful. Again, it is probably not in the public's interest to dog the companies' heels and adjust rates immediately whenever some small cost saving is achieved. If they could not look forward to even temporarily high profits, the utilities would have no incentive to increase efficiency. Yet, if this point of view is carried far enough, there is very little regulation left.

Individual consumers seldom have enough interest in the outcome of particular regulatory hearings to pay much attention to them, but the affected industry finds it worthwhile to devote its best talent to those proceedings. The regulators are apt to hear one side more loudly than the other as a result. If they do not, the regulated industry may turn to the legislature or the chief executive, hoping to change the law or the regulators or both. Just as the manipulation of public-utility franchises con-

---

[19] FPC, *State Commission Jurisdiction* . . . , *op. cit.*, p. 43.

tributed to the corruption of city governments at the turn of
the century, so present-day regulation has generated powerful
lobbies from affected industries that tend to lessen the effectiveness of state and federal democratic process. Once such a
lobby is established, it becomes difficult to prevent regulation
from reflecting the interests of the industries being regulated.

Probably most commissioners have sought what they felt was
the public interest, but they often turn out to think that what
is good for their industry is good for America.

V. PERFORMANCE

A. *Production*

The experience of the electric power industry during this century
is indicated in the output, price, profit and productivity series
shown in Figures 3-8, 3-9, 3-10, and 3-11. In each case, they are
compared with similar series for all manufacturing.

Figure 3-8 shows the electric industry's output record. The
generation of electric power is a new industry which has grown
much faster than the economy as a whole. This is to be expected.
Not only were the power companies supplying the needs of a
growing country; they also provided a convenient substitute for
the human, animal, and direct steam power that had been the
main source of energy previously.

The growth in electric power production has been much more
steady than the growth in most of industry. Once electricity had
won new users, it never lost them again. Even in major depressions, demand barely declined. This was due in large part to the
character of the product. In household use, at least, the income
elasticity of demand must be very low. Once the high fixed costs
of wiring the house and buying the refrigerator have been incurred, few people will pull out the plug to save the small marginal cost—the electric bill—even if their incomes fall. Moreover,
electric power is the most fleeting of perishable commodities.
Consumers and businessmen can use last year's refrigerator or
last year's power lines when a depression hits, but they cannot
use last year's power. The stability of electricity demand is
definitely not a matter of rate policy. Rates just do not fall in
response to temporary declines in demand due to depressions.

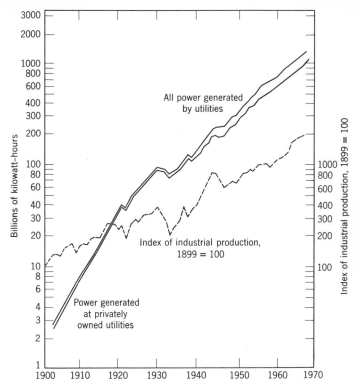

Figure 3-8. *Source. Historical Statistics of the United States;* FPC, *Statistics of Electric Utilities in the United States,* 1963 and *Statistical Abstracts.*

B. *Rates*

The performance of electric utility rates is shown in Figure 3-9. Of course, electric rates depend on who pays them and how much he consumes. The solid line shows the average rate paid in cities (over 50,000 to 1958 and over 2500 thereafter) by residential consumers buying 100 kwh per month expressed as a percentage of its 1957-9 level.

Electric-power rates were among the few prices that fell consistently over the first half of this century. Their stability during the inflationary 1940's should really be counted as a further decline. Their record was closer to the average in the

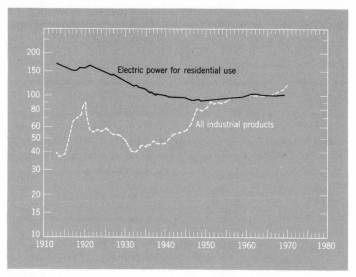

Figure 3-9.   Indexes of electric-power rates and wholesale prices of industrial products, 1957-59 = 100. *Sources. Historical Statistics of the United
States*, p. 116 and 129; FPC, *Typical Electric Bills*, 1969; *and Economic
Report of the President*, 1970. The BLS composite index for electricity was
spliced with an index for 100 kwh residential bills at 1923.

1960's, when neither power rates nor industrial prices rose or
fell by much.[20]

In part, the long price decline occurred simply because electric power was a new industry with decreasing costs and an expanding market. In the 1920's, technical progress and increasing
scale resulted in continuously falling rates even though that was
the period when the regulatory commissions were most weakened
by judicial decisions. A number of rate reductions at that time
were made voluntarily without orders from the commissions,
implying that the commissions were ordering rates *higher* than
the levels that seemed most profitable to the companies!

---

[20] The average rate paid by the average consumer is still declining because
we are buying more and more electricity, whereas Figure 3-9 assumes 100
kwh per month in every year since 1923 (before that, the BLS used a
"composite" index). In 1945 revenue per kwh of residential demand was
3.4¢. By 1968 it was 2.12¢ and still falling. (Derived from *Statistical Abstracts*, 1962, p. 535, and 1969, p. 516.)

In the depression years of 1931-35 and 1937-39, utility rates fell more slowly at a time when most prices were falling drastically.[21] In part, this was the result of the rate-making formula. When output declined, the overhead had to be carried by a smaller number of kilowatt-hours so that average cost increased. This was offset in part by reductions in labor and fuel expenses, but commissions were in no position to require rate reductions using their old standards.[22] Some firms in highly concentrated industries maintained stable prices during the depression years also and, in such cases, it was interpreted as monopolists exercising their monopoly power to protect themselves. It is interesting that commission regulation resulted in a similar policy.

The rate stability in times of rising prices since 1940 is a common characteristic of public utilities. It is a result of regulatory practices. The machinery of rate changes is so slow-moving that upward adjustments are apt to lag behind general price increases. As a result, regulated firms are often unprofitable during periods of rapid inflation. Moreover, rate regulation permits very little upward adjustment in many cases. If plants are evaluated at their original cost, then depreciation, property taxes, and a stable return on the company's investment cannot increase except as new plant is added and even then they will creep up slowly. Labor and fuel costs can rise rapidly, but in the power industry these are less than half of the total.

C. *Profits*

Figure 3-10 shows electric utility profits compared with those of all manufacturing corporations. The FPC required all electric utilities falling under its jurisdiction to adopt uniform accounting

---

[21] The sharper drop in 1936-37 coincides with the mild recovery and the introduction of tougher regulation in those years. Even then, rates fell no faster than in the 1920's.

[22] On the basis of reduced traffic and high overhead, the railroads were actually permitted to raise rates during these years. In retrospect, this was probably not a very wise move on the part of the regulators or the railroads. The demand for their service was certainly not inelastic in view of the alternative means of transportation available. A rate reduction might have increased railroad earnings more.

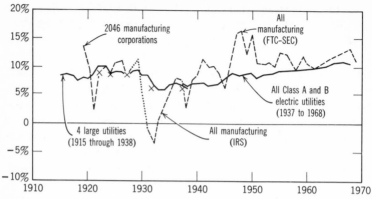

Figure 3-10. Profits after tax in electric utilities and manufacturing. *Source.* Electric utilities: 1915 to 1938, Annual reports of Boston Edison, Consolidated Gas and Electric Light and Power of Baltimore, Detroit Edison, and Pacific Gas and Electric as presented in *Moody's Public Utilities Manuals;* the X's represent returns from the 1922, 1927, 1932, and 1937, Censuses of Electrical Industries. 1937 to 1968, all Class A and B utilities, FPC, *Statistics of Electric Utilities. . . , op. cit.* All manufacturing: 1919 to 1928, R. C. Epstein, *Industrial Profits in the United States,* National Bureau of Economic Research, 1934. The 1929 and 1930 profit rates are estimated by the author. 1931 to 1947, Internal Revenue Service, *Statistics of Income.* 1947 to 1969, FTC-SEC, *Quarterly Financial Reports, United States Manufacturing Corporations.*

practices beginning January 1, 1937. Earnings shown for electric firms from that date onward are reported by the FPC.

For earlier years the figures are poor. Public utility accounting was colorful at times during the 1920's. The FPC required the companies of write off or amortize about 20% of the assets they claimed in 1937, and to increase greatly the rates at which they depreciate their equipment. It is clear that company accounts for earlier years exaggerated the value of the firms so that reported rates of profits before 1937 are too low.

Even with some understatement, the reported profits of these companies were as good as those of the average manufacturer in the 1920's. In the 1930's, when their sales fell less than most firms' and their prices stayed up, the electric companies did much better than most of industry. The electric utilities did not participate in the high profits common in inflationary years like

1941-42, 1946-8, and 1950 because they did not participate in the inflations, but they were normally prosperous even in those years.

Over the whole period in Figure 3-10, the most remarkable thing about electric utility earnings is their stability. The character of demand and the standards of regulation seem to assure a regular return. Since there is apparently less risk in this sort of industry, earnings need not include such large risk premiums as elsewhere. In other words, the utilities are really quite prosperous when they show only average rates of profit.

D. *Productivity*

Figure 3-11 compares estimates of the increase in output per man-hour in manufacturing and electric power. Productivity has

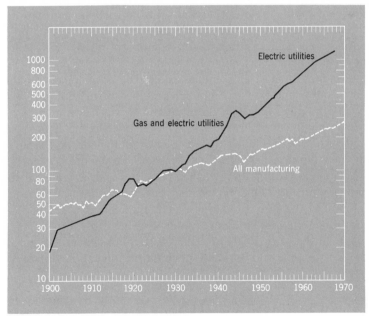

Figure 3-11. Output per man-hour: Electric utilities and all manufacturing, 1929 = 100. *Source.* J. W. Kendrick, *"Productivity Trends in the* United States, Princeton, 1961, pp. 465-6, 590; BLS Bulletin 1612, "Indexes of Output Per Man-hour: Selected Industries, 1939 and 1947-1967," p. 100; and *Economic Report of the President,* 1970, p. 216. 1954-1967 data refers to gas and electric utilities.

grown much faster in the utilities than in manufacturing. This is to be expected in the first years of an industry, especially where economies of scale are apparently very great. The continuation of the trend in productivity for two-thirds of a century without slowing up is quite impressive, nevertheless. The rapid increase in productivity in the electric utilities is an important reason, along with the commissions' emphasis on original costs, for their declining or stable rates when most prices were rising.

The electric power industry can hardly be charged with any failure to make progress in spite of the monopoly positions of its members. On the other hand, the utilities have an exceptionally standardized and unchanging product. Their innovations have been primarily cost-saving changes, which show up in increased productivity, rather than product-improving changes, which do not. The utilities had rapidly expanding markets with a demand that was quite stable during short-run fluctuations and with no threat of competitors, who might make their plants prematurely obsolete. In such a setting, the installation of usually well-tested new equipment and techniques would be far less risky than the innovations in most of manufacturing. The development of this new equipment was an impressive achievement, but this was done primarily outside of the industry. It was firms in the electrical equipment industry such as General Electric and Westinghouse that developed the huge new equipment, and firms in the metallurgical fields that were responsible for the new metals which made possible the high temperatures and pressures of the new equipment. The equipment manufacturers have also carried on most of the early private research on atomic power. The utilities cooperated by building a number of high cost, experimental plants in the early 1950's and 1960's. Many observers thought of this as an effort to forestall government operation of atomic power.

VI. UNPROFITABLE UTILITIES

A. *The Goals of Regulations Once More*

Electric power production has experienced an almost continuous boom during the last 80 years, but not all regulated industries have been as fortunate. Some, including many railroads in the last century and the airlines until the 1950's, were built in advance of demand and had to wait many unprosperous years until the markets they were designed to serve caught up with them. Some were just poor ideas to begin with. Finally, many of the once prosperous railroads and urban transit systems have simply fallen on hard times as new means of transportation have taken their place.

Regulation in cases of this sort involves very different problems from the regulation of prosperous utilities like electric power. The main goal is no longer the elimination of monopolistic profits—there are no profits to eliminate. In fact, the problem becomes one of keeping the company afloat and the service available.

Figure 3-12 illustrates the regulatory problem in the case of a railroad where demand has fallen off. Since the plant (roadbed, track, bridges, and tunnels) is already installed, the short-run cost for that plant is shown. Average cost inevitably declines as the large overhead of the railroad is spread over more and more service. The demand in this particular case is such that there is only one rate that would cover costs. At any higher or lower rate, the firm would take losses. The regulatory commission try-

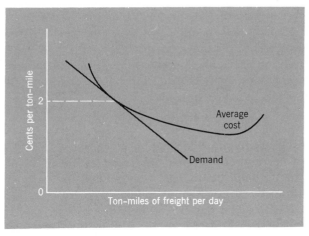

Figure 3-12

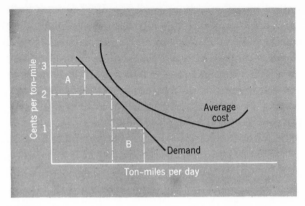

Figure 3-13

ing to set rates that yield a normal profit *must* approve a price of 2¢, just what the most exploitative of monopolists would charge.

Of course, there may not be any rate that would be profitable. This is the case in Figure 3-13. If the commission is to keep *losses* at a minimum it must again set the most exploitative possible price, 2¢ in this case.

B. *Rate Discrimination Once More*

It might be possible to completely avoid losses in a situation like that shown in Figure 3-13 by rate discrimination. Instead of charging all customers 2¢, the railroad might set a rate of 3¢ per ton-mile for those who would pay it (customers with more valuable freight, at least if they have no alternative means of transportation), and 1¢ a mile for other groups who cannot or will not pay 2¢ (perhaps shippers with very bulky products or those at ocean or lake ports). The additional revenues indicated by rectangles A and B make up all the losses that the company would suffer without discrimination.

It is difficult to object to discrimination when it keeps a company in operation that would otherwise go under. It might be better not to build the railroad from scratch starting today, but with it already in existence we might as well use it. If, by discrimination, we can get the facilities used closer to the point where the last carload of freight is just worth its extra costs, the public as well as the firm may be better off.

Some of the railroads would probably *never* have been profitable if no discrimination had been allowed. In these cases, discrimination was a way of subsidizing an unprofitable enterprise. Ordinarily, such a policy means encouraging businessmen to make the wrong investments, but if there are social gains that do not accrue to the railroad, it may make publicly desirable projects possible. Many of the nineteenth century railroads that opened up new regions obviously did offer rapid economic development that in many cases made the investment worthwhile for society even if not for the companies.

Discriminatory rates are universal on the railroads and are so complicated that hardly anyone can understand the entire structure. The law does not allow railroads to discriminate between individuals within the same class, but classes are defined minutely, and the railroads have been permitted to discriminate among groups of customers according to "what the traffic will bear." There are special rates for hundreds of different commodities. Rates are sometimes more in one direction than in the other, and more in one part of the country than in another. In Canada, where the waterways freeze up, there are even higher rates in winter than in summer. Of course, the marginal costs are not the same for all services rendered by the railroads, but freight rates and marginal costs show no consistent relationship.

C. *Competition*

In the days before the ICC, unregulated rate discrimination sometimes got the railroads into trouble. As good monopolists, they set low rates where elasticities were high (that is, where they had lots of competition) and made up for it with high charges on noncompetitive business. Since most of their competition in those days came from other railroads, this sometimes meant spectacular rate wars. Agreements among the roads to prevent such rivalry were common and caused much discontent among shippers, especially in the farm belt.

One of the main effects of regulation on the railroads was the suppression of rate competition among the different lines. Wholesale discrimination continued, but the ICC coordinated rate policies between lines. Some observers have concluded that the suppression of rate competition was a major goal of the ICC from the start.

After trucking became a serious competitor of the railroads that, too, was brought under ICC control. In 1935, the ICC was empowered to license interstate truckers (with some major exceptions such as those handling farm products and those hauling their own freight) and to regulate their rates. In 1940, its authority was extended to common carriers on inland waterways. In both cases, the government provides the roadbeds (highways and waterways), and the carriers pay for them only in license fees and gasoline taxes. As a result, the investments necessary to start business are relatively small so the two industries are potentially very competitive. With federal regulation, however, the number of common carriers is limited and price competition is suppressed.

When the ICC became responsible for the rates of these other freight carriers, it had the unpleasant job of deciding on each group's share of the market. At rates that have prevailed over the last two decades, truck and barge traffic has increased enormously in spite of obvious railroad overcapacity but, whenever railroads have sought rate reductions on traffic in competition with the trucks and barges, the other carriers have objected that such changes would be discriminatory. Actually these rate reductions have generally been moves away from discrimination. The truckers tended to take over the high value freight on which the railroads had set high rates. Railroads had to reduce these rates or lose the business. Demand had become more elastic, so high discriminatory rates were no longer profitable. The ICC has often intervened to prevent such rate reductions.

D. *Subsidies*

Even the most advantageous level and structure of rates may not be enough to make some utilities profitable. If not, the firms must either be subsidized or go bankrupt ultimately. Both have happened. In the early years of the railroads, the federal and state governments made large land grants to firms that built lines across the West. State and local governments often offered tax exemptions and even built some of the facilities for the railroads in the early days. Similarly, the Federal Government subsidized the airlines, built many airports and air navigation aids, and still subsidizes the feeder lines.

Subsidy has also appeared in the case of declining industries. Many cities have taken over their municipal transit utilities, not because of a trend toward socialism but because they were too unprofitable for private firms to operate. The service could not be abandoned because downtown business depended on it and because it was the main means of transportation of the lower income group.

The cities had to run some of these lines at a loss. A subsidy in this case was unavoidable, but there was still the question of how much subsidy. The city might keep its losses at a minimum by taking full advantage of its monopoly position. It could set rates at 25¢ in a case like Figure 3-14, experience only a small loss (area A), and run half-empty busses. Alternatively, the city could set a rate such as 15¢ in Figure 3-14. The busses would be more fully used, and the price would meet the marginal cost standard, but the city would be involved in a more substantial loss (area B). In fact, the higher fare might actually be more expensive to the city overall. This could happen because the city would have to build more parking lots and widen more streets

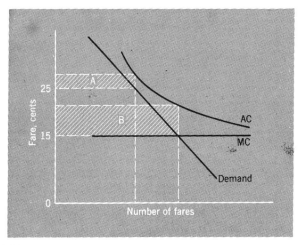

Figure 3-14

for people who drove to work instead of riding the busses or subways.

The case for subsidies to mass transportation is especially strong because private commuting seems to involve heavy social costs that do not fall upon the individual commuter. One more car does not contribute enough to the rush hour congestion to keep that car off the road. Yet, when several hundred thousand individuals each disregards his contribution to the congestion and drives into the city, everyone loses an extra half hour, and driving within the city may become almost impossible.

E. Reorganizations

The alternative to subsidy in some cases is for the company to go broke. Although this is a pretty drastic remedy, it can sometimes solve the problem. Usually the firm will not go out of business at a result; it will simply be reorganized. Stockholders will lose their claim on the company, and creditors may accept a reduced claim as better than nothing at all, or the facilities will be sold for what they will bring, and the new buyer will operate the firm. The buyer will not pay the full original cost, of course, but only a price that seems warranted in view of the prospective returns. After the reorganization, then, only a part of the original fixed costs must be borne by the firm. Figure 3-15 shows the cost curves of a railroad that took $100 million to build and that went into receivership. After it was sold for $50 million, or its obligations were scaled down to that level, it could again operate without losses.[23]

There is not enough revenue here to cover the cost of a complete railroad. If the old railroad ever wears out, it will not pay to build a new one; but until then, if receipts cover operating expenses, the trains can be kept running. This is another illustration of a point made in Chapter 2. A firm will keep in operation so long as it at least covers its variable costs. It does not have to cover fixed costs as well. Reorganizations of this sort are far

---

[23] If the reorganized firm is to be workable, the claims must be scaled down to a suitable level. Since this means that someone must lose out, it has not always happened. In the case of railroads, the ICC as well as security holders must now approve any reorganization plan.

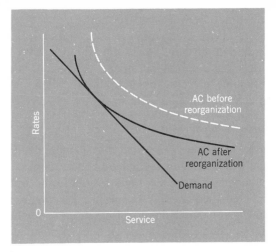

Figure 3-15.

from rare. Most railroads in the country have passed through re-ceivership, some of them several times.

F. *Mergers*

In the 1960's, the ICC became quite receptive to proposals for mergers among the railroads as a less painful solution to the problem of excess capacity. Some of the railroads that com-bined were probably too small to be efficient even when demand was high, but the ICC encouraged combinations among very large railroads as well. The most striking was the merger of the Pennsylvania and the New York Central, the nation's largest and third largest railroad, both serving the Chicago-New York route. To go by anti-trust policy elsewhere, such mergers would not have been permitted in unregulated industries.

The goal of these mergers was to eliminate duplicate, under-utilized track, stations, and other such facilities. Savings in the hundreds of millions were claimed for some of the mergers, though most did not produce nearly the predicted gains, and some produced none at all. The Penn-Central went bankrupt in 1970, largely *as a result of* the huge merger that had formed it only two years earlier.[24] At the same time, however, any possibility of competition between the formerly competing lines was also eliminated. Price competition among railroads is prevented by ICC regulation anyway, but freight shippers have often benefited from service competition among the lines. The possibility of "deregulation" of railroads is reduced when most of the chances for competition among railroads are removed by mergers.

G. *Abandonment of Service*

In the case of a declining industry, the abandonment of service is a difficult problem. The regulatory commission cannot make a company keep operating if it takes overall losses, but it can require a firm that plans to stay in business to continue some unprofitable service. Commissioners often listen sympathetically to the objections of home owners on bus lines to be abandoned and of small towns on unprofitable railroad branches. A common result is the grudging continuation of poor service with nobody very happy.

H. *The Railroads and the Trucks*

But why be concerned to keep the railroads afloat at all? In unregulated fields, if demand is inadequate to cover total costs, the industry will simply disappear in the long run and the economy will be more efficient as a result. The resources in the dying industry will produce more valuable services somewhere else. When the railroads began, we could reasonably argue that they offered large external benefits that accrued to society as a whole over and above those direct benefits from which the railroads themselves could profit, but at that time they were the only effective means of transportation. Their whole problem today is that alternative means of transportation abound. The external benefits of railroads are much less obvious than they once were.

A group of economists who have carefully examined this question have concluded that there still is a strong economic case for the railroads.[25] They found that the long-run marginal cost of

---

24 See "The Penn-Central Bankruptcy Express," *Fortune*, August, 1970. pp. 104-109.
25 J. Meyer, M. J. Peck, John Stenason, and Charles Zwick, *The Economics*

long distance freight (more than 50 miles) is distinctly lower for railroads than for trucks, that it is the long line truckers rather than the railroads that are inefficient and probably should be going out of business. The reason that they thrive is the railroad's old price discrimination against high value merchandise. Long line truckers took over a large part of this business, but the ICC has, in large part, prevented the railroads from responding to the new situation by cutting rates on high value goods. The ICC has also consistently opposed the development of short line trucking as a part of the railroad service, another step that would enhance the competitive positions of the railroads.

Perhaps the best bet for improving the prospects of the railroads and for increasing the efficiency of the American transportation system generally is to reduce the regulation of transportation and to rely much more on competition in that area than we have done in the past. The wholesale mergers that the ICC has permitted in the last decade have considerably reduced the possibility of such a policy.

VII. GOVERNMENT ENTERPRISE— POWER TO THE PEOPLE?

One alternative to the less than perfect success of regulation outlined to this point is government operation of utilities or transportation industries. This is usual in much of the world. In the United States, the government has operated the post office since the start of the country and has provided water, sewer, and highway services very widely, though all of these are capable of private operation. Most American utilities are privately owned, but about a quarter of our electric power comes from publicly owned generators today. That quarter is highly controversial.

A. *Federal Power Projects*

Public power today takes three main forms: federal power projects, municipal utilities, and Rural Electrification Adminis-

---

of Competition in the Transportation Industries, Harvard University Press, Cambridge, 1959.

tration (REA) co-ops.[26] The federal projects are the most obvious and have caused the greatest controversy, though the municipals and co-ops are now growing faster.

The role of the Federal Government in power production dates mainly from the 1930's and centers around the development of large hydroelectric projects. About half of federal generating capacity (and 6% of all U.S. capacity) is accounted for by the Tennessee Valley Authority (TVA), a government corporation established in 1933 that took over and developed the entire power system of most of Tennessee, important parts of Alabama, Mississippi, and Kentucky, and bits of three other states. The Tennessee River is the main stream draining the southern Appalachians, an area with some of the heaviest rainfall and highest elevations in the eastern half of the country, so it had one of the largest power (and flood) potentials in the nation. The TVA area included some of the poorest parts of the country—in the southern Appalachians and much of the south central farm region. There was a need for improved methods of agriculture and for local industrialization to draw excess farmers into the city. The valley therefore provided an ideal setting for a large-scale experiment in economic development.

The TVA spent almost $4 billion between 1933 and 1968 building or acquiring 29 hydroelectric plants and 11 large steam-generating plants with a total capacity of more than 18 thousand mw. It established the Tennessee Valley as one of the main centers of low-cost power, it put a check to heavy floods that had been common in the region, it provided a 650-mile navigable channel into the southern Appalachian coal fields, and it engaged in extensive programs of agricultural improvement and reforestation. The region has experienced a rapid growth under TVA. Per capita incomes have risen much faster there in the country as a whole, though the same is true in most of the South.

The other half of federal power comes from projects built by the Army Corps of Engineers and the Bureau of Reclamation

---

[26] There are also a few state projects, notably the statewide system of Nebraska and the Niagara and St. Lawrence River projects of the State of New York Power Authority. Technically the REA co-ops are privately owned, but they are sponsored by a federal agency.

since the early 1930's. They are scattered all over the country, but the most important group is in the Pacific Northwest. The Bonneville Power Authority is by far the most important power source in the area, though private utilities still exist there. Federal power is no longer growing very rapidly outside the TVA area because we are running out of large, unexploited power sites.

B. *The Municipals and Co-ops*

The municipal utilities and REA cooperatives are less spectacular, but they distribute about 22% of the power sold in the country. They are given a preferential right to the low-cost power available at most federal projects. And they pay exceptionally low interest rates. Interest on municipal bonds is exempt from federal income tax, so corporations and high-income persons will buy such bonds at interest rates a quarter to a third less than on corporate bonds. The co-ops are subsidized directly. The REA lends to them at 2% regardless of market interest rates (though it puts a limit on the amount of such cheap capital it will provide). Because of the high capital requirements of electric utilities, interest is a large part of their costs, so the municipals and co-ops have a substantial financial advantage over private utilities.

Except for a few large cities such as Los Angeles and Seattle, the municipals and co-ops are quite small. They commonly buy power and distribute it. Privately owned companies sell to them at wholesale prices, but are seldom willing to let them buy capacity in new plants at long-run marginal cost. As a result, the municipals and co-ops are apt to have high wholesale power costs compared with privately owned utilities, except in areas where they can buy large amounts of federal power. Faced with wholesale prices higher than the lowest attainable production costs and given their interest rate advantages, municipals and co-ops have installed increasing amounts of generating capacity in recent years, much of it of suboptimal scale.

C. *Public Power—Pro*

Defenders of public power put great emphasis on the multiple purposes of many federal projects. Private firms might never have undertaken them because the power produced was not enough to pay for the entire investments, but the public gained in many ways where full remuneration was not feasible. It would be virtually impossible to collect flood protection fees downstream, though the economic gain in some instances is obvious. Similarly, irrigation projects are usually not directly self-financing and inland waterways and the recreational facilities yield no revenue at all. Even if electric power production were enough to pay for some of these other services, private firms might not build the facilities that best meet the public needs. The FPC, in licensing private projects, can require specific facilities, but in practice there is a limit to the extra expense it can ask private firms to bear without remuneration.

Some of the projects in the 1930's can be defended as means of accelerating economic development. Like the railroads of the nineteenth century, the power projects were enormous investments that had to be in place before their users could develop. Unless heavily subsidized, private capital was not available to finance such large undertakings when the potential market was far in the future if it existed at all.

Most of the early large-scale projects were undertaken as fiscal policy measures to help get the country out of the Depression. However, in prosperous and sometimes inflationary years, projects certainly could not then be defended because of the stimulus they gave the economy. The largest part of federal expenditures on power development has occurred in the years since World War II. The government installed or acquired 4.8 thousand mw of generating capacity between 1933 and 1945 compared with 27.7 thousand mw since.

The purpose of public power, in many minds, is to offer power at lower unit costs, thus eliminating monopoly profits. In practice, TVA and the Bonneville Power Administration have very low rates compared with their predecessors and other private utilities. Their rate structures are also simpler. If nothing else, TVA and the Bonneville Power Administration have shown very little inclination to exploit their monopoly positions, something that cannot be said of every producer of electricity.

D. *Public Power—Con*

Critics of public power hold that many projects are clear misallocations of the nation's resources. Not all creeks are worth developing, but if political conditions are right many of them will be developed anyway. Private investments are subject to the standards of the market place and, unless promising, will not be undertaken. Public funds are likely to go to states with powerful congressmen, whether or not the projects are economically worthwhile. The pork barrel is an old American institution and is well worth watching.

Some critics have doubted the value of many multipurpose projects. It might well be cheaper to have only partial protection against the sort of flood that comes once in a century than to build a dam across every creek in Kansas. Again, how much are inland waterways worth to a country well supplied with half-idle railroads, and how valuable is new irrigated cottonland when the Department of Agriculture is restricting acreage on what we already have? This does not mean that flood control, navigation, and irrigation projects are all worthless, but it is not always easy to determine their true social value.

One social value that probably gets underrated is recreation. In a nation that puts several billion dollars a year into television, bowling, professional sports, and the like, considerable public expenditure for forests, campgrounds, and just open space is probably warranted. Power projects have inundated or threatened to inundate substantial sections of such public preserves as Glacier Park, Grand Canyon, and Dinosaur National Monument. Many feel that the power and water just are not worth the permanent loss of some of our scarce, undeveloped countryside.

E. *Cost-Benefit Analysis*

Some early public power developments were justified on a fairly haphazard basis, but, more recently, the public power agencies have developed a technique known as *cost-benefit analysis,* which has brought the agencies closer to the criteria of the market place. An attempt is made to put dollar values on the expected benefits included in flood control, transport, and additional downstream water and power as well as directly saleable water and power at the site. The project is supposed to be undertaken only if the estimated benefits exceed the total cost. For this purpose total costs include dollar estimates of the nonmarket social costs and are computed using an interest rate in line with the rates applicable to taxpayers. Such analyses have worked reasonably well with power and water projects where market values downstream or at the site are pretty straightforward. They are at least within the realm of possibility for many other civilian public expenditure programs such as education, highways, and urban renewal. Even in areas where dollar estimates of benefits are not feasible, as in defense, it is possible to evaluate the "cost effectiveness" of various projects—that is, to compare the costs of various means of attaining specific goals.

The estimates of benefits can seldom be precise but, to the extent that dollar values can be assigned, we can decide among private and public products on the same basis that we decide between shoes and phonograph records. We add to total public services (or to privately produced goods) so long as another unit is worth more than the opportunity cost of the resources used in producing them. Cost-benefit and cost-effectiveness studies became a regular part of Washington life for a while in the late 1960's, with the leadership of such persons as Secretary of Defense McNamara. Less was heard of them under Nixon.

F. *Public Power and Private Enterprise*

Much of the criticism of public power is a matter of ideology. A large part of the American public clearly believes that private enterprise is superior to public and that government should stay out wherever private business can serve. Some are seriously concerned about the future of personal freedom as government grows larger and acquires increased control over a greater segment of the economy. Those who see no danger to our democracy from government-owned instead of government-regulated utilities may still fear the power of a government monopoly. In the electric industry, this may be a minor consideration, but in other fields, such as transportation, a government-owned enterprise might be in a better position to suppress competition than a private firm or its regulatory commission.

Probably more widespread than either of these concerns is

doubt about the efficiency of government-operated enterprises. The slow-moving bureaucracy that is tangled in red tape and staffed by uninspired civil servants is a familiar caricature. Private business, subject to the threat of competition, is usually supposed to be forced onto a higher level of efficiency. Private utilities are certainly on the border line between government and competitive business, however. Government regulations that set rates on the basis of cost plus a reasonable profit is a very imperfect substitute for competition when it comes to forcing producers to innovate and increase efficiency.

Government enterprise is probably more workable in electric power than in most lines of business. Electricity is a single, very uniform product requiring only small amounts of labor and depending on a technology supplied by other industries. Where these conditions do not apply, our awkward government decision-making machinery may produce less acceptable results. Some of the possible creaks and groans of public enterprise have appeared dramatically at the post office. Investment has been minimized and technological progress has been slow. Productivity has risen far more slowly than in manufacturing. In some cases, Congress has provided expensive services at no additional charge (for example, rural mail delivery) and has prevented the offering of other services that could be profitable (such as electronic transmission of mail). Postal rates have little relationship to the marginal costs of the various services being offered. A rigid and narrow set of job specifications has kept postal labor discontented and has badly weakened incentives. The result has been deteriorating service, increasing costs, and labor unrest. Public enterprise may be unavoidable in the post office, but its poor performance there does not recommend it for wide application elsewhere.

VIII. SUMMARY

It is not an easy job to eliminate the undesirable effects of monopoly by direct control of private business. Under the best of conditions in prosperous industries such as electric power, regulation is necessarily imperfect simply because of the mechanical complexities of rate making. Conditions have often been less than the best owing to interference from the courts and to the inadequacies of regulators. Moreover, even the most efficient commission is apt to set rates that are too high if it applies the usual standards to firms with decreasing costs. While discrimination or the undervaluation of utility property may make up for this to some extent, both are subject to criticism themselves.

In unprofitable industries, regulation is even less likely to eliminate monopolistic pricing. Rates set to keep losses or subsidies to a minimum automatically exploit the monopolists' positions. The commission in such circumstances is likely to use its power to reduce competition both within the industry and with other industries. Regulation in such fields does protect the public against abandonment of service, but we might be better served if more of the abandonments were permitted.

Government operation avoids some of the faults of regulation, but introduces others. Prices and services tend to reflect political influences. There is something to be said for subsidizing the development of depressed regions but less for subsidizing regions with powerful senators. The pressure for minimum costs may be even less than in regulated industries, and cost itself is difficult to determine when the government absorbs the risks, distorts interest rates, and provides direct subsidies, as is often the case. Public enterprise is not an impossible solution, but it is seldom clearly superior to regulation.

Another alternative is to depend on unregulated competition. This may well be superior to either government operation or regulation by the ICC and the CAB in the case of intercity transport. With trains, barges, airlines, and private cars all competing for the business, no carrier has the monopolistic position that the railroads occupied when the ICC began 80-odd years ago.

There is even room for some competition in such industries as electric power. At the local level, competition between gas and electricity is possible, except in those areas where the regulators permit the continued operation of both utilities by the same company. And a good deal of competition is now possible at the generating level, if many producing and distributing utilities have access to the same transmission grid. Most observers would probably feel that this competition is too limited to warrant the abandonment of regulation in electric power, but such competition can at least serve to reenforce regulation and bring us closer to its goals.

IX. FURTHER READINGS

The study of public utilities is a major subdivision of economics. A number of good texts are devoted to the subject including C. E. Troxel, *The Economics of Public Utilities*, Rinehart, 1947, which emphasizes the analytical aspects of the subject and P. J. Garfield and W. F. Lovejoy, *Public Utility Economics*, Prentice-Hall, 1964, which emphasizes operating policies. A comprehensive treatise on the subject is A. E. Kahn, *The Economics of Regulation Principles and Institutions*, John Wiley and Sons, 1970. The journal *Land and Public Utility Economics* contains many articles on regulated industries and regulation. An interesting collection of recent articles on the subject appears in W. G. Shepherd and T. G. Gies, *Utility Regulation, New Directions in Theory and Policy*, Random House, 1966. L. M. Kohlmeier Jr., *The Regulators*, Harper and Row, 1969 is a dissection of the foibles of regulatory agencies by a well-known journalist.

The suggestion that marginal costs be used in setting public utility rates is ordinarily attributed to Harold Hotelling, "The General Welfare in Relation to the Problems of Taxation and of Railroad and Public Utility Rates," *Econometrica*, July 1938. It was widely debated in the 1940's. A good summary of the debate appears in two articles on marginal cost pricing by Nancy Ruggles in the *Review of Economic Studies*, Nos. 42 and 43, 1949 to 1950. An interesting set of essays on French experiments along this line appears in J. R. Nelson, *Marginal Cost Pricing in Practice*, Prentice-Hall, 1964.

Transportation is yet another subdivision of economics in which specialized texts have appeared. C. E. Troxel, *Economics of Transport*, Rinehart, 1955, is an analytical one and D. P. Locklin, *Economics of Transport*, 6th Ed., Irwin, 1966, is an institutional book. A thorough evaluation of the alternative transportation industries and our present allocation of resources among them is J. R. Meyer, M. J. Peck, John Stenason, and Charles Zwick, *The Economics of Competition in the Transporta-*

tion Industries, Harvard University Press, 1959. The Universities-National Bureau Conference on *Transportation Economics,* Columbia University Press, 1965, contains papers on a wide variety of pertinent subjects.

The public versus private power issue is examined in a number of specific cases using the cost-benefit analysis in J. V. Krutilla and Otto Eckstein, *Multiple Purpose River Development,* Johns Hopkins, 1958. A good summary and evaluation of the debate over cost-benefit analysis appears in Ralph Turvey, "Cost-Benefit Analysis, A Survey," *The Economic Journal,* December 1965.

A good way to learn more about the imperfections of public enterprise in the case of the post office is to read the report of the President's Commission on Postal Organization, *Toward Postal Excellence,* June, 1968.

4

Oligopoly—Steel

While monopoly is rare outside of regulated industries, *oligopoly*, where a few firms dominate, is a common situation in the American economy. Steel, automobiles, oil, chemicals, aluminum, tires, farm equipment, and many other important industries fall into this category. Steel has probably received more attention than any other oligopoly. It is the perennial subject of investigation by Congress, the courts, and economists. In the eyes of the American public it has long been the symbol of big business, and it is the symbol of industrial prowess and economic growth throughout the whole world.

I. INTEGRATION

A. The Steel-Making Process

Steel making is a complicated process. The steel industry consists of hundreds of firms performing any or all of the tasks shown in Table 4-1.

While there are at least a few firms specializing at each step, the bulk of the steel produced in the United States today comes from great *integrated* companies that combine at least steps 2 through 6 and often go farther.

By 1969 about 98% of the United States pig iron capacity and about 89% of its steel capacity was owned by 22 *integrated* firms. The rest of the country's steel capacity was in 69 *semi-integrated* companies which bought pig iron and scrap, and produced and

Table 4-1.

Process	Product	Plant
1. Mining	Coal, iron ore, and limestone	Mines, quarries, steamships, docks, railroads
2. Preparation of materials	Coke Ore concentrates (pellets and sinter)	Coke ovens "Beneficiation" plants (pellet plants)
3. Smelting	Pig iron	Blast furnaces
4. Refining	Steel	Steel furnaces: Open hearth (50% of total 1968 production), basic oxygen furnaces (37%) electric furnaces (13%)
5. Rolling	Semifinished steel (blooms, billets, bars, slabs, tube rounds, and rods)	Rolling mills
6. Finishing	Finished steel products (sheet, strip, plates, bars, rails, tin plate, pipe, wire, structural shapes)	Rolling mills, tin plate mills, pipe mills, and a great variety of other finishing mills.
7. Fabrication	Manufactured steel products (ships, woven fence, buildings, bridges, oil field equipment)	Manufacturing plants and contracting offices of all sorts
8. Distribution		Warehouses (18% of sales) and salesmen

finished steel. In addition, the industry included some 130 *nonintegrated* steel companies which purchased ingot steel or semifinished steel and finished it.[1] These semi-integrated and

---

[1] The numbers of firms shown here are derived from the American Iron and Steel Institute, *Directory of Iron and Steel Works in the United States and Canada,* 1967, adjusting for mergers since. Percentages of capacity are based on the 1960 *Directory* adjusted for mergers, abandonments, and new construction that has occurred since. A fourth type of firm that was once important is the "merchant furnace" which produced pig iron only. Only seven independent pig iron producers remain and they have only about 2% of the pig iron capacity.

non-integrated firms are quite important in some lines that do not require great size—such as, concrete reinforcing rod, electric-weld pipe, and wire—but they are generally unimportant in most rolled steel products which constitute the most important output of the steel industry. Some of the leading semi-integrated firms produce "special steels" such as high alloy tool steel or stainless steel. This is almost a separate field from the high tonnage "carbon steel" industry which supplies the materials for tin cans, automobiles, appliances, buildings, machinery, and thousands of other products. There has been a persistent trend toward full integration in the mass-production industry that most people think of as "steel."

Integration offers definite advantages in steel production. If blast furnaces, steel furnaces, and rolling mills are at one site, pig iron and steel can be kept at high temperatures as they move from one stage to the next, and gasses and waste heat from the coke ovens and blast furnaces can be used elsewhere in the mill. Open-hearth furnaces, the main type of steel furnace installed down to the late 1950's, used large amounts of scrap or purchased ingots, but the basic oxygen furnaces that are now replacing them require at least 70% of their charge to be "hot metal" (molten pig iron from the blast furnace), so that integrated steel mills now have an even greater advantage over steel producers who do not have blast furnaces.

B. *Economies of Scale*

Integrated steel mills are unavoidably big. The most efficient blast furnaces being installed today can produce 1 to 1½ million tons of pig iron per year, and there are some economies in having two such furnaces. Open-hearth and electric furnaces are much smaller than this, but the most efficient basic oxygen furnace seems to have an annual capacity of about 3 million tons.[2] Roll-

---

[2] These estimates are based on interviews by the author with representatives of seven steel companies and steel equipment suppliers in 1966 and on written replies from nine integrated steel producers received during 1965 and 1966. The estimates correspond closely to equipment sizes now being installed—32-foot hearth blast furnaces with daily capacities around 4000 tons and basic oxygen furnaces with capacities of 300 tons per heat and roughly 10,000 heats per year. A mill that used electric furnaces and scrap

ing mills may be even larger. A continuous hot strip mill may cover 40 acres and be capable of rolling sheet or strip for auto bodies or tin cans at rates up to ten tons per minute—something like 30 miles an hour! The capacities of such mills usually exceed one million tons a year and some of the newest are as large as 4 million tons.

Demand is apt to be strong for sheet today and for tube or structural shapes tomorrow. Most steel producers sell a variety of steel products to avoid the instability that may be associated with serving a single, specialized market, and this means other finishing mills in addition to the rolling mills. Most steel mills have more finishing capacity than steel-making capacity. To keep all their equipment busy, integrated steel plants typically have several blast furnaces and coke ovens in the hundreds.

All this adds up to steel plants with capacities of 3 or 4 million tons. A careful study of costs for new integrated steel mills in Britain seemed to show that average costs fall by about 10% with each doubling of capacity from 250,000 tons to 2 million tons per year and that there are some further economies up to 4 million tons.[3] Officials of sixteen steel companies contacted by the author in 1965 and 1966 estimated that an average of 3.8 million tons capacity were needed for minimum costs. At present price levels, such a plant would cost something like three quarters of a billion dollars to build. Bethlehem's new 2.0-million-ton plant at Burns Harbor, Indiana had already cost more than a billion dollars in 1969.[4] It is laid out to accommodate ultimate expansion to something like 10.0 million tons capacity—which would apparently cost several billion dollars in all.

It does not follow that simply because the most efficient steel mill is in the billion dollar range, the steel industry must inevitably be dominated by a few giants. The total steel capacity

---

(so that the blast furnace is avoided) could be a good deal smaller and still be efficient, but electric furnaces are still high cost means of producing the major tonnage items. If power costs are reduced sufficiently and if the problem of scrap impurities can be solved, steel producers may be able to attain low costs with much smaller plants in the future.

[3] C. Pratten and R. M. Dean, *The Economics of Large Scale Production in British Industry,* Cambridge University Press, Cambridge, 1965, p. 80.

[4] *Steel,* May 5, 1969, pp. 30–31.

of the country in 1967 was about 162 million tons, large enough to include 40 or 50 optimal plants. The integrated steel producers actually had 49 integrated plants. Yet, three companies accounted for just under half of total capacity. Control of steel production is far more concentrated than the industry's plants require.

It is an open question whether steel producers gain in *efficiency* by operating more than one plant. Steel men themselves differed on the question when surveyed in 1951–1952.[5] They can attain greater diversification and geographically wider sales with more plants. Yet, some of the most successful steel producers have been one- and two-plant firms.

C. *Raw Materials*

Most major steel companies today own raw material sources and product outlets as well as integrated mills. The savings that can be accomplished by combining mine, mill, and warehouse in this way are less obvious than the economies of mass production within the steel mills.

One gain that is sometimes claimed is simply not there. Students often conclude that if a company acquires its suppliers or outlets it can avoid paying their profits and thus cut costs. The trouble with this is that the mill will have to put as much capital into mines, steamships, and warehouses as the independent firms did. This investment must earn a return, whoever makes it. The businessman who thinks he is saving money by making the investment himself is just not allowing a return on his own money. Of course, the suppliers and outlets might have more profitable businesses than the mill, but this would be a good reason for investing in other industries, even if no vertical integration were involved.

There is perhaps something to be gained in coordination of operations at various levels by combining them all under one management. The qualities of ore and coal may be carefully controlled and levels of output at various stages can be kept in line. Steel firms gain little in timing by acquiring ore because ore shipped on the Great Lakes must move during the ice-free

---

[5] J. S. Bain, *Barriers to New Competition,* Harvard University Press, 1956, p. 254.

months and be stockpiled at the mills, regardless of when the steel is produced.

Whether or not they gain anything in efficiency, steel companies certainly gain in security by owning their own ore and outlets. It is understandable that steel men want to be assured of supplies in boom years and outlets in bad before sinking hundreds of millions into a permanent plant. The raw materials suppliers may have a similar point of view. An independent iron mine may not be a very attractive investment if the potential customers are few and powerful. An active competitive market could also give such assurance. Textile mills do not worry about being shut off from their cotton supplies, nor meat packers from shipments of cattle and hogs. They can always buy on the same basis as their competitors.

In the early days of the steel industry, the mills bought most of their supplies from independent coal mines and ore "merchants." Then in 1896 Andrew Carnegie, the largest steel producer, acquired a substantial part of the northern Minnesota ore reserves under a long-term lease. While this assured him of an ore supply, it meant that other steel producers had to make similar arrangements or expect trouble. There followed a race to buy up ore lands and companies that owned ore lands until practically all useful domestic ore was either owned by, or under long-term contract to, major steel producers. The few merchants that remain today have close ties with major steel companies. Most of their output goes to the majors because of the steel companies' rights to jointly owned mines or because of long-term contracts.

In some cases, steel firms may have to invest in raw material production simply because no one else will. This has not been true of Appalachian coal, Great Lakes shipping, or high-grade Minnesota iron ore, where large numbers of independent firms exist, or at least existed until the steel companies came along. In the 1950's however, the industry had to turn to other sources as the high-grade Lake Superior ore approached exhaustion. Most of the new projects have been on a scale that only very large firms could handle. USS's ore deposits at Cerro Bolivar are in a largely undeveloped section of central Venezuela and required a 90-mile railroad, a 150-mile deep sea channel on the Orinoco River, and a tropical city. The mines on the Labrador-Quebec border were financed jointly by six large steel and two ore companies and involved a 360-mile railroad, a large hydro-electric development, and another city, this time in the northern wilderness. (They were also one of the main reasons for the St. Lawrence Seaway.) The low-grade taconite ores of Minnesota require large scale pellet plants which have again been cooperative ventures of major steel and ore companies. Each of these ore developments required an initial investment of more than $100 million dollars. Some came as high at $300 million.[6]

D. *Outlets*

The forward integration of steel companies into such fields as construction ship-building, oil field supply, fencing, steel drums, and warehousing makes sense mainly from the point of view of security again. By acquiring outlets, an individual steel company could assure itself of markets. Logically, it was in the depression years of the 1930's that the forward integration movement really got under way, though it has continued since. Of course, what one firm gained the others lost, so the forward integration movement became another race. In the 1930's and 1940's the eight leading steel companies absorbed 104 fabrication and warehouse companies, including some of the largest in their respective fields.[7] Forward integration into such fields as construction and warehouses has continued since, but it has not been carried far enough to threaten new competition for major steel customers. Any steel company that starts making tin cans or appliances is likely to lose the business of existing tin-can or appliance firms.

E. *Vertical Integration and Competition*

Whatever the purpose, expansion of steel companies back to the raw materials and forward toward the consumer reduced the

[6] The cost of the various projects came from *Moody's Industrial Manual,* 1960; Federal Trade Commission, *op. cit.;* and testimony of several witnesses at the Subcommittee on Anti-Trust and Monopoly, *Administered Prices,* 1957 (hereafter *Administered Prices*), esp. p. 841.

[7] House of Representatives, Select Committee on Small Business, 81st Congress, 2nd Session, *Steel—Acquisitions, Mergers, and Expansion of Twelve Major Companies, 1900–1950,* 1950, *passim.*

chances of new competition.[8] The number of companies that can build such empires is certainly limited. Once the empires are built, such nonintegrated raw material producers and steel outlets as remain can hardly be very independent. They are beholden to the major steel companies for markets in bad times and for supplies in good.

The control of iron ore by the major steel producers has traditionally been a particularly serious barrier to new entrants. As far back as 1911, a very knowledgeable steel man predicted that further development would be by firms already in the industry "for the reason that the possibility of a new company getting a sufficiently large supply of raw materials would make it exceedingly difficult, if not impossible."[9] Actually, new entry has occurred since then, some of the firms acquiring ore by merger or long-term contracts with the few remaining ore merchants and others, depending on local deposits in new regions such as the South and the Southwest.

The problem of ore supplies may be less of a barrier today than it has been over most of this century. Taconite reserves were much more widely available than direct shipping ores had been, so ore merchants and new steel companies were able to acquire additional reserves more easily when the high-grade ores ran out and the industry switched to taconite. Many of the new foreign ore developments were projects of existing major steel companies, but iron ore is now available on a worldwide basis, some of it from independent suppliers. The Japanese mills now buy most of their ore from a variety of independent sources on an oceanwide market. Steel men report that ore was available on good terms throughout the 1960's. Nevertheless, most firms still try to assure themselves of 50 to 100 years' supply of ore for any addition they make to capacity.

---

[8] Vertical integration need not reduce competition in all industries just because it seems to in steel. The possibility that large-scale retailers may become their own wholesalers or suppliers is a potent source of competitive pressure in many fields.

[9] Charles M. Schwab (then president of Bethlehem Steel and former president of USS) at Stanley Committee Hearings, Vol. 2, p. 1291. Quoted in Federal Trade Commission, *op. cit.*, p. 27.

II. CONCENTRATION AND ANTITRUST

A. *Steel Before 1900*

Until the 1860's steel was an expensive specialty product used by tool markers. The Civil War was fought with wrought iron rifles and cast iron or bronze cannons. The development of the Bessemer and open-hearth furnaces in the 1860's offered industry cheap steel for the first time, and the new metal rapidly displaced other materials. The market that steel took over grew spectacularly in the subsequent period with the building of the railroads and the industrialization of much of America. Steel production doubled about every six years from 1880 to 1905. It was growing as fast in that quarter century as did electric power from 1905 to 1930 or aluminum from 1930 to 1955, and faster than either of these have been able to grow in more recent years.[10]

In the early years steel, like wrought iron before it, was produced on a very small scale. The advantages of integration led to the construction of huge steel mills in the 1870's and 1880's by men such as Andrew Carnegie, but even then the industry was not very concentrated. In 1894 the four largest firms accounted for only 28% of the country's steel-ingot capacity.[11] The industry was about as concentrated then as the textile industry is today. The steel industry was noted for sharp competition in those days. Wide price fluctuations occurred, and large rebates were often given to big buyers. Agreements to fix price or output or to divide up the market were common, but they were notable mainly for the frequency with which they were broken.[12]

B. *The Sherman Act—Collusion*

Steel has since become a highly concentrated industry where the leading firms can generally control the terms on which they sell.

---

[10] Based on *Historical Statistics of the United States*, series M-251, P-203, and S-28 and corresponding data in *Statistical Abstracts* since 1962.

[11] Derived from American Iron and Steel Institute, *Directory,* 1894, and *Historical Statistics of the United States,* p. 418.

[12] See Peter Temin, *Iron and Steel in Ninteenth-Century America,* The M.I.T. Press, Cambridge, 1964, Chapter 8 for a picture of structure and conduct in that era.

This transformation has occurred *since* the passage of the Sherman Anti-Trust Act in 1890. The growth of the big steel companies and the announced public policy of preventing monopoly power were not always as inconsistent as they seemed.

The Sherman Act has two major provisions. In Section 1 it prohibits collusion:

Every contract, combination in the form of trust or otherwise, or conspiracy, in restraint of trade or commerce among the several states, or with foreign nations is declared to be illegal. . . .

In section 2 it prohibits monopolization:

Every person who shall monopolize, or attempt to monopolize, or combine or conspire with any other person or persons, to monopolize any part of the trade or commerce among the several states or with foreign nations shall be deemed guilty of a misdemeanor . . . .

The reader may be excused if he is not sure what those provisions mean. The very broad language in the statute left the exact content of the law up to the courts.

The meaning of Section 1 was established quite early in the Addyston Pipe and Steel Case.[13] A group of cast iron soil pipe manufacturers were charged with having made agreements to reserve particular cities for individual firms, to sell at agreed-upon prices in certain other areas, and to submit bids on public contracts according to a prearranged plan. Similar practices had been common in the steel industry. The firms under indictment argued that the prices agreed upon were reasonable and that they were merely preventing ruinous competition. However, Judge (later President) Taft decided that Section 1 forbids any overt agreement with the primary purpose of restricting competition, regardless of the purported "reasonableness" of the prices that resulted.

While the courts have changed their interpretation on other aspects of the antitrust law, Taft's decision on overt agreements in restraint of trade set a precedent that remains virtually intact today. The prohibition was often violated. Collusion cases have come before the courts quite regularly from industries of all shapes and sizes. For instance, in 1964 and 1965 members of the

---

[13] U.S. v. Addyston Pipe and Steel Co., 85 Fed. 271 (1898).

steel industry were charged with rigging bids in the sale of structural steel in one case and in the sale of pressure pipe in another, and with meeting to agree on the charges for "extras" (special sizes, shapes and finishes) on steel sheet and strip in a third case. The firms involved pleaded *nolo contendere*[14] and paid their fines in all three cases. The most spectacular collusion cases, however, were those in the electrical equipment industry where officers of such firms as General Electric and Westinghouse went to jail, and settlements were in the hundreds of millions of dollars before the cases were finished.

C. *United States Steel*

At about the time of the Addyston case, the steel industry, like many others, contracted merger fever. Some economists believe the decision played a role. It was now definitely illegal to enter an agreement with your competitor but, for the next few years, it looked as if you were free to buy him out.

Steel companies did just this in the late 1890's. Table 4-2 lists some of the important steel mergers that occurred between 1898 and 1901. Then, in 1901, a group of citizens led by J. P. Morgan contrived to merge the mergers. They brought all of the combinations listed in Table 4-2 plus the lion's share of Minnesota iron ore reserves under a single roof entitled United States Steel (USS).[15] The corporation was the largest of its kind ever organized in the United States up to that time. It was America's first billion-dollar corporation. It controlled 44% of the country's reported steel ingot capacity,[16] and 66% of output. Its subsidiaries

---

[14] A plea of nolo contendere means "no contest." The firms did not admit guilt, but they chose not to fight the case. The court may refuse to hear such a plea. The cases mentioned here are listed in the CCH *Trade Regulation Reporter.*

[15] There were a number of other mergers of the same period (1898 to 1901) that were not included in USS. Two that are still important are Republic Steel (1899), which combined 30 rolling mill companies, and Crucible Steel (1900), which combined practically all of the nation's crucible steel capacity.

[16] It seems likely that USS's share of ingot capacity at that time was understated because other firms overstated their capacity. George Stigler, "Monopoly & Oligopoly by Merger," *American Economic Review,* Proceedings, May 1950, p. 30.

Table 4-2.

Year and Company		Number of Companies
Basic steel producers		
1898 Federal Steel	15% of ingot capacity	a
1899 National Steel	12% of ingot capacity	8
1900 Carnegie Steel	18% of ingot capacity	a
Steel finishers		
1898 American Tin Plate	About 75% of tin plate output	36
1898 American Steel and Wire	About 80% of wire and wire products	19
1899 National Tube	75% of wrought tubing	13
1899 American Steel Hoop	Barrel hoops and cotton ties	9
1900 American Sheet Steel	About 70% of sheet steel capacity	17
1900 American Bridge	About half of structural steel business	26
1900 Shelby Steel Tube	About 90% of seamless tube output	13

a Federal Steel combined two major steel producers and a number of ore and transportation firms. Carnegie Steel was a reorganization of an earlier group of affiliated firms.
Source. Derived from the Commissioner of Corporations, *Report of the Steel Industry,* 1911, Pt. I, pp. 2–5. Select Committee on Small Business, *op. cit.,* and Gertrude G. Schroeder, *The Growth of Major Steel Companies, 1900–1950,* "Johns Hopkins University Studies in Historical and Political Science," Series LXX, No. 2, Johns Hopkins University Press, Baltimore, 1952, pp. 36–38.

had even greater predominance in some finished lines such as pipe, wire, and rails. Moreover, the ingot capacity of USS was regionally concentrated. When originally organized, the corporation had no important basic plants east of the Pittsburgh area, south of the Ohio, or west of the Mississippi, so that within the lake states it was even more powerful than in the country as a whole. In 1907 it acquired the Tennessee Coal, Iron and Railroad Company and thus became the dominant producer in the South. It only began producing steel in the West in 1930 and it started building its first fully integrated eastern plant in 1951.

USS was a holding company somewhat like the public utility holding companies of the 1920's or the new conglomerates of the 1960's. Owners of the operating firms and of the combinations of 1898 to 1900 exchanged their stock for securities of the new corporation. They were willing to do this because they usually received securities worth more than those they surrendered. Owners of a $1 million firm would receive stock and bonds with a face value of $2 million.[17] Of course, a share of stock need not sell at its par value. On the stock market a share with $100 printed clearly on its face may sell for $200 or $20 or $2. However, the securities issued by USS held up in value, and the owners of the old companies prospered.

By what alchemy were J. P. Morgan and his friends able to change a $1 million asset into a $2 million asset? Buyers must have been convinced that USS combined had much better profit prospects than USS in bits and pieces. This is hardly surprising. A near monopoly is likely to do much better than its parts in competition with one another. The owners of the original firms whose participation made the combine possible were able to take most of the prospective extra profits in one lump by selling out at a large gain. Buyers of USS stock[18] bid its prices up until it yielded only normal returns *to them.* Incidently, the organizers did not go unrewarded. Morgan and the other firms that participated in these mergers received securities worth more than $60 million as their fees.

The chairman of the board of the new corporation was Judge Elbert H. Gary, not a steel man but a Chicago attorney who played an important role in the earlier consolidations and had the confidence of Morgan. He led the corporation for its first

---

[17] The Commissioner of Corporations attempted to estimate the value of USS's components at the time of its organization. He arrived at $676 million by a historical study of the tangible assets of the component firms, $682 million by an attempt to measure replacement costs, and $792 million by adding up the market value of the securities of the component firms. Against this, USS had securities outstanding with face values of $1402 million in 1901. Commissioner of Corporations, *op. cit.,* p. 15.

[18] The stock market might also have anticipated profits due to economies of scale, but it is doubtful whether USS could realize many economies not already available to its component firms. An optimal, fully integrated mill producing rails (the product that then required the largest capacity) seems to have involved four blast furnaces, two Bessemer converters, a blooming mill, and several rail mills. With the equipment then in use, such a mill would have a capacity of 500,000 to 1 million tons. Altogether USS had 10 million tons capacity when formed.

three decades, and more than any other man he set the tone of business in the steel industry.

He was convinced that the only policy for USS was to avoid acts of aggression and to cooperate with other steel producers for the good of the whole industry.[19] As America's biggest company in a basic industry with a spectacular organizational history, USS was always in the public eye, and its prospects for survival in the trust-busting days of the 1900's would have been dim if it had followed the aggressive policies of the tobacco and oil trusts. Instead, Gary sought stability and good public relations.

D. *Price Policy—The Gary Dinners*

Judge Gary is best known for the pricing policy he inaugurated. USS had not absorbed everyone in the industry. There were still a number of producers of a workable size, though the largest had only about 5% of the nation's steel capacity.[20] The corporation sought the cooperation of these smaller firms.

In 1907 there began a famous series of "Gary dinners" which all the important steel producers attended. They were repeated often. Permanent committees were appointed to deal with specific products such as steel bars, ore and pig, and rails and billets. The participants made no formal agreements because to do so would have been illegal. They did make declarations of policy and each felt honor bound to notify his dinner associates if he chose to change. The members of the industry turned out to be very cooperative. Judge Gary reported in a speech made October 24, 1910:

---

[19] His attitudes are well documented. See Ida M. Tarbell, *The Life of Elbert H. Gary,* Appleton and Co., 1925, especially pp. 124, 126-151, and 240, and Arundel Cotter, *The Authentic History of the United States Steel Corporation,* Moody Magazine and Book Co., 1916, pp. 171–186. Tarbell presents Gary as an evangelizer preaching cooperation and public relations to the formerly buccaneering steel men.

[20] In 1904 Lackawanna Steel and Jones and Laughlin each had about 4.1% of reported industry steel-ingot capacity. Pennsylvania Steel and Maryland Steel were commonly owned. Between them they had 5.8% of reported steel capacity. These market shares may be understated because of the inclusion of obsolete capacity in the industry total. Derived from American Iron and Steel Institute *Directory* for 1904 and *Historical Statistics of the United States.*

Since 1907 . . . we have in large measure at least worked together; we have secured as a rule the maintenance of fair prices; we have avoided injuring our neighbors who are in competition with us; we have helped one another almost daily and have secured and maintained conditions that are much better than they were during the times many years ago when, regardless of public sentiment, contracts were actually made though not kept, to establish and maintain prices.[21]

For the most part, USS set the pattern and the others followed. It sold all of its products at their Pittsburgh price plus rail freight from Pittsburgh, regardless of where they were actually produced, and all the other steel producers did the same, even those whose only plants were in the Chicago or Philadelphia areas.[22] The major steel companies published identical lists of "extras" to cover the various specifications to which steel was made. When USS changed the prices of its products, other manufacturers of the same items made equivalent changes.

The Gary dinners ended in 1911, but cooperation among steel makers did not. Established pricing practices such as Pittsburgh-plus, uniform lists of extras, and price leadership continued. This was understandable. Small firms, one tenth the size of "big steel," were not likely to challenge its position of leadership. Generally they had no reason to. Why should they be eager to return to price competition? In a subsequent antitrust case against the corporation, the other firms had nothing but good to say about USS.

The corporation had unquestioned control over steel prices most of the time, and presumably it set them with an eye to its own profits. However, a profitable price for USS was apt to be a profitable price for the smaller firms that had not been absorbed and for prospective new ones as well. If the corporation took full advantage of its powerful position, it would provide a strong incentive for new firms to enter the industry and for old ones to

---

[21] Addresses and Statements by Elbert H. Gary, 1904–1927 (pamphlets, speeches, and statements collected by J. A. Farrell and bound, in Baker Library, Harvard), quoted in Louis Marengo, *Basing Point Pricing in the Steel Industry,* unpublished doctoral dissertation, Harvard University, Cambridge, June 1950, p. 300.

[22] This system of pricing, known as the basing point system, will be discussed more fully on pp. 180–182.

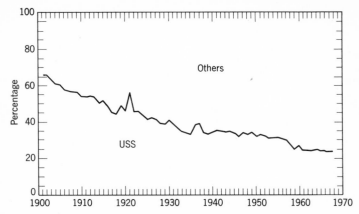

Figure 4-1. USS's share of national crude steel production. *Source.* USS, *Business—Big and Small—Built America* (materials presented at Celler Committee Hearings, 1950), *Moody's Industrial Mannual,* 1969, and American Iron and Steel Institute, *Annual Statistical Report.*

expand. Actually it had little choice. It had to take fairly substantial economic profits in view of the great amount of securities that had been issued at its birth. If it had not it would have offered very low returns to the holders of those securities.

The new conditions in steel did attract new steel producers. Many of the leading companies of the industry today either were organized or built their first major plants in the decade after the emergence of USS, which seemed to offer stable and profitable prices to anyone who could get under its big umbrella.[23] In the nineteenth century the corporation might have tried to keep the newcomers out with price wars or by excluding them from ore supplies, but such tactics were not consistent with Judge Gary's new policies. The policy resulted in an almost continuous decline in the corporation's share of steel production (Figure 4-1). The

---

[23] This was true of Inland Steel, Bethlehem Steel, Youngstown Sheet and Tube, Weirton Steel (predecessor of National Steel), and to a lesser extent, Armco. The other two major firms besides USS are Republic Steel, formed at the height of the merger movement in 1899, and Jones and Laughlin, the only firm in the group that was a major producer in its present form in the nineteenth century.

corporation's share of ingot production has gone from two thirds at its birth to one fourth in the 1960's! USS has grown, but the steel industry has grown considerably faster.[24]

E. *Monopolizing*

Why wasn't USS just one big continuous violation of Section 2 of the Sherman Act? Was it not "monopolizing" a very substantial "part of the commerce . . . among the several states?" The courts had a difficult time deciding, but they finally concluded that it was not.

The basic issue was the definition of the verb "to monopolize." It was established in the early years of this century that overt predatory acts to get and maintain monopoly—such as price wars designed to drive competitors out of business—were illegal under Section 2. Standard Oil and American Tobacco were convicted of "monopolizing" in 1911 and were ordered broken up by the courts. They had controlled the great bulk of their respective industries, but the language of the Supreme Court's decisions made it clear that it was their unreasonable behavior that convicted them. What about a monopolistic firm that avoided such behavior?

The government brought a case against USS a few months after the Standard Oil and American Tobacco decisions, charging it with violation of both Section 1 and Section 2 of the Sherman Act. The case took nine years, but the Supreme Court finally decided in favor of USS in 1920.

On the question of collusion, the court acknowledged that the "pools, associations, trade meetings, and . . . social dinners" in which USS led the industry during the first decade of its life had perhaps been illegal, but they had been discontinued nine months before the antitrust case began. Informal price leadership was apparently within the law. The court dismissed the government's attack on the "universal imitation" of the Corporation's policy. It cited the testimony of a large number of competitors, dealers,

---

[24] There were other reasons for USS's declining share of the steel market. As part of his public relations policy, Gary seems to have decided to limit the size of his corporation to less than 50% of the industry (Tarbell, *op. cit.*, p. 257) and to avoid absorbing further competitors after 1907. Location and managerial efficiency were also important; they are discussed later.

and customers that "no adventitious interference was employed to either fix or maintain prices."

The corporation's large share of the steel market did not make it guilty of monopolizing either:

The Corporation is undoubtedly of impressive size and it takes an effort of resolution not to be affected by it or to exaggerate its influence. But we must adhere to the law and the law does not make mere size an offense or the existence of unexerted power an offense. It, we repeat, requires overt acts and trusts to its prohibition of them and its power to repress or punish them. It does not compel competition, nor require all that is possible.

In other words, so long as a firm seemed to behave well—that is, so long as it did not abuse its rivals or appear to exploit the public—it was legal under the Sherman Act, even if it comprised half of a basic industry. Since it is difficult to establish that a price is too high, this amounts to an injunction to keep the other firms in the industry happy and to maintain good public relations. Judge Gary's policy had been vindicated.[25]

The court's decision in the steel case probably reflected the sentiments of a large part of the American public at the time. Some practices of big business in the past were certainly reprehensible. Reasonable men could see something wrong with Jim Fisk stealing a railroad by stock manipulation, or American Tobacco getting out a special brand of cigarettes for the sole purpose of conducting local price wars with its rivals. Gary and his associates had done none of these things. USS acted in the interests of other steel companies rather than undermining them. It kept honest records and made them public. Its leaders were responsible businessmen protecting the interests of their stockholders and stabilizing the industry. It was difficult for many people to find their actions criminal. Of course, the interests of

---

[25] All of the quotations in this section come from U.S. v. United States Steel, 251 US 416 (1920).

Only four justices supported the decision. Three felt that USS was an illegal combination and should be dissolved. Two justices, Brandeis and MacRenolds, did not take part in the decision. Moreover, there has been considerable criticism of the government's presentation of the case. USS seemed particularly public-spirited in the inflation of 1919 to 1920 anyway. It maintained a stable price when it clearly could have charged much more.

big steel's stockholders and of the smaller steel companies are not always the same as the interests of the consuming public, but it is difficult to understand and evaluate the effects of monopoly.

The decision in the steel case set the tone of antitrust in the 1920's and early 1930's. It was clearly illegal for independent firms to enter formal price-fixing or market sharing agreements, but it was seldom illegal for them to merge. Moreover, if the formation of one or a few dominant firms led naturally to parallel price policies without formal agreement, this too was within the law. The point of view expressed in the steel case was not basically changed until World War II.

The courts' interpretation of "monopolizing" has changed substantially since the 1930's. Overtly predatory behavior is still illegal, but the courts have gone much farther. In a few cases involving nearly pure monopolies, the courts have come close to finding the mere possession of monopoly an offense. In many more cases they have outlawed restrictive practices such as long-term exclusive contracts or the accumulation and restrictive licensing of patents in cases in which the firms involved are dominant within their markets. The restrictive practices attacked are far more subtle than old-style predatory pricing.

III. MERGERS AND THE LAW

A. *Mergers among the Independents*

Steel is no longer an industry of one dominant seller. USS is still the largest producer, but it is one of eight big firms. While USS was declining to one quarter of the industry, new giants were arising. Most of these were the result of more mergers.

Bethlehem Steel was the child of Charles M. Schwab, an executive of Carnegie Steel and first president of USS. In 1904 he left USS and acquired the United States Shipbuilding Company which comprised several unprofitable shipyards and the small Bethlehem Steel works. He built up Bethlehem by exploiting the new Grey process for making wide flange structural shapes. Then, in 1916 he merged it with Pennsylvania Steel and Maryland Steel and in 1922 and 1923 he acquired the plants of Cambria Steel and Lackawanna Steel. Bethlehem thus acquired the third, fourth, sixth, and eighth ranking steel producers of 1904[26] and combined the bulk of the basic steel capacity east of Pittsburgh.

Republic Steel was the result of a merger of 30 small producers in 1899. From then until the late 1920's its main concern was the replacement of obsolete equipment and the unification of its enterprise. In 1927 it represented 2.2% of total ingot capacity. In that year Cyrus S. Eaton, a Cleveland financier, acquired control of the company and proceeded, over the next ten years, to engineer mergers with nine major steel producers. By 1937 Republic was the third ranking steel maker with 9.0% of capacity.

The growth of many of the smaller companies has also been by merger, though there are some exceptions. One study of 12 large companies concluded that about 30% of their assets' growth through 1950 was attributable to merger rather than new construction. Inland Steel acquired only 4.3% of its assets from the outside, but Republic acquired a full 50% that way.[27]

All the important increases in market shares have been due to mergers. No firm has increased its share by more than 4 percentage points by any other means since the turn of the century. Among the big three, only Bethlehem has been able to increase its share by as much as 2 percentage points by internal growth. Steel companies seem to have found it more profitable to grow by acquiring and expanding old facilities than by building new plants because (1) it was quicker, (2) it usually required less cash, (3) there was a ready-made set of customers with every newly acquired plant, and (4) in periods when the industry had excess capacity, it permitted firms to grow without unnecessary additions to capacity. From the public point of view, the results were not always so good. Mergers that permitted inefficiently small firms to move more easily toward efficient scale rather than leaving the business may have been in the public interest, but mergers that combined large and viable firms meant less opportunities for competition in the future.

B. *The Clayton Act*

The government made repeated efforts to check the merger movement in steel, all of them unsuccessful until the 1950's. The

---

[26] Bethlehem itself was fifteenth in 1904. Schroeder, *op. cit.*, p. 96.

[27] Schroeder, *op. cit.*, pp. 93–94.

Clayton Antitrust Act was passed in 1914 to spell out particular offenses that might have gone uncontested under the Sherman Act. Among these were mergers. No corporation is to acquire the stock of another competing firm "where the effect of such acquisition may be substantially to lessen competition."[28] The Federal Trade Commission (FTC) filed a complaint under this provision against the Bethlehem mergers of 1922 and 1923. However, it was unable to bring about a dissolution because of a Supreme Court ruling in 1926. The court concluded that the law had prohibited the acquisition of the stock but not of the plants, mines, and other assets of competing companies.[29] This loophole was only removed by an amendment to the Clayton Act in 1950.

In 1935 the Justice Department contested one of the Republic mergers, but this was no more successful. This time, the court concluded that the combination involved did not lessen competition "substantially."[30]

During World War II the Federal Government financed most of the expansion in steel plant. By the end of the war it owned 6% of total steel capacity.[31] For the most part these new facilities were sold to firms already in the industry. Some of them were so-called "scrambled" facilities, built as part of existing plants, which had only one likely buyer, but there were also four separate, fully integrated plants, all of which went to large steel producers. The most significant of these was the Geneva plant in Utah. Bids were made by several firms, but the Surplus Property Board finally accepted the offer of USS. It took a substantial loss in doing so, though the loss would have been greater if it had insisted on another buyer. On the other hand, by this one move the government made USS the largest producer in the West and extended the corporation's dominant position into a new section of the country.

When USS subsequently acquired Consolidated Steel, a West Coast fabricator, the Justice Department took another tack, this time challenging the move as a case of "monopolizing" under the

---

28 Clayton Act, Section 7.

29 Thatcher Manufacturing Co. v. FTC 272 US 552 (1926).

30 US v. Republic Steel Corp., 11 F. Supp. 5152 (1935).

31 *War Plant Disposal—Iron and Steel Plants*, Joint Hearings, Subcommittee on Surplus Property and Special Committee on Post War Economic Policy and Planning, 1945, p. 5.

Sherman Act. The courts ruled against the government once more, however, arguing that the merger was too small to constitute "monopolizing." A minority of the court dissented, arguing that if a firm the size of USS were free to make small mergers, the decision might result in the gradual elimination of competition.[32]

C. *The Antimerger Act*

The government's long history of failures in its attempts to check mergers seems to have ended with the passage of the Celler-Kefauver Antimerger Act amending the Clayton Act in 1950. For the first time mergers of every form were covered and the government could stop a merger if there was a reasonable probability that it might "substantially lessen competition." It did not have to prove "monopolization" to prevent a merger, the way it did in Sherman Act cases.

One of the first cases to be tried under the new act was the proposed merger of Bethlehem Steel with Youngstown Sheet and Tube, then the second and fifth ranking steel producers. Combined, they would have produced more than a fifth of the nation's steel. The companies argued in defense of the merger that they did not compete significantly, since Youngstown's plants were in the Midwest while Bethlehem's were on the two coasts. The avowed purpose of the merger was to permit Bethlehem to expand Youngstown's plants, especially those in the Chicago area. They argued that the merger offered the public the benefits of additional structural shape and plate capacity in the Chicago area and a firm capable of offering "challenging competition" to the USS.

The court rejected these arguments. It found that the two firms did ship substantial amounts of goods to common markets, especially in Michigan and Ohio. It also doubted that the merger was necessary to create additional Chicago capacity. Both companies had proved quite capable of rapid growth by internal expansion. At any rate, the supposed virtues of the merger were irrelevant since the law made no exceptions for "good mergers" if they could reasonably be supposed to "substantially lessen competi-

---

[32] US v. Columbia Steel, 334 US 495 (1948).

tion." Finally, the trial judge argued that if the merger of these two huge firms could be allowed, the door would be open to practically any other conceivable merger in the industry. The merger was therefore enjoined.[33]

The government has been very aggressive in prosecuting the new law since the Bethlehem case. By the mid-1960's it was well established that the law prohibited mergers between substantial rivals in even moderately contentrated markets (such as Los Angeles food stores) or vertical mergers in which a series of acquisitions by major firms could conceivable foreclose an important part of the market (such as acquisitions of shoe-store chains by shoe manufacturers). The government finally has the clear power to prevent mergers of the sort that created the steel giants.

D. *Conglomerate Mergers*

We succeeded in having yet another merger wave in the late 1960's, in spite of the tough new law. This time the mergers were *conglomerate* in character—that is, they combined firms from unrelated or only distantly related industries. Such mergers had been on the rise throughout the post-World War II period, but they took on the proportions of a frantic rush after 1965. Large firms were created almost from scratch as they exchanged complex bundles of their own stocks and bonds for one after another corporation.

Several of the integrated steel companies were involved. Lone Star Steel was acquired by Northwest Industries—Northwestern Railroad in disguise. Crucible Steel became part of the Colt Industries, which had also acquired makers of pumps, scales, diesel engines, machine tools, television sets, and firearms. Youngstown, facing possible takeover by several alternative conglomerates, agreed to an acquisition by Lykes Brothers Steamship Company, a much smaller company that had acquired a quarter of its stock. Jones and Laughlin (J&L) was bought up by Ling-Temco-Vought (LTV), a new company that had combined an electronics firm, two aircraft companies, Wilson and Company (meat packing, drugs, and tennis balls), Okonite Corporation (wire and cable),

---

[33] US v. Bethlehem Steel Corporation and Youngstown Sheet and Tube Company, 168 F. Supp. 576 (1958).

National Car Rental Systems, Braniff Airlines and assorted smaller firms into one of the most ungainly giants of the age. The LTV-J&L merger was the largest industrial merger in dollar assets to that date over all of American history, combining a 3-billion-dollar conglomerate with a billion-dollar steel company.

The purpose of many of these mergers seemed to be short-term financial gain. A firm that bought up another with a low stock price relative to earnings would add more to its earnings than to its stocks and bonds outstanding and thus increase its earnings per share outstanding. The original low price probably meant that investors did not expect much increase in earnings in the future, but the acquiring firm could make its own profits grow further by yet other acquisitions of the same sort. Some of the most active conglomerates enhanced their apparent profits further by changing the accounting practices of firms they acquired, by issuing great amounts of debt, and by taking advantage of favorable tax rules. For a while in 1967 and 1968 the stock market seemed to judge conglomerates on their prospects of additional acquisitions, but clearly this could not go on forever. When the chain letter ran out in 1969, the value of the stock in most such companies sank, and the game was over, at least for a while.

E. *Conglomerate Mergers and the Law*

The effect of the conglomerate mergers on competition was not completely clear, and for some time no legal action was taken against them.[34] By the start of 1969, however, the mergers had become so large and frequent that much of the public became convinced that something had to be done. The number of mergers more than doubled and the value of acquired assets almost

---

[34] Several mergers between firms in related markets were successfully challenged in court on the argument that potential competition is reduced if one of a few most likely entrants into a market is allowed to buy a leading firm in that market (for example, the acquisition of Clorox by Procter & Gamble). The aftermath of the Bethlehem-Youngstown merger case provides some support for this argument. When prevented from merging its way into the Midwest, Bethlehem proceeded to build a new plant from scratch near Chicago. The Midwestern steel market is clearly more competitive than it would have been if the merger had been permitted.

tripled from 1966 to 1968. Twice as many mergers were recorded in 1968 as in either 1899 or 1929, the peaks of our two previous merger waves. By 1968 manufacturing and mining mergers were occurring at an average rate of 67 per day and very large mergers (assets of a quarter of a billion or more) were being announced at a rate of one a month.[35]

A suit was begun against the LTV-J&L merger early in 1969. The government charged that the merger would permit large-scale reciprocity, would eliminate potential competition, and would increase aggregate concentration.

Reciprocity means inducing your suppliers to buy from you. Presumably, LTV could have used auto purchases by National Car Rental to fence off some auto steel sales for J&L. The reciprocity involved in this one merger could not have foreclosed much of the steel business by itself, but the you-scratch-my-back-and-I'll-scratch-yours aspect of all conglomerate mergers of the time taken together may have been important. The number of situations in which two companies met as competitors in more than one market, as competitors in one market and as supplier and buyer in another, or as supplier-buyer in one market and buyer-supplier in another increased very rapidly as the mergers occurred. There was danger that such increasingly interrelated firms would become inhibited from competing hard in market A for fear of what would happen in market B.

There was probably some chance that LTV would enter the steel industry or that J&L would enter one of LTV's multifarious line of business, but neither could be described as one of the leading threats of new competition (unlike Bethlehem, which surely was one of the most likely entrants in Chicago at the time of its attempt to merge with Youngstown). However, if the government prevented *all* very large mergers and if the apparent drive to diversify persisted, the government might induce a good deal of new entry into concentrated industries, with more competition as a result.

The increase in aggregate concentration that seemed to result for the conglomerate merger wave worried many people. The

---

[35] Federal Trade Commission, *Economic Report on Corporate Mergers,* published by Antitrust and Monopoly Subcommittee, Senate Judiciary, 1969, pp. 665, 667 and 674.

share of the largest 200 firms in manufacturing increased from about 45% in 1947 to 60% in 1968. What would become of the country if these large firms came to control the whole lot? This concern was probably more with the political and social consequences of bigness than with competition. Large firms certainly alter the democratic process, but many of LTV's acquisitions were big business even without LTV. It is not clear that LTV would have had more political power than J&L, Braniff, and Wilson taken together.

F. *The Case for Conglomerate Mergers*

There is something to be said for the conglomerate mergers, however. They may serve as means of changing managements in large firms or of shifting capital from one industry to another. Stockholders in large firms are seldom able to remove poor managements, short of all out disaster. But if the firm is not taking full advantage of its opportunities, it will be worth less on the stock market than it is to another management. This is especially true if the current management holds a large amount of cash, a safe but usually unprofitable investment. If a Lykes Brothers Steamship Company has better use for the money, it can buy Youngstown away from the current stockholders at a price above market, making everyone better off—except the previous management. One of the most common faults of old managements is likely to be a commitment to the wrong industry. One reason why the steel companies were such common targets of takeover in the 1960's was that they kept investing in the relatively unprofitable steel business. If the new firm uses the resources it acquires in another, more profitable industry, we may get more out of our capital resources after the merger than before. Of course, during the merger wave, the most aggressive acquirers were apt to use any cash they got to buy up yet other firms.

One sort of merger that the government should definitely *not* attack is the "foothold" acquisition, in which a major outsider acquires a minor firm in a concentrated industry. This would seem to be one of the most likely ways of effecting entry. For instance, National Steel acquired a large interest in Southwire Co., an aluminum fabricator, in 1968, and with that beginning and lots of cash it proceeded to build a primary aluminum plant. The merger therefore served to direct capital from steel to aluminum and to create a powerful new competitor in one of our most concentrated industries.

The LTV-J&L merger case never went to trial. LTV had incurred enormous debts during its acquisition binge. At the peak it had debts equal to 85% of its assets. When recession came in 1970 it faced the same sort of problems that many of the grand mergers at the turn of the century and the public-utility holding companies of the 1920's had experienced. It sold off National Car Rental and Wilson Sporting Goods, and the government then settled the case on condition that it also dispose of Braniff and Okonite.

The government still has several cases pending that will test the applicability of the merger law to conglomerates. No decision has been handed down in any of these cases at this writing. For the time being the Department of Justice has announced a policy of closely examining and probably challenging mergers in which large firms (among the top 200 industrials or firms of equivalent size) acquire leading firms in concentrated industries. Such a policy would not prevent takeovers of the Lykes-Youngstown variety or footholds like National-Southwire, but would prevent another LTV-J&L merger. The number of large conglomerate mergers fell sharply after the announcement of this policy, but this may have been more a matter of low stock prices than of the antitrust threat.

IV. OLIGOPOLY PRICING

A. *The Oligopolist's Two Demand Curves*

The steel industry with several large firms is apt to behave much as it did with one dominant one. The position of an oligopolist of the sort found in steel today is illustrated in Figure 4-2. The price of steel just happens to be $100 a ton. We will decide later how it got there. The firm can be thought of as having two different demand curves, depending on assumptions made about the reaction of other firms. D_1 is drawn on the assumption that no one else does anything when this firm changes its price. D_1 is very elastic because steel is a standardized product. Steel is made to specifications, and anyone with the necessary plant can meet

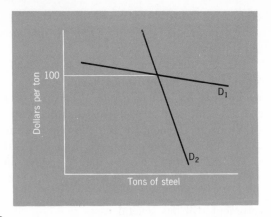

Figure 4-2

them. A firm may be able to win some loyal customers by filling orders promptly and accurately, meeting their needs when steel is scarce, and entertaining their officers when they come to town, but that loyalty would be badly strained if the firm raised its prices by a few dollars and the rest of the industry did not.

The other demand curve, D_2, shows the amounts of steel this firm could sell if all its rivals moved their prices up and down right along with it. D_2 slopes downward and to the right like all good demand curves, but it is much steeper than D_1. The only way in which this firm can sell more at $50 than at $100 is for the public to buy more steel in general at the lower prices. This company will not gain at the expense of the other steel firms, because the others cut prices as much as it does. D_2 is roughly this firm's share of the total demand for steel.

B. *Oligopoly Price Policy*

What policy a firm would follow with a demand situation like that in Figure 4-2 depends on its assumptions about the other companies. In view of the standardized character of steel, a very plausible assumption is that any price reduction by this firm will be promptly met by the rest of the industry. Steel executives have testified repeatedly that they think along these lines. For instance, Ernest T. Weir, then chairman of National Steel, told a congressional committee in 1950:

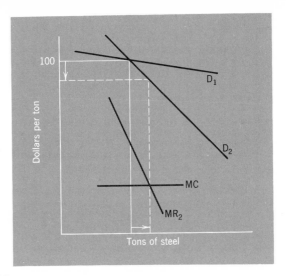

Figure 4-3

Practically every steel consumer buys material from more than one producer. Most consumers have a number of steel suppliers. When one producer lowers a price, the other producers learn about it immediately from customers. If consumers can get a lower price from one producer, they want that same price from all producers. If one producer raises a price, that becomes known too. If other producers do not follow, the consumer naturally switches his buying to the producers with lower prices.[36]

On such an assumption, the firm would have to use D_2 in considering any price reduction. It might still decide that a reduction was worthwhile. Figure 4-3 shows such an instance. Even counting the D_2 curve here, marginal revenue is greater than marginal cost. However, since this firm's D_2 curve is approximately a scale model of the industry demand curve, a steel *monopolist* with the same marginal costs as this firm would find a price reduction profitable in these circumstances also. If the other firms in the

---

[36] Hearings before Subcommittee on Study of Monopoly Power, House of Representatives, 81st Congress, 2nd Session, Serial No. 14, Pt. 4A, *Steel* (hereafter Study of Monopoly Power), pp. 810–811.

industry have similar cost and D_2 curves, they will gain just as the price cutter did. If this firm finds it worthwhile to cut prices, it will be increasing the profits of the whole industry just as a monopolist would.

A price increase is more difficult to analyze. The firm is bound to lose if others do not follow. It will find itself moving up its very elastic D_1 curve. On the other hand, a price increase may well be in this firm's best interest if the others can be counted on to follow. They are most likely to follow if the price increase is plainly in their interests also. At any rate, if they do not follow, the initiator is usually free to retreat. Figure 4-4 shows a case where a price increase is worthwhile, presuming that other companies have similar costs.

It is the D_2 curve, again, that indicates that a price increase is called for. In other words, in increasing prices an oligopolist is also likely to follow in the monopolist's footsteps. It would seem that oligopolists can arrive at the most profitable price for the whole industry by just following their individual best interests. It would certainly pay to get together and work out the price

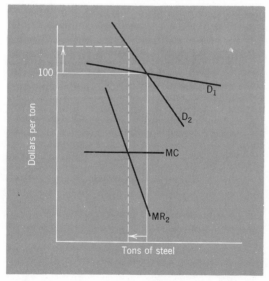

Figure 4-4

among themselves, but they can have a similar effect without directly communicating at all.

Things are not usually this easy. Someone may misinterpret his costs or industry demand. After all, the most profitable price can only be roughly estimated at best. Or someone may misinterpret another company's actions. Or one of the firms may not understand the rules of the game very well. Then the industry may wind up with prices lower than the optimum (from its point of view).

Steel men (and some economists) have often emphasized the dangers of price competition in steel.[37] Demand for their product is apt to fluctuate violently. They have fairly high fixed costs, though nothing like those of the public utilities. When demand gets down to half of capacity, which is not uncommon during recessions, individual firms are tempted to try to pick up a bit more business and spread their overhead by shading prices. Steel men feel that they are almost bound to lose from such "ruinous" competition.

C. *Price Leadership*

The steel industry has been able to accomplish necessary price changes with few lapses into price competition. Until the 1960's this was widely attributed to USS's continued leadership. It was no longer a giant among many small firms, but, as a rule, the other companies still followed its price decisions. It led in most general changes in list prices in the 1920's and 1930's and in every such change from the end of World War II to 1958.

Other steel companies have often led since then. The transitional case is interesting. On July 1, 1958, a substantial automatic wage increase occurred under union contracts. Everybody's marginal cost curve had shifted upward by a uniform amount. There was general agreement that a price increase was indicated. The press was full of speculation about it. There were comments about USS's responsibility to the industry. But nothing happened. USS simply did not lead. One small producer (about 0.3% of the

---

[37] A number of statements to this effect are collected in George Stocking, *Basing Point Pricing and Regional Development,* University of North Carolina Press, Chapel Hill, 1954, Chapters I and II.

industry's capacity) raised his price but he had to retreat when nobody followed him. The rest of the steel producers milled about for a whole month. Finally Armco (with 4.4% of ingot capacity) announced a price increase and the others, including USS, fell into line.[38] It is doubtful whether the ultimate price resulting from this minuet was very different from what would have occurred if USS had led right off.

Steel no longer has a price leader, and we no longer see general price increases for all steel products at once. Instead, Bethlehem might announce a change in sheet prices today, Republic might change plate prices next week, and USS might adjust tube prices later on. In most cases the rest of the industry will quickly move to the new price levels. Such price changes are less likely to get into the headlines than a single loud announcement by USS, but they are no less likely to be made with the purpose of enhancing steel profits. Armco, Bethlehem, and Republic are almost certain to set price with an eye to their D_2 curves, just as USS had done for the previous half century.

Neither the old price leadership pattern nor the new system of passing around the lead with the rest of the industry generally going along necessarily implies formal conspiracy. Several companies with a standardized product are bound to have the same

---

[38] A running account of this price change is available in *Iron Age* for the weeks June 26 to Aug. 7, 1958. The comment about USS's "responsibility" appeared in the June 26 issue. An interesting explanation for the price increase appeared in the Aug. 7 issue (p. 95): "Meanwhile steel earnings reports for the second quarter and the first half showed why steel prices had to go up. While profits were somewhat better in the second quarter than the first, six-months' earnings for most firms were still far below the same period in 1957." The argument was further reinforced by a statement that at least five steel firms were taking losses in 1958. This is clearly the thinking of an oligopolist. The low profits of early 1958 were due mainly to decreased demand during the sharp recession of that period. In a highly competitive industry where price is set by supply and demand, this would certainly have meant a decrease in price, not an increase. In short-run situations, competitive prices do not conveniently go up just because producers are having a tough time. Of course, wages would not be very likely to rise during a recession in a competitive market either.

A better advertised "failure" of USS price leadership occurred in 1962. It will be discussed on pp. 179–180.

prices if they all expect to sell. Any changes must be made by someone, and the others are automatically followers.

The pricing practices of the steel industry are not any the less monopolistic even if they come naturally. Regardless of how innocent modern steel executives may be of latter-day Gary dinners, USS or any other major firm that initiates a change in list price still must set its price with an eye to its demand curve, which is a near replica of the whole industry's.

D. *Cost Differences*

That does not necessarily mean that the price arrived at by steel oligopolists is the price they would set if they were combined into a single monopoly. Prices may be unsatisfactory for many in the industry if cost or demand differs from firm to firm.

For example, in the early 1930's a regular source of price cuts was National Steel, a combination of Weirton Steel, Great Lakes Steel, and some properties of the M. A. Hanna Company. It was organized just one week after the market crash in 1929. Weirton was a rapidly expanding firm which had installed one of the first continuous strip mills just before the Depression. Great Lakes was not only one of the newest firms in the industry (its plant was completed in 1929) but also the only integrated steel producer in the Detroit area. M. A. Hanna was one of the major ore companies so that National Steel, like USS and unlike many of the others, was able to meet all of its own iron ore needs. With efficient new plants, its own ore, and an aggressive management, National was in a better position for independent action than most steel firms.

Most steel prices declined during the Great Depression, but the price cuts were much greater on some steel products than on others. On the average, finished steel prices fell about 20% from 1929 to the low in 1933, but the prices of heavy steel products such as rails, plates, and structural shapes fell less than this while prices of sheet and strip fell more. Rail prices went down only 9% while cold rolled strip prices fell by 39%.[39]

---

[39] TNEC Hearings, *op. cit.*, pp. 10719–10721. The composite price of finished steel products published in *Iron Age* fell a little less than 20%; the prices actually realized by USS subsidiaries fell slightly more than that.

Part of the explanation for the lower prices on sheet and strip is that firms like National, which had installed the new continuous strip mills, experienced great reductions in costs and could afford lower prices. The high-cost producers had no choice but to go along with their prices.

When the National Industrial Recovery Act was passed (1933) permitting industries to work out "codes" to control competition and providing government enforcement, the steel industry was one of the first to participate. Its code went into effect seven weeks after the Act was passed. It formalized the old pricing rules of the industry and provided fines for those who did not observe them. To guarantee against secret price concessions, producers were required to file their minimum prices with the American Iron and Steel Institute and to give ten days notice prior to price changes. Since this almost guaranteed that price cuts would be met, in effect the code was forcing members of the industry to operate on their D_2 curves. Most firms filed simultaneous, identical prices, but even under the conditions set by the NRA code, National Steel refused to go along with several price increases and it initiated some important price cuts.[40]

National Steel was probably acting in its own best interests when it took the role of price cutter in the 1930's. The price competition that it inaugurated may have been "ruinous" for the others, but not for National. It was the only major steel company to make profits in every year during the depression. Its average rate of return over the whole decade was second only to Inland Steel's,[41] an amazing record for a company whose first years of business coincided with the nation's greatest depression.

The explanation is only partly secret price concessions. Others could and did do the same, though some companies with large and inflexible organizations were at a disadvantage in making individual price bargains. Even considering its D_2 curve, as it had to under the NRA code, National preferred lower prices than the others. With its new plants and good locations it had some of the lowest costs in the industry. Figure 4-5 illustrates such a case.

---

[40] C. R. Daugherty, M. G. De Chazeau, and S. S. Stratton, *Economics of the Iron and Steel Industry*, McGraw-Hill, New York, 1937, pp. 667–671.
[41] Schroeder, *op. cit.*, p. 175.

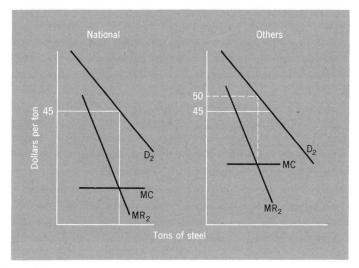

Figure 4-5

The optimum price for National Steel, on the left, might be $45, but for the older firms with higher costs $50 would be preferable. The firm that sets the lower price is apt to win the argument.

E. *Public Pressure and the Elasticity of Demand*

The best advertised breakdown in traditional steel price policies since World War II occurred when several major independents refused to follow USS in a general price increase in 1962. President Kennedy had intervened in the steel labor negotiations in 1961–62 to limit union demands, and had felt that he had a moral commitment from the steel companies to hold their prices constant if the union accepted a moderate settlement. As it happened, the union settled without a wage increase for the first time in thirteen years. Four days later, USS announced a 3.5% price increase anyway. The President brought every pressure at his command to bear on the steel companies. Some firms hesitated, and 3 days later Inland, followed by Kaiser, announced that they were not following. In an almost unprecedented situation, USS had to back down.

The immediate reaction of much of the business community

to the White House strong-arm tactics was anger. At the same time, some businessmen were critical of the price increase, not only because of the bad political timing,[42] but because it was bad business.[43] The Chairman of the Board at Inland Steel, where the price rise had been stopped, had opposed such a change well before USS had moved. He had said earlier:

Profits can be improved either by raising prices or by lowering costs. Of these alternatives I would much prefer the latter. Price levels which would further weaken the American steel industry's competitive position in relation to foreign producers would not be in the interest of the United States or of the employees, customers, and stockholders of the steel industry.[44]

If this statement is taken literally, it would seem that Mr. Block believed that the demand for *American* steel was quite elastic because foreign steel is such a good substitute. The leadership of USS seems to have felt otherwise. The situation might be illustrated by Figure 4-6. The seller who thinks the demand is relatively elastic (D_e) will choose a lower price than the one who believes in D_i. The first man is likely to win the argument.

F. *Freight Absorption*

Steel has a fairly low value per ton, so freight is an important cost. The price would naturally be higher the farther the buyer is from the mill. However, steel mills are not all at the same location, so a systematic policy of charging a single price f.o.b. mill[45] plus freight would result in price differences. Buyers would naturally choose the closest mill unless the badly located mills made up the difference with a lower f.o.b. price. But this comes perilously close to open price competition.

Historically, the steel industry has found various ways around this problem. For years everyone in the industry sold at the Pittsburgh price plus freight from Pittsburgh regardless of where

---

[42] *Steel* magazine, April 23, 1962, pp. 24–27.

[43] R. A. Smith, "Behind U.S. Steel's Price Blunder," *Fortune,* August, 1962, p. 75.

[44] *Ibid.,* p. 77.

[45] F.o.b. mill means "free on board." An f.o.b. mill price is the price of a shipment ready to be hauled away from the mill.

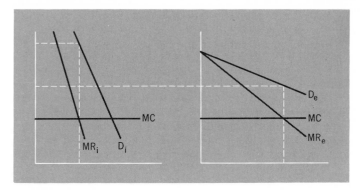

Figure 4-6

they were located. This was known as the *basing-point system.*
It was one of the subjects of the Gary Dinners and the NRA
code. It resulted in buyers in Chicago paying freight from Pittsburgh even though the steel was made right next door in a plant
with costs no higher than Pittsburgh costs. Other basing points
were established in 1924, though they really made little difference
until 1938. The whole system was abandoned after a successful
antitrust case against another basing-point system in the cement
industry in 1948.[46]

Today the steel mills do announce f.o.b. plant prices. If they
want to sell to customers near another mill they "absorb freight"
—that is, they try to match the nearest mill's price including
freight from that mill. The best profits are made on sales to
nearby customers, so there is a temptation in shortage periods to
stop shipping to distant buyers. When excess capacity appears,
steel mills reach out for customers where they can find them, and
absorb lots of freight in the process.

Some mills have to absorb freight most of the time. In Andrew
Carnegie's day the best place to make steel was in Pittsburgh, and
Pittsburgh, Youngstown, and environs still have much more ca-
pacity than would be needed to supply the nearby customers.
They operate at respectable levels without giving up profits on

---

[46] F.T.C. v. Cement Institute, 333 vs. 683 (1948).

neighboring sales and without unseemly price wars against their rivals in other cities by absorbing just enough freight to get their steel into markets throughout the Midwest and the East.

In times of excess capacity the steel companies really do forego profits in the struggle for sales. A representative of a midwestern steel producer told the author that the entire price increase from 1959 through 1967 had disappeared into freight absorption. Their mill net realizations were no higher than in 1959, though the price of steel was 6% higher. Freight absorption, though painful to the company, does not reduce the price to the customer. He pays the same amount that he would have paid to a closer supplier. What the steel company gives up in freight absorption goes to the railroad or trucker rather than to the buyer. Freight absorption is not completely worthless to the customer, however. He gets a wider choice of suppliers and probably better service, but it is doubtful whether he gets a dollar's worth for every dollar given up by the steel company.

G. *Happenings Under the Counter*

Once in a while straightforward price competition also appears in the steel industry. When they find themselves operating at far less than capacity, individual steel companies sometimes attempt to gain customers by making secret price reductions. They try to slide down their flat D_1 curves by not letting the others know what they are doing and thus avoiding retaliation. If such price cutting becomes widespread, the industry leaders may see fit to adjust official prices to reflect it.

Sub rosa price competition occurred during the depressions of 1921–22, 1931–33, and 1938. The steel industry avoided such price cutting over most of the post-World War II period. A recent study compared list prices with those actually paid by large buyers from 1957 through 1967 for many industrial goods, including steel. The actual price and the list price moved very close together for most steel products, with the exception of steel wire, where list price remained the same from 1959 through 1965 while transaction prices fell 15%. In wire, unlike most steel products, the integrated companies produce less than half of total output, concentration is low, and imports were already important in the 1950's. None of the many small wire producers needed to worry much about retaliation from his rivals, especially when the price concessions were secret. Undercover price competition seems to be much more common in other industries. The same study revealed many price fluctuations that did not appear in list prices for such goods as petroleum products, electrical equipment, and industrial chemicals.[47]

Price competition in such products of the large integrated companies as sheet and strip finally broke out in 1968. Imports at less than domestic prices had been a growing problem for some time, but they increased particularly rapidly in 1968. Rigid adherence to list price by U.S. mills made it easier for foreign steel producers to pick up U.S. customers, because the American mills seldom met foreign prices. Steel users imported especially large amounts in anticipation of a strike in August, 1968. The strike never came off, but with all the inventory that had been accumulated, demand fell. As a result, output ran at about half of capacity for the rest of the year.

At that point the steel industry caught one of its rare cases of price competition. List prices had been raised by about three percent with the wage settlement, but the trade press reported that the prices people really paid fell. The secret price cutting continued until November when Bethlehem announced a 20% cut in list price for steel sheets. The new price was reportedly near average variable cost, so that further price cutting would reduce the receipts of anyone trying to pick up more business that way more than it reduced his avoidable costs. That stopped the malaise. After a month the price was raised substantially, and a few months later, as capacity utilization increased, the August prices were restored and exceeded.[48]

Even in steel, outright price competition is possible if excess capacity becomes large enough, but it is not a regular habit.

---

[47] G. Stigler and J. Kindahl, *The Behavior of Industrial Prices*, Columbia University Press, New York, 1970, Chapter 6.

[48] This description is based on various articles in *Iron Age*, especially Nov. 14, 1968, pp. 57–59; Nov. 21, 1968; and Dec. 12, 1968; and in the *Wall Street Journal*, including those on Oct. 7, 1968, p. 1, Nov. 20, 1968, p. 3, Dec. 4, 1968, p. 6, and Dec. 24, 1968, p. 4.

V. THE MARKET POWER OF STEEL

Although the half-dozen leading steel producers are almost bound to set prices with an eye to the industry demand curve, it does not *necessarily* follow that their prices will be terribly exploitative. If good substitutes are plentiful or entry is easy, an industry with only a few sellers will not be able to take excessive profits. The only two hotels in town probably will not engage in violent price competition, but if the suburbs are full of motels, their oligopoly cannot result in exorbitant prices or excessive profits.

The ability of steel producers to agree tacitly on price *is* significant, because the firms in the industry have more monopoly power as a group than the hotels in this illustration. They have definite limitations on their power, nevertheless.

A. *Entry*

The three quarters of a billion dollars entry fee and the limited access to ore have made entry into steel production difficult though not impossible. The birth of a new, integrated steel producer, starting from scratch seems to occur about once per generation—Kaiser Steel, built near Los Angeles at the start of World War II, and Henry Ford's captive plant in Dearborn, Michigan built just after World War I are the latest examples.

The more common route into the steel industry is for a firm to start as a semi-integrated producer and to gradually build or merge its way to integration. Many of the major firms today began this way, and new capacity in the tonnage steel industry continues to appear from this source. Since World War II, four such firms—McLouth Steel (Detroit), Granite City Steel (St. Louis), Interlake Steel (Chicago), and Lone Star Steel (Dallas) —have joined the ranks of the integrated steelmakers. McLouth had some financial support from General Motors, Lone Star had government loans at its start, and Granite City and Interlake both attained integration by merger.

Several new semi-integrated steel producers appear each decade. A large proportion produce special steels or supply isolated markets such as Florida, Arizona, or Hawaii, but every once in a while one of them turns into a McLouth or Interlake.

Altogether, entry is not insignificant in steel production, but barring something revolutionary, the members of the industry can generally expect its pace to be stately.

The rate at which entry appears depends on the profit prospects as well as the barriers to entry. It was in the aftermath of the Korean War, when steel was often in short supply and when profit prospects at locations far from Pittsburgh were particularly good, that most of the entry in the last 40 years occurred. The share of capacity accounted by the 8 leaders fell from 80% at the start of World War II to 75% in 1959. It has hardly changed at all during the relatively unprofitable 1960's.

B. *Substitutes for Steel*

The leaders of the steel industry must also consider the competitive position of their product compared with other industrial materials—that is, they must consider the elasticity of demand for steel. Traditionally this elasticity was supposed to be low. Steel is a raw material that seldom accounts for much of the cost of final products. For instance, steel accounts directly or indirectly for about 16% of the cost of making a car. If steel companies were to shave 10% from their prices they might cut the price of cars by 1.6%—hardly enough to bring new auto buyers clambering at the dealers' doors.

The catch in such calculations is that the automobile producers and other steel users are likely to respond to changes in steel prices relative to prices of other materials, even if buyers of the final product do not.

An economist retained by USS in 1938 estimated that the elasticity of demand for steel was approximately 0.3 to 0.4.[49] This was a short-run elasticity—he was trying to evaluate the usefulness of price cuts in dealing with excess capacity during a depression—and he explicitly qualified his estimate by saying that at drastically higher prices the elasticity might be very different. Even in his day the elasticity would almost certainly have been more than 0.3 if the steel companies had doubled or tripled their

---

[49] USS, *TNEC Papers,* Vol. I, *Economic and Related Studies,* USS, 1940, p. 170.

prices, especially if the price changes promised to last long enough for users to substitute other materials.

As it happened, the steel companies did come pretty close to tripling their prices in the following twenty years (1938 to 1958). During the same period cement prices just about doubled, aluminum prices rose by a quarter, and the price of plastic materials actually fell. In other words, steel prices doubled or tripled relative to the prices of some competing materials and, as they did, the steel industry was regularly embarrassed by the appearance of aluminum truck bodies, plastic window screen, and prestressed concrete beams. Of course, technical changes in the competing products were part of the reason for these market losses, but those changes, in turn, were at least partly due to the high price of steel.

Today, with the technical possibilities for substitution much greater than in 1938, and with the prices of cement, aluminum and plastic much more competitive than they had been, the long-run elasticity of demand for steel must be far greater than 0.3!

C. *Imports*

A particularly good substitute for American steel is Belgian or Japanese steel. Until the late 1950's imports of steel were minor, but since then the U.S. steel mills have faced substantial competition from abroad. Foreign mills were becoming relatively more efficient. Between 1951 and 1959, American steel prices rose by half; British, Belgian and French steel export prices rose by about a quarter; and Japanese prices actually fell.[50] By the early 1960's Japanese domestic prices were 67% to 90% of U.S. mill prices, depending on the product. American import tonnage, which had been less than 2% of steel supply up to 1958, rose to 6% in 1959 and 17% by 1968.[51]

It was plain throughout the 1960's that American steel manufacturers could rapidly lose much of their market if they increased their prices relative to those in foreign sources of supply.

---

[50] CEA, *Report to the President on Steel Prices,* April, 1965, p. 18.
[51] American Iron and Steel Institute, *Annual Statistical Reports.*

D. *The Character of the Market*

One important limitation on the steel industry's monopoly power has been the type of buyers with which it deals. A number of its customers are huge firms such as the automobile companies and the tin can manufacturers. Such buyers are good matches for the big steel companies in any negotiations. In depression times they were such important customers that steel suppliers were ready to make price concessions to win their business. Moreover, even though entry was difficult for other would-be steel producers, these huge steel consumers are quite capable of breaking into the field if they feel it necessary.

Not all of steel's customers are giants, but most of them are well-informed businessmen. They know the products they are buying very well and generally have much better ideas of the prices available to them than the typical consumer buying shoes or toothpaste. Steel companies have very few opportunities to divert customers to high-priced sources of supply with advertising or superficial frills; and it is next to impossible to keep steel users in the dark about real differences in price or quality. The well-informed character of the customers contributed to the breakdown of tacit collusion in depression years and has deprived the steel makers of profit opportunities available to some consumer goods manufacturers.

E. *Public Opinion*

USS and the other large steel companies have had to keep public relations in mind when setting policy. USS has long been famous for its concern about public opinion. In the early days the continued existence of the corporation was probably at stake. In the years after World War II, the industry had to explain its periodic price increases to congressmen in their almost annual investigations.

It is clear that this public pressure kept the steel companies' prices below their most profitable levels in some instances. This is especially true of the inflationary years after World War II. Steel was in very short supply and some distributors were able to resell such steel as they did acquire at great profits on the "grey" market. Yet announced steel prices remained stable or increased only moderately, and the companies rationed steel by administrative decisions rather than price.

The steel companies' concern for public opinion was intensified, if anything, after their showdown with President Kennedy in 1962. Price increases in the next six years were small and applied to only limited groups of steel products. Moreover, they were largely offset by price reductions on other steels. Yet these "selective price increases" received thorough newspaper coverage and official scrutiny by Senate committees or administrative agencies.

F. *The Demand for Steel Reconsidered*

Altogether, the major steel companies, although they have a good deal more control over their prices than hog farmers or textile manufacturers have, are definitely limited in what they can charge. The demand curves we have been using in this chapter have resembled D_1 and D_2 in Figure 4-7, but taking into account the probability of entry, substitutes, and imports if the price reaches certain levels, the long-run D_2 curve must really look more like the broken line in Figure 4-7. The steel companies probably can raise price somewhat above long-run marginal cost, at least in those lines where they have a comparative advantage over foreign steel producers, but if they should push prices too

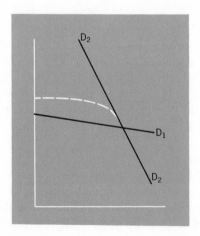

Figure 4-7

high they can expect to see their markets progressively disappear to new steel producers, new materials, and foreign suppliers. Anyone who invests in the long-lived equipment of the steel industry must expect to be around for a long time. If he expects to keep selling for a long time, he must keep himself within the bounds set by the revised D_2 curve in Figure 4-7.

VI. IMPORT CONTROLS

Imports were the most significant element of competition in the steel industry during the 1960's. The steel makers did not accept the loss of a sixth of their market to foreign mills lying down. They went straight to their Congressmen and demanded action. After the disastrous year of 1968, they got it in the form of quotas that put limits on the tonnage that European and Japanese mills could send in. Quotas of one sort or another had already been established on oil, cotton textiles, and meat, and more have since been sought on a wide variety of goods, so the steel-quota controversy is symptomatic of a serious general issue.

A. *Steel Tariffs*

Steel, like most American industries, had been protected by high and generally rising tariffs over most of its history, until the Reciprocal Trade Agreements Act of 1934 reversed this direction. Under that act, its various extensions, and the Trade Expansion Act of 1962, we have regularly reduced steel tariffs and those of many other industrial products in negotiations with our main trading partners. Inflation reduced the effect of many steel tariffs further, since duties, expressed in cents per pound, became less significant as prices rose. By 1968 the duties on various sorts of steel ran from 3% to 13% of import prices. They had run from 12% to 45% in 1933 when the tariff was at its peak.[52]

In the years since World War II the tariff reductions were negotiated on a multinational basis with most of the important non-Communist trading countries under the General Agreement on Tariffs and Trade (GATT). In these we were able to win

---

[52] U.S. Code, Chapter 19, Schedule 6, Part 2, Subpart B. The 1933 percentages were estimated using 1933 price levels and Class 2 Tariffs.

large concessions by many countries, covering the bulk of our industrial exports. The removal of most of the post-World War II quotas and exchange controls in Europe was particularly important.

The movement toward freer trade won wide support. With greater freedom to import and export, both the United States and its trading partners could specialize in the industries in which they were most efficient. The increased trade encouraged the shift of labor and capital in all countries concerned into fields in which they could be relatively most productive. The world was richer as a result. In addition, the tariff reductions increased competition in most advanced countries and probably contributed to more satisfactory international relations. The postwar support for freer trade was partly an attempt to avoid the disastrous effects on economic activity and international good will that had resulted from the spiraling increase in trade barriers in the 1920's and 1930's.

B. *American Steel and International Trade*

The United States was a consistent net exporter of steel from the turn of the century until the late 1950's. The steel industry stood to gain from trade expansion in those days. It had a clear cost advantage over foreign producers due to its superior ore and coking coal, its large scale, and its advanced technology. While Americans in the 1930's were worrying about the inefficiency induced by monopolistic practices, many Europeans were impressed by the efficiency of the American steel industry, especially after the "dazzling speed" with which it converted to continuous rolling during the depression.[53] In general, the United States had and still has a comparative advantage in industries that depend heavily on natural resources (iron, oil, and cotton then, and coal and feed grains now) or in which its large market and heavy expenditure on education and research yield large returns (automobiles and steel then, and aircraft, computers, and nuclear energy now).

The American steel mills' advantage had eroded badly by the

---

[53] Duncan Burn, *The Steel Industry, 1939–1959*, Cambridge University Press, New York, 1961, pp. 476–7.

1950's. European and Japanese producers were able to win many economies of scale and to adopt more advanced techniques as they rebuilt their industries after World War II. The price and wage policies pursued by the American industry in the 1950's only made its weakened international competitive position worse.

The events of 1968 led the industry into a concerted effort to get import quotas. Imports had skyrocketed during the inventory buildup in anticipation of an August strike, rising from 12.2% of apparent supply in 1967 to 16.7% in 1968. For a short while in August and September imports exceeded a quarter of total supply.[54] During the fall of that year heavy imports coincided with and played a large role in serious American excess capacity and significant price cutting.

C. *"Voluntary" Quotas*

With this episode as the background, the Johnson administration, as one of its last acts, persuaded the steel makers of Japan and the Common Market to agree to "voluntary" quotas limiting their exports to the United States for the years 1969, 1970, and 1971.[55] The foreign firms seem to have agreed for fear that Congress would pass more stringent mandatory quotas if they did not. These negotiations were followed by demands for similar arrangements in many other industries. The Nixon administration tried hard to negotiate such an agreement on synthetic textiles, and Congress pressed for other agreements on such products as shoes, apparel, electronic products, and glass.

Although the quotas were presented to the public as temporary, it seems doubtful that they could be. Protection will normally induce businessmen to invest too much in an industry and induce too many young people to learn trades there. After a few years it becomes much harder to remove the quotas, since to do so would impose serious losses on these individuals. Once we create vested interests, it becomes very difficult to change the policy that supports them.

---

[54] American Iron and Steel Institute, *Annual Statistical Report,* 1968, pp. 8, 31, and 45.

[55] Joint press release by House Ways and Means and Senate Finance Committees dated Jan. 14, 1970.

D. *The Arguments for the Quotas*

It is clear enough why the industry wanted quotas, but why should the rest of us go along? Proponents make several arguments.

They point out that wages are much higher in the American steel industry than in Japan, where the largest part of the imports originate. The presumed implication is that we cannot compete, but our wage rates are higher in virtually all industries. Yet we export as much to Japan as the Japanese do to us. Our high wages merely reflect the fact that labor is relatively scarce in the United States. In industries where our rich natural resources and large scale and advanced technology offer sufficient offsetting advantages, we can compete very well. If we cannot in steel, it means that our resources have less productivity advantage in that industry than in others.

A second argument has to do with our balance-of-payments deficit. Presumably it would be reduced if we bought from domestic rather than foreign sources. Perhaps that would be so, temporarily, though even that would not work if other countries impose restrictions on our exports at the same time. They are quite likely to do so because we are the world's leading importer of steel and of many other commodities. Even if we do get away with the restrictions without retaliation, we may not improve the balance of payments much because steel is an important cost for many of our export industries. Our machine-tool, diesel-engine, and farm-machinery makers will have a harder time competing abroad if they have to pay high prices for steel. Whatever adjustment in the balance of payments is attained must be weighed against the reduced competition and less efficient allocation of resources that follow from the trade restrictions. The balance of payments can be adjusted without such misallocations by changing price levels or exchange rates. A reduction in the international value of the dollar (or an increase in the value of the yen and of European currencies) would improve the market position of our steel industry as well as our balance of payments.

The most common argument for steel quotas is that we need a domestic steel industry for military security, even if it costs us something in inefficiency. Maybe this is so, though it could hardly make any difference in one of the 48-hour nuclear wars that the press talks about, and we seem to have regular access to foreign steel during limited wars of the Korean or Vietnam variety. Anyway, imports are not likely to put the entire American steel industry out of business. At least in the 1960's, foreign suppliers merely absorbed a large part of the growth in American demand. The domestic industry was able to maintain previous output levels and even grow. Perhaps we need some steel capacity for military security, but do we need enough to meet 85% of all our peacetime needs? The voluntary quotas reserve about that much of the market for American mills. There is something to the military self-sufficiency argument, but we should recognize how much it costs. Quotas involve consumers paying a hidden subsidy equal to the difference between import and domestic prices to the steel industry. Steel sales come to about $20 billion a year, so even a 5% subsidy might cost a billion dollars a year. The present oil import quotas are estimated to cost consumers $6 billion per year.[56] It seems extremely doubtful whether Congress would appropriate anything like those amounts to maintain such large domestic steel and crude oil industries as military reserves. Yet the government seems to find it quite easy to impose quotas that have the same effect.

Steel men sometimes allege that foreign suppliers are dumping on our markets. That is, they are supposed to be exporting steel at much lower prices than they charge at home. This would mean that they were discriminating in favor of us and against their domestic customers. Under the Trade Expansion Act and also under GATT we can raise tariffs to offset the effect of dumping, and we have done so for some other commodities. However, only very limited steel-dumping complaints have been presented to the Tariff Commission, and not all of these have been accepted.[57] If the Japanese really are systematically discriminating in favor of our fabricators, perhaps we should relax and enjoy it. The

[56] Cabinet Task Force on Oil Import Control, *The Oil Import Question,* Feb., 1970, pp. 259–263.

[57] Antidumping tariffs have been imposed on steel reenforcing bars and shapes from Canada and cast iron soil pipe from Poland. The only antidumping case against Japan was one concerned with wire rods in 1963. The tariff commission held extensive hearings on that matter but took no action.

United States will be richer and our fabricators will be better able to compete with Japanese steel users as a result.

E. *Faults in "Voluntary" Quotas*

Whatever case can be made for protecting the steel industry, "voluntary" quotas seem a poor way to do it. They create a cartel under which foreign private firms allocate the American market among themselves and between themselves and the American industry. This is an unseemly arrangement for the world's leading advocate of competition to sponsor!

Quotas, if effective, would isolate the American market from the rest of the world. Regardless of how prices change abroad, no more steel can come into the country, so American steel prices would be free to rise to any level that the domestic producers conceive to be in their best interests. This is especially serious in the case of steel because of the industry's proven ability to control domestic prices. A tariff designed to permit the same level of imports would still put limits on domestic prices. They could not exceed foreign prices plus the tariff.

All effective quota systems involve awkward problems concerning who is to have the valuable and limited right to import. This does not arise with a tariff because the difference between foreign and domestic prices is taken by the government rather than the private trader in that case. "Voluntary" quotas tend to break down and become mandatory because of disagreements about each importer's share. And for the same reasons, long lines tend to form outside the offices of persons who attempt to administer mandatory quotas.

In general, most economists would probably favor a higher tariff over the introduction of import quotas, if we must protect the steel industry.

F. *Why We Have Quotas*

In spite of our long commitment to freer trade and the obvious faults in the "voluntary" quota system, we seem at this writing (late 1970) to be headed down that road. Why?

One reason is that quota proposals have been considered one commodity at a time. The loss to consumers and exporters from any one new restriction is too widely diffused to generate much opposition. A steel quota might raise cost of living $30 or $40 a year. Most of us did not find that prospect serious enough to warrant a letter to our Congressmen when quotas began in 1969. On the other hand, the prospective gain from the quotas was sufficiently concentrated and large that it paid steel companies to twist almost every arm on Capitol Hill.

Another reason for the growth in quotas is that other countries still seem to believe the word "voluntary" and do not formally retaliate as they would against tariff increases or the introduction of mandatory quotas. It appears to Congress and the administration that they can respond to determined pressure groups in this way without our exports losing access to any foreign markets. This situation seems unlikely to last if we negotiate many more "voluntary" quotas. And even if the rest of the world never does retaliate directly, the precedents that we have set are likely to result in other countries' adopting similar arrangements, thus restricting our trade as well as theirs.

Is there a way to avoid the new protectionism? Perhaps the most promising proposal[58] for a way to check the growth in quota systems is to negotiate their revision or removal on a multinational, multiproduct basis, as the world did so successfully in the case of tariffs. We would have to acknowledge that our quotas were imposed by us and were not merely voluntary actions of inscrutable Japanese and European businessmen. Then we could propose to remove or weaken our controls on steel imports if the Europeans would ease their restrictions on our coal and feed grains and the Japanese would remove their quotas on our machinery exports. This would make it clear that American restrictions limited our exports as well as our imports. Important industrial groups would stand to gain just as much from the removal of the quotas as our steel companies stand to lose. Of course, the consumers on both sides of the ocean would be better off as well.

G. *Adjustment Assistance*

The removal of the steel quota at this point (1970) would probably not require much adjustment on the part of the indus-

---

[58] See Robert Baldwin, *Non-Tariff Distortions of International Trade,* Brookings, 1970, pp. 44–46.

try. As luck would have it, world steel markets turned out to be tighter in 1969 and 1970 than they had been for a decade. Prices rose rapidly abroad, to the point where the American industry was able to export substantially for the first time in years. It is doubtful whether the quotas really restricted trade much as a result. Such periods of prosperity are the best times to eliminate protection, because no one needs to leave the business in order to adjust. Removing protection at such a time simply directs new workers and new investment into other industries with better long-run prospects.

Removing protection from oil or cotton textiles now or from steel if we maintain the quotas until they make a real difference, would be much more difficult. The workers and investors who went into these industries in response to the quotas would then be forced to make large sacrifices to improve the standard of living of the rest of us. A case can be made that we have some moral obligation to the losers, and it is not politically very realistic to expect to pass legislation that would impose billion-dollar losses on such groups in any case.

There are two ways to deal with such situations. The easiest is to keep the protection intact. The industries involved will be helped, but the old, inefficient allocation of resources will be passed on to the next generation.

Alternatively, we can try to ease the adjustment of those displaced, by means of unemployment compensation, retraining programs, and relocation payments for displaced labor and government loans and tax writeoffs to facilitate the transfer of capital. In cases like oil, where resources often cannot be transferred to other uses, it would even pay to buy up and cap many of the high-cost oil wells if we could remove or weaken the restrictions in the process. With such programs the consumers, who gain from liberalized trade, can compensate the workers and investors who lose, and we will then all be better off because of our more efficient economy.

The Trade Expansion Act of 1962 provided for "adjustment assistance" of this sort, but it has not been used very much because such assistance becomes available only when it can be shown that an industry is suffering primarily because of imports due to the removal of a tariff. The administration has asked Congress to broaden this provision, permitting adjustment assistance when imports are a major cause of hardship, whether or not the removal of a trade restriction is involved. Although Congress seems ready to impose new trade restrictions with only moderate urging, it has not yet been ready to make this small expenditure to facilitate once-and-for-all cost reductions.

VII. PERFORMANCE

How has the industry actually fared in the presence of domestic oligopoly and growing international competition?

A. *Capacity and Output*

Figure 4-8 shows the ingot capacity and ingot production of the American steel industry since 1901. Steel capacity has grown a little more slowly than total industrial production and much more slowly than electricity. This does not necessarily mean that steel was dragging its feet. It was well established as one of our key industries at the turn of the century, while electric power was only then beginning.

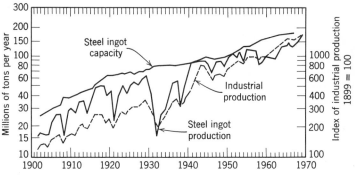

Figure 4-8. *Source.* Steel capacity and production: USS, *TNEC Papers,* Vol. II, and American Iron and Steel Institute, *Annual Statistical* Reports, 1968. Industrial production: National Bureau of Economic Research and Federal Reserve Board. Capacity estimates for 1961 through 1967 based on Jon P. Nelson, "An Inter-regional Recursive Programming Model of the U. S. Iron and Steel Industry: 1947-1967." Ph. D. thesis, Univ. of Wisconsin, 1970, pp. 384-7.

B. *Instability*

The most notable feature of Figure 4-8 is the instability of steel production. Output has been as low as 20% of capacity in one year, and it has often dropped below half capacity.[59]

This volatility is the result of the market for steel. Steel and things made from steel are durable, so purchases can be postponed in bad years. Moreover, a large proportion of the steel that is produced goes into capital goods such as machinery and buildings. Demand for such items is particularly unstable because it depends upon *changes* in the demand for ultimate consumer goods.[60] For instance, a shoe firm may normally need to replace 20 machines per year. In a recession when sales drop by perhaps 10%, it may be able to get along with no new equipment at all, and in a boom when shoe sales increase by 10% it may have to install 40 new machines instead of just 20. A 10% rise or fall in demand for shoes may lead to a 100% rise or fall in machinery (and steel) orders.

C. *Excess Capacity*

The steel industry had a long history of excess capacity. Even in prosperous years like 1909 to 1913 and 1923 to 1929, the industry as a whole ran at well below capacity, though there were individual plants with much better records. In view of the unstable demand, not all of this excess capacity can be looked upon as waste. Enough plant to meet demand in peak years means excess capacity at other times. Ten steel companies surveyed by the writer in 1965 and 1966 reported that the "normal operating rate" that they could expect in reasonably prosperous years was from 75% to 92% of capacity with an average of 81% of capacity. They have not done this well in practice. Steel output averaged less than 80% of capacity in the decade before World War I, in

---

[59] Since Figure 4-8 gives annual production figures, it does not show the extremes that occur in some months. Such years as 1958, 1961 and 1968 included months when the steel industry was at 50% of capacity. On the other hand, there were periods in a number of the postwar years when steel output exceeded 100% of *rated* capacity!

[60] Readers with a good economic vocabulary will recognize this as the accelerator effect.

the 1920's, in the 1930's, and in the 1960's. The rapid growth after the consolidations at the turn of the century and during World War I provided more than enough plant for subsequent years, and the conservative pricing policies of the industry protected obsolete plants that would probably have been eliminated in more vigorously competitive industries.

Because of this excess capacity, there were fairly long periods with little expansion in steel facilities. More than half of the relatively small expansion during World War II was undertaken by the government and not all of that was retained after the war. In the period from 1945 to 1950 there were only modest additions to plant. This was a period of steel shortage, and pressure was put on the industry to expand. President Truman once proposed that the government build facilities if private firms would not. After the Korean War, the industry finally made up for the previous 30 years' slow growth, and by 1958 was once more suffering from excess capacity. From 1958 on, imports took an increasing share of U.S. steel demand. The industry adjusted by adding only slowly to its capacity. By the late 1960's its operating rate was back near 80%, which it seems to consider normal.

The slowness of the industry to grow in the 1920's, 1930's, and 1940's cannot be interpreted as monopolistic restriction in the usual sense. A monopolist seeking maximum profits would build plant if he could sell its output at prices selected by him. However, the monopolistic position of the steel industry did permit it to make decisions on the safe side. There were few impatient upstarts to force its hand. When a race for additional capacity finally did occur in the 1950's, it went too far, but by the late 1960's the industry was again adding capacity at a prudent rate.

D. *Price Rigidity*

Steel prices are compared with wholesale prices of all manufactured goods in Figure 4-9. Steel prices proved somewhat more stable during the twenties and thirties than industrial prices in spite of the extreme loss of sales by steel firms. Prices of steel products where concentration was high, such as rails and heavy structural shapes, were particularly rigid.

Price rigidity is a common characteristic of oligopolies. An ingenious explanation has been developed. The effective demand

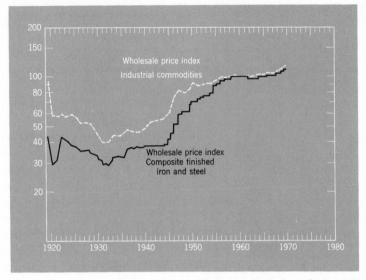

Figure 4-9. Wholesale prices of steel and of all industrial products, 1957-9 = 100. *Sources.* American Iron and Steel Institute, *Annual Statistical Reports, Surveys of Current Business, and Statistical Abstract.*

curve of a conservative oligopolist is a combination of D_1 and D_2. If he cuts his price he must count on the other companies following, but if he raises his price they may not. If he is a careful man, the oligopolist will consider D_2 on the way down and D_1 on the way up. In other words, the demand curve that concerns him is the dark portions of D_1 and D_2 in Figure 4-10.

With such a demand curve, the oligopolist is apt to leave well enough alone. If a price rise leads to rapid loss of market and a price drop means small additional sales, circumstances will have to be extreme before a change is in order.

Price rigidity would make sense even disregarding this "kinked" demand curve. If nothing else, price changes mean work. New catalogues have to be prepared and thousands of new prices have to be determined. Small changes are likely to be fruitless anyway. Steel makers cannot really tell if conditions would be better or worse at a price of $100 instead of $101.

Consumer reactions to price changes also encourage rigid prices. If low demand means low prices and high demand high

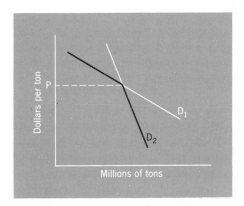

Figure 4-10

prices, buyers are apt to hold off ordering on a declining market and vice versa, thus making the industry's instability worse. At any rate, temporary price reductions in time of depression probably will not increase steel sales very much because the short-run demand for steel is certainly inelastic.

From a public relations point of view, price flexibility has its disadvantages. If Congress investigates whenever the price goes up, increases will occur only when they are obviously worthwhile and preferably when there is a good excuse such as a wage increase or a change in the tax law. Similarly, sellers will want to be very sure before cutting prices because it is so unpleasant getting them back up again.

Finally, in an oligopoly where every seller's welfare depends on a tacit agreement, every change may be dangerous. The industry may be better off taking decent profits at a long-established price that is accepted by everybody than trying to wrest the last penny from the market by changing price often and risking a price war each time.

The relative stability of steel prices during periods of depression gives some indication of the steel companies' control over price. They were not able to keep their prices up as well as the electric utilities in 1931 to 1933, but prices in purely competitive fields could hardly have remained as stable as steel prices in the face of a 75% drop in demand, especially in a field with fairly high fixed costs. The steel industry displayed steadfast tenacity in maintaining both announced and transactions prices stable from 1959 until 1968, even though output periodically went down to 50% of capacity. It finally succumbed in 1968, as we have seen (p. 183).

E. *"Creeping Inflation"*

In the 1950's, steel prices increased more than most. The annual steel price increase became something of a national institution and was widely damned as a major source of our "creeping inflation." The mere fact that a price is rising is not necessarily a basis for criticism. Some prices would always be going up and others down in a purely competitive economy depending on where shortages and surpluses appeared. In the early 1950's steel was undoubtedly in short supply, but this was not the explanation of price increases in the latter half of the decade when there was usually some excess capacity in the industry.

The price increases usually coincided with increased wages, which were themselves rising faster than in most industries. Steel prices rose proportionately with steel wages for a decade. Since steel productivity was also going up, this meant that steel prices were rising faster than labor cost per ton of output.

A plausible explanation of this behavior on the part of the steel companies might be that they had not been able to take full advantage of their position earlier because of public pressure and were just getting their prices up to what they felt was an optimum level. Steel makers defended their profits in 1956 and 1957 along these lines:

We started out through the war with a control on prices, and unfortunately control was not exercised to the same extent on wages or other things we had to buy, and we found ourselves at the end of the war in a position where we had been squeezed down to the three percent profit on our sales dollar . . . and we have spent the next decade trying to catch up.[61]

The rapid rise in steel wages had a somewhat similar explanation. They had increased less than most wages from 1939 to 1949, and

---

[61] Statement of Robert C. Tyson, Chairman of the Finance Committee, USS, *Administered Prices, op. cit.*, p. 278.

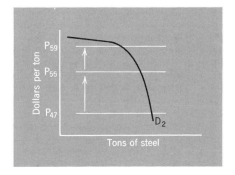

Figure 4-11

their more rapid rise in the 1950's brought them back to their 1939 level relative to other wages.[62] In both 1939 and 1968 steel wages were well above wage rates in manufacturing generally.

The new stability of steel prices and the new moderation of steel increases after 1959 has been interpreted by some economists[63] to mean that the steel companies and the steel unions had finally fully exerted their market power. The unusual expansion of new steel firms in the late 1950's, the influx of imports after 1958, and the stagnation of steel demand at less than 1955 levels for a decade while manufacturing as a whole grew by a third certainly suggest that the steel companies had precious little unexploited power left by the end of the 1950's. Figure 4-11 seems to fit the situation fairly well. A major steel company in 1947 could obviously increase price (and/or let unit labor costs go up) without losing much business. Until about 1955 he had more orders than he could handle. After that, further price increases seemed to push steel prices into a more elastic range of the steel companies' D_2 curve. By 1959 it may have looked to many major steel companies as if another rise in unit costs could mean disaster. At least it was then that they finally chose to fight the longest strike in the industry's modern history—the first that ended without a price increase. If this interpretation is correct, the spectacular government interventions in steel wage and price

---

[62] See Chapter 6, pp. 321–322.
[63] M. Adelman, "Steel, Administered Prices, and Inflation," *Quarterly Journal of Economics*, January 1961.

decisions in the 1950's and 1960's were of secondary importance. Until 1959 they represented a failing cause, and after that they may well have influenced the steel companies and the steel union to do what they would have done anyway. When imports were finally checked in 1969 and a world steel boom led to rising import prices, the industry finally pushed prices up once more.

F. *Steel Profits*

Figure 4-12 shows rates of return in the iron and steel industry compared with all manufacturing concerns. The steel companies have not earned particularly high profits in most years. The excess capacity of the 1920's and 1930's made steel one of the low profit fields. Government and public pressure did the same in the 1940's. The industry was finally able to get its profits into line with those of most manufacturing in the 1950's, but as the excess capacity reappeared in the late 1950's, the steel industry found itself back at the low profit end again. Steel profits are probably understated in the 1950's and 1960's compared with other industries because depreciation was exaggerated and steel had more to depreciate than most manufacturing industries. Even allowing for this excess depreciation, however, steel has not been very profitable in recent years.

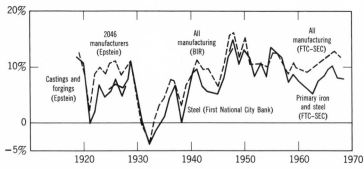

Figure 4-12.   *Source.* 1919 to 1928, R. C. Epstein, *Industrial Profits in the United States,* National Bureau of Economic Research, 1934. Steel 1925 to 1947, First National City Bank, *News Letters.* All manufacturing: 1931 to 1947, Internal Revenue Service, *Statistics of Income;* 1947 to 1968, FTC-SEC, *Quarterly Financial Reports, United States Manufacturing Corporations.*

From the point of view of the economy as a whole, the crucial question is whether the steel industry has access to enough capital to finance investments required for expansion (if economically justified) or modernization (and this should be justified too). In the 1950's there could be no doubt about it. The ability of relatively small and new firms like Kaiser and Granite City to double their plant in a decade, often with debt capital, meant that the industry profit prospects were easily good enough to attract as much capital as was needed. To judge by the excess capacity after 1958, it very possibly attracted too much. From 1958 on, the steel industry was a far less attractive place to invest, yet it spent more than a billion dollars on plant and equipment every year from 1958 through 1969. Perhaps some of the smaller steel producers were unable to invest as much as they thought would be profitable from 1958 on, but most of the firms with plants of efficient scale were able to do so. This implies that the steel industry's profits were not far from normal profits, even though it ostensibly earned a good deal less than the average for all manufacturing. Partly, this is because "all manufacturing" includes a lot of firms with a good deal of monopoly power.

G. *Profitability and Size*

Not all the steel companies did as badly as Figure 4-12 suggests. Over much of the 1920's, 1930's, 1940's, and 1960's USS had rates of return a good deal lower than the middle-sized steel companies such as Armco, Inland, and National. Prices and market conditions that won USS good returns in peak years like 1955 (14%) resulted in almost embarrassing returns for some of the middle-sized steel companies in the same years (22% for National and 25% for Inland). The slow growth of USS and to some extent of Bethlehem, Republic, and Jones and Laughlin relative to the middle rank firms points in the same direction.

When USS first saw the light of day it was by far the largest industrial corporation in the world. In 1970 it was considerably surpassed by such well run and profitable firms as General Motors, Standard Oil of New Jersey, Ford, General Electric, and IBM. Perhaps when USS was founded it was simply too large to be efficient. With the rapid development of modern statistics, accounting, and management techniques, however, this disadvantage of large organizations seems no longer necessary. Firms that are larger than USS have become the low cost, technically most progressive leaders of their industries.

Periodically USS has announced its renaissance. When the author first examined the industry, in 1958, he was just about convinced that USS was at last on the right track. It was selling about one third of the country's steel then. Since then USS's share has declined to less than a quarter of domestic output and not much more than a fifth of total U.S. sales including imports. The big steel companies have not done as well as the next group. Perhaps this is bad luck or bad management, but at the very least, Armco, Inland, and National have proven every bit the equal of their very large competitors.

H. *Progressiveness*

American economists who have looked closely at USS and its rivals have sometimes depicted the steel industry as prone to slow growth and nonpioneering. At the same time, European observers have sometimes marveled at the efficiency attained by American steel producers. The truth seems to lie somewhere between.

Figure 4-13 shows the pattern of productivity trends in steel and in all manufacturing. Both series are expressed as percentages of 1957–1959 levels and are plotted against a logarithmic scale, so the same slope anywhere in the figure represents the same rate of growth. Steel productivity has increased at about the same rate as in manufacturing generally. It grew a little faster during the 1920's and mid-1930's when the industry was introducing continuous rolling, and it has grown a bit more slowly since then.

Productivity growth measures only one aspect of progressiveness. It says nothing about quality change. At least as important as the increase in output per man-hour in the 1930's was the industry's new ability to roll wide strip in coils which, in turn, permitted the fabrication of such products as all steel auto and appliance bodies. The most serious difficulty with the productivity measure as an indicator of progressiveness, however, is that it asks the wrong question. Industries differ in their potential for further progress. It would be wrong to criticize the shirt industry for not advancing as rapidly as electronics. What we really want

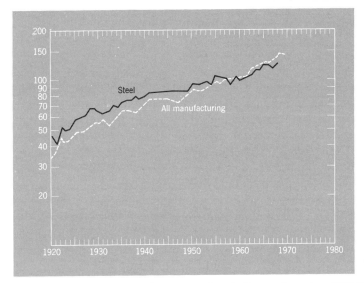

Figure 4-13. Output per man-hour in steel and all manufacturing, 1957-9 = 100. *Source.* Kendrick, *Productivity Trends in the United States*, Princeton, 1961; BLS Bulletin 1200, "Man Hours per Unit of Output in the Basic Steel Industry, 1939-1955"; BLS Bulletin 1612, "Indexes of Output Per Man-Hour, Selected Industries, 1939 and 1947-1967"; and *Economic Report of the President*, 1970.

to ask is how well the industry exploits its opportunities for technical progress compared with other industries.

I. *Innovation in Steel*

A striking number of the technical changes occurring in steel have come from independent companies and were only adopted by the leaders after they proved successful. The most important change of the first half of the century was continuous rolling, patented by Armco, then a quite small firm. A decade before its merger spree, Bethlehem Steel had made its name with the Grey process for making heavy structural shapes. National led in electrolytic tin plating. Republic and the smaller specialty steelmakers did the most with alloys.

The established steel producers have often been pictured as stodgy in their approach to innovation. Basic techniques, except for the rolling mill, were not very different in the mid-1950's than they had been at the turn of the century. The industry made many useful engineering improvements in existing methods, but there were no revolutionary changes.

Since the mid-1950's, however, the steel industry has experienced a technological revolution. In 1957 a Senate committee attempting to evaluate the prospects for further advance heard a series of enthusiastic witnesses describe changes that would, altogether, revolutionize steelmaking: (1) the production of iron directly from the ore, thus bypassing the blast furnace and permitting the use of other fuels besides coking coal, (2) the basic oxygen furnace that would make steel to specifications as exacting as those attained in the open hearth in about one eighth as much time, (3) the continuous casting of steel that would save more handling time and would permit the mills to use a much larger proportion of the raw steel they were producing than they had in the past, and (4) the Sendzimer rolling mill that would permit continuous rolling on a far smaller scale. The committee foresaw a major change that would permit the efficient operation of steel mills on a much smaller scale in local markets throughout the country.[64] Some of the steelmen were more doubtful. Indeed, they were at that moment completing a momentous expansion in steel capacity—an increase by 40% in six years—most of which was open hearth.

Taking the stance of Monday morning quarterbacks, we can now say that both the committee and the industry were wrong. Many of the innovations were introduced, but they *increased* the scale needed for minimum cost and they made the producers *more* dependent on assured access to iron ore than they had been. But the industry was wronger! Direct reduction of iron is still in the pilot plant state (though it was being reannounced as a great breakthrough for the umpteenth time in 1970), but the basic oxygen furnace (BOF) is now unquestionably the low cost method for mass production steel, and continuous casting is well established for many products. The Sendzimer mill is also in operation, though it is limited to special steels. For carbon steel, the change in the rolling mill was to even larger, wider, and faster, computer-controlled mills.

---

[64] *Administered Prices*, Hearings, Part 3, passim.

New firms were again the main innovators. It was Kaiser Steel that obtained the American patent on the BOF and McLouth installed the first American BOF shop. McLouth was also the first mass production steel producer to build a working continuous casting machine. By the late 1960's, the BOF's had risen to almost half of total steel output here and more abroad. By a combination of bad luck and bad timing, the industry was once again forced to invest heavily during a dull market to remain competitive.

VIII. CONCLUSIONS

The steel industry is unavoidably one of the very large firms, at least with present techniques. However, it need not have been as concentrated as it has been in practice. The industry would probably have been no less efficient if the big merger of 1901 had never occurred or if the government had won the dissolution suit of 1920. It might well have been more efficient.

An oligopolistic industry like steel is apt to display a price policy similar to a monopolist's. Some price competition may occur if costs differ among firms if firms estimate demand elasticities differently, or if some firms are in desperate condition as in time of severe excess capacity. It is likely to be sporadic and undercover, however.

The price policy of the steel industry has been oriented toward stability and good public relations. Profits have been excessive compared with other manufacturing, but established firms have seemed to take the safe position. They have often been slow to develop new techniques or locations. As a result, profit prospects have at times been good enough to encourage the rise of relatively small firms in spite of obstacles that have seemed prohibitive to some observers. By taking advantage of opportunities not grasped by the large firms, a number of small ones have become important.

In the past some economists have proposed the dissolution of USS as the most likely means of accomplishing more competition and innovation in the steel industry. Such a change is now unlikely in view of the corporation's declining share of the industry. Further combinations among the leading firms of the industry can be prevented, however. These firms are all of a size clearly capable of efficient operation and progress, as their histories indicate. This does not mean that all merger within the industry is of necessity against the public's interest. Such combinations as the merger that established National, have sometimes led to increased rather than reduced competition in the past.

The main barriers to new firms are the large initial investment and the concentrated control over ore reserves. The first can only be altered by a change in the basic techniques of the industry. The raw-material barrier may have been reduced by the increasingly international market in ore and coking coal, but new entrants are still rare. The main prospect for increased competition is still imports. The "voluntary" quotas eliminate much of this competitive effect, distort the allocation of resources internationally, and encourage the spread of trade restrictions to other products.

IX. FURTHER READINGS

A good history of the leading steel companies which has been used extensively in this chapter is Gertrude G. Schroeder, *The Growth of Major Steel Companies, 1900–1950,* "Johns Hopkins University Studies in Historical and Political Science," Series LXX, No. 2, Johns Hopkins University Press, Baltimore, 1952. A good analysis and evaluation of the steel industry in all respects, not just the basing point system, appears in George W. Stocking, *Basing Point Pricing and Regional Development,* University of North Carolina Press, Chapel Hill, 1954. There are great quantities of official materials on the industry arising from its perennial investigations. The four most complete studies were the hearings and monographs of the Temporary National Economic Committee (1938 to 1941), the Subcommittee on the Study of Monopoly Power (Celler Committee, 1950), the Subcommittee on Anti-Trust and Monopoly (Kefauver Committee, 1957), and the Joint Economic Committee (*Steel Prices, Unit Costs, Profits, and Foreign Competition,* 1963).

The classic on the oligopolist and his two demand curves is Edward Chamberlin, *The Theory of Monopolistic Competition,* Harvard University Press, Cambridge, 1933. Part of the analysis of price leadership and of location in this chapter was based on

Kenneth Boulding, *Economic Analysis,* 4th ed., Vol. I, Harper, New York, 1966. The kinked demand curve was the invention of Paul Sweezy, "Demand Under Conditions of Oligopoly." It is criticized in George Stigler, "The Kinky Oligopoly Demand Curve and Rigid Prices," both reprinted in *Readings in Price Theory,* Irwin, Homewood, Ill., (for American Economic Association), 1955. A good source on oligopoly theory in general is William Fellner, *Competition Among the Few,* Knopf, New York, 1949.

On the question of mergers see J. F. Weston, *The Role of Mergers in the Growth of Large Firms,* University of California Press, Berkeley, 1953, R. L. Nelson, *Merger Movements in American Industry,* Princeton University Press, Princeton, 1959, and George Stigler, "Monopoly and Oligopoly by Merger," reprinted in *Readings in Industrial Organization and Public Policy,* Irwin, Homewood, Ill., 1958. The Bethlehem-Youngstown merger case was well discussed in L. S. Keyes, "The Bethlehem-Youngstown Case and the Market Share Criterion," *American Economic Review,* September 1961, and comments in the June 1962 issue by D. D. Martin. The FTC's *Economic Report on Corporate Mergers,* 1969, is the most complete study on conglomerate mergers yet published.

Steel price policies in recent decades have been explored by a variety of persons from many points of view. Otto Eckstein and Gary Fromm, "Steel and the Post War Inflation," *Joint Economic Committee,* 1959, emphasize the relationship between steel market power, steel unions and capacity utilization during the creeping inflation of the 1950's and its impact on other industries. Morris Adelman, "Steel, Administrated Prices, and Inflation," *Quarterly Journal of Economics,* January 1961, presents the view that the industry was re-exerting unexploited market power during the 1950's and was stopped by market forces from 1958 on. The Council of Economic Advisors' *Report to the President on Steel Prices,* April 1965, contains the administration's case for stable steel prices as well as a very useful set of data.

On import quotas see Robert Baldwin, *Non-Tariff Distortions of International Trade,* Brookings, 1970. American economists engaged in a lengthy debate during the 1960's over whether the American steel industry had dragged its feet in adopting the BOF. See Walter Adams and Joel Dirlam, "Big Steel, Invention, and Innovation," *Quarterly Journal of Economics*, May, 1966 and discussion with McAdams, same journal, August, 1967; and G. S. Maddala and P. T. Knight, "International Diffusion of Technical Change—A Case Study of the Oxygen Steel Process," *Economic Journal*, September, 1967.

5

Monopolistic Competition—Retailing

A large part of American industry does not fit very well into any of the pigeonholes used in this book so far. This is true of many service industries and much of distribution and light manufacturing—for the most part the sort of enterprise that congressmen and men in the street call "little business." Conditions in these fields are not very well represented by either the pure competition of agriculture or the oligopoly of steel. Like many oligopolists such as the auto makers and unlike the farmers, these businessmen often advertise and employ salesmen, and they ordinarily must make their own decisions about prices. But landlords, shopkeepers, and apparel makers, like farmers, come in great numbers and more are usually available whenever profit prospects are good.

I. MONOPOLISTIC COMPETITION

The fields which combine some of the features of purely competitive and of monopolistic industries have been described as *monopolistic competition*. Table 5-1 shows where this category fits in. The distinction between monopolistic competition and oligopoly lies in the number of sellers. In oligopoly each seller is so large that he must expect his rivals to notice his policies and react to them. In deciding on price or design or advertising, Ford must always take the reaction of GM into account. In monopolistic competition, however, individuals are small enough so that any

Table 5-1. Types of Industrial Organization

	Many Sellers	Few Sellers	One Seller
Standardized product	Pure Competition (agriculture)	Pure oligopoly (steel)	Pure monopoly (electric power)
Differentiated product	Monopolistic competition (retailing)	Oligopoly with differentiated product (automobiles)	

one of them can adopt a policy on its own merits without worrying about the direct reaction of others. If it looks profitable for any one of 100 storekeepers to improve his service, change his prices, or move his store to a new location, he can usually do so without the rest of the shops in town retaliating. Both purely competitive and monopolistically competitive markets are often described as *atomistic*. The "atoms" of which they are composed are individually too small to have any significant impact on market conditions.

A. *Product Differentiation*

The other feature that distinguishes monopolistic competition is the character of its products. The industries studied so far in this book sell largely *standardized* products. Of course, not all wheat or steel is alike, but the customers—usually expert industrial buyers—draw few distinctions between the products of individual firms. They are unwilling to pay a tenth of a cent per bushel more for farmer Brown's number two red winter wheat than for wheat of the same quality grown by anyone else. They are equally ready to buy 80 inch .002 gauge cold rolled carbon steel sheets from any company that can meet their specifications if the terms are right.

By contrast, many products sold to relatively uninformed household consumers are *differentiated*. Buyers of cigarettes or automobiles often develop strong loyalties to particular brands. Such differentiated products may or may not differ physically. Two gasolines may be identical in the test tube, but if some consumers swear by the one brand and some prefer the other, the effect on competition between the two will be the same as if technical differences did exist. Cigarettes, gasoline, and automobiles are all produced by oligopolies, but product differentiation also occurs in atomistic markets. Individual dentists, barbers, apartment houses, restaurants, or drug stores each enjoy a particular circle of customers, even as individual brands of cigarettes and gasolines do. It is such markets which combine large numbers and differentiated products that have been labeled as *monopolistically competitive*. Much of retailing probably belongs in this category.

In a sense each retailer, because of his location, the geniality of his sales-people, or just the habits of his customers, has a mild sort of monopoly on his particular product—for example, groceries sold at Fifteenth and James Streets. His monopoly is mild because of the many fine substitutes for his product, such as groceries sold at Tenth and James.

The distinctions among the various market classifications are represented by the demand curves in Figure 5-1. The demand for farmer Brown's number 2 red winter wheat is like that in the first diagram. The price is the same regardless of how much he chooses to grow. The James Street Supermarket faces a demand more like the second curve. Its proprietor would still have some business if he raised prices, and he can increase sales sharply by cutting them. A tobacco company might have demand curves like those in the third part of Figure 5-1. Its quite elastic D_1 curve is similar to the demand at the James Street store. Its sales would be very responsive to price changes if the other cigarette companies ignored its actions, but of course they would not. It must, therefore, price with an eye to the demand for cigarettes

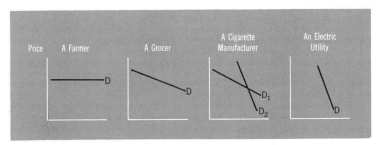

Figure 5-1. Demand curves faced by firms in pure competition, monopolistic competition, oligopoly, and pure monopoly.

generally as reflected in the D_2 curve. Finally, the power company, with the only generator in town, need consider only the overall demand for electricity as shown in the last diagram. The James Street Supermarket faces a more elastic demand than those of the power company or of the cigarette company (as long as it considers its rivals' reactions) because the substitutes for electricity or for cigarettes are much more remote than the substitutes for groceries at a particular location. It has a less elastic demand than the farmer would have because no one can exactly duplicate its services in the eyes of its customers.

II. THE STRUCTURE OF THE RETAILING INDUSTRY

A. *Types of Retailing*

Retailing is not just one field of enterprise, but a whole collection of fields. Most retail outlets are fairly small, with sales on the order of $250,000 per year, but even our largest cities can support only a few department stores. Chains are all-important in some lines (variety stores) and unimportant in others (auto dealers). Some outlets (such as restaurants) have highly differentiated products, while others seem to be practically cases of tweedledum and tweedledee to the customer. Most retailing is highly competitive but there are legal limitations on price competition in a few lines and restrictions on entry set by law or the manufacturer in some.

To cover all these features as well as many aspects of monopolistic competition, this chapter discusses several different cases: (1) retailing in general—food and dry goods stores; (2) standardized products—gas stations; (3) restrictions on price competition—drugs; and (4) restrictions on entry—liquors.

B. *The Revolution in Retailing*

The trade of shopkeeper is an ancient one. At the end of the nineteenth century it was still the province of small proprietors for whom retailing, like farming, was a way of life. The shop was often part of the family home, and the family ordinarily supplied most of the labor. The typical shop was unrelated to other outlets except for the independent wholesale firms supplying them all. There are still large numbers of these stores but they account for a shrunken share of retail sales. Every decade since the turn of the century has seen some major new type of retailing grow at the expense of the family store.

The first great changes were the department stores and mail order houses, the former made possible by the concentration of transportation lines at the nodes of our large new cities, the latter by the development of reliable mail and express service.[1] The scale of such institutions permitted them to purchase in large quantities using specialist buyers and winning discounts from the prices paid by the small dry goods and hardware stores of the day.

The chain stores developed in the early part of this century. Some had their origin in the nineteenth century, but most of the growth occurred between 1914 and 1930. They brought large-scale buying—the advantage of Macy's and Sears—to the variety, food, and drug fields, all of which sell in relatively small local outlets. Their spectacular growth in the 1920's and their advantages in price competition won them a place among the popular villains of the day.

The supermarket was the great innovation of the 1930's. By cutting out credit and delivery, letting the customer serve himself, and operating on a large scale, they were able to offer the buyer low prices at the worst of the Depression when he was extremely price conscious. The first supermarkets were converted garages and warehouses and seemed to be fly-by-nights or poor people's stores. Only after several years did it become clear that standard brands, modern packaging, and the family car had made the old grocery clerk and the delivery wagon obsolete. Since the 1930's the supermarket idea has spread to the hardware, drug, and variety fields.

The years since World War II have produced the shopping center, the discount house, and franchising. The first is a sort of latter-day, multifirm extension of the department-store idea. With

---

[1] The United States did not really participate in an earlier "revolution in retailing," the rise of the cooperative, which did much to undermine the traditional retailers in England in the 1860's and 1870's. The very modest development of coops in the United States has been widely attributed to our relative lack of class consciousness and to the development of other innovations in retailing.

its acres of parking lot and convenient location, it provides an alternative to "downtown" well suited to suburbia. Discount houses extended minimum-service, low-margin retailing to consumer durables. Like the supermarkets, they were greeted as barely legitimate at first, but when it became clear that much of the public preferred to provide its own service and not pay for large inventories and salesmen, the department stores, variety stores, and appliance dealers went into the discount business too. The franchise boom of the 1960's brought the advantages of chains to many of the fields still run by little business—hamburger stands, pizza parlors, ice-cream stores, specialty stores, and convenience food stores (what remains of the corner grocery), not to mention employment agencies, day nurseries, dance studios, car washes, various sorts of auto repair, and motels. Franchises offer broad promotion, centralized buying, and, sometimes, good planning to local businessmen who supply some capital and much effort, and "own their own businesses."

C. Concentration in Retailing

Ever since the revolution in retailing began, there has been much viewing with alarm over the supposed destruction of competition that accompanied it. For decades a substantial portion of our people have pictured the A&P or Sears when they used the word "monopoly." Observers have regularly foreseen the extinction of the independent store and a retail trade dominated by a half-dozen giants.

Actually, retailing remains one of our most competitive lines of business. Until about 1930 the larger firms did seem to have a growing advantage, but they were probably increasing competition rather than destroying it. The mail order houses and chains, combined with improved means of transportation, undermined the quasimonopolistic positions of the few local merchants in thousands of formerly isolated small towns. The new institutions certainly emphasized price competition to the embarrassment of the traditional firms. Some of the innovations since 1930 have helped to preserve the independents, rather than destroy them. By becoming supermarkets, independent food stores could achieve enough scale to keep up with the chains, or even become local chains themselves. The discount houses were independent stores almost by definition, to start with, although many have developed into chains or large department stores by now. In many lines, franchising has given a substantial advantage to local businessmen who were at least quasi-independent.

The shares of the chains in total sales of lines in which they are important and of department stores and mail order houses in the fields where they compete are shown in Figure 5-2.[2] p. 221. Down to 1954 the shares of the large retailers generally remained fairly stable or actually declined. The striking exception was department store chains, but the department stores, which are large retailers with or without chains, were experiencing a sharp relative decline in the same period. Food chains grew somewhat at the expense of independents, but drug and variety (dime store) chains were declining relatively.

The share of large retailers has risen rapidly in most of the lines covered by Figure 5-2 since 1954. However, half or more of the business is still in the hands of independents in most types of retailing. Chains do account for the bulk of variety store (dime store) and department store sales, but both must compete with many other types of stores selling similar merchandise. All department stores together still make only 42% of the apparel, furniture, appliance and general merchandise sales. Moreover, some of the food store chains are local organizations that started out as supermarkets in the 1930's, and some of the census "depart-

---

[2] "Chains" in this case are retailers with 4 or more stores. The Census switched from a 4- to a 10-store cutoff in 1954, but the 4-store definition has been retained here for continuity. Chains with 10 or more stores show the same relative growth patterns in the 1948 to 1967 period as those shown in Figure 5-2. For 1967, the 10- and 4-store chains' proportions of total sales are as follows:

	10 Stores	4 Stores
Variety store chains	79.4	81.6
Department store chains	78.8	90.6
Food chains	48.4	53.1
Drug chains	30.0	33.7

Sales of *all* department stores and of mail order houses are compared in Figure 5-2 with total sales of department, general merchandise, apparel, shoe, furniture, house-furnishings, and appliance stores and mail order houses.

ment store" chains are the more successful of the discount houses from the 1950's. Both still behave as "independents" in many cities.

There are some enormous firms in retailing, but they are seldom large enough to dominate their fields. Table 5-2 shows the 1968 sales of the four largest firms in the two lines that contain seven of the eight largest retailers. It compares the sales of the four largest chains with totals for the whole country in their lines. The billions of sales of the four largest food chains came to only 19% of total retail food sales.[3] The four largest general-merchandise retailers do about 18% of the business in the main lines that they sell. The four largest limited-price variety store chains (not shown) had a little more than half the business of such stores in 1954 and 1963, but they compete with the department and drug stores as well. By 1968 it was impossible to tell how much of the dime-store business they did, because Woolworth's and Kresge's had both gone into the department-store business and were mak-

Table 5-2. Total Sales of the Four Largest Firms in Two Retail Fields, 1968, in Millions of Dollars

Food Stores		General Merchandising Stores	
Great Atlantic and Pacific Tea Company	5,436	Sears Roebuck	8,199
		J. C. Penney	3,323
Safeway Stores	3,686	Montgomery Ward	1,986a
Kroger Stores	3,161	Federated Department	
Food Fair	1,372	Stores	1,813
Total, four largest	13,855	Total, four largest	15,321
Total, all food stores	73,267	Total, all general merchandise, apparel, furniture, appliance, and mail-order sales	90,298
Percentage	18.6	Percentage	17.0

Source. Annual Reports and 1969 *Statistical Abstract,* p. 760.
a Excludes Container Corporation, another part of Marcor Corporation.

---

[3] The Census found that the four largest chains accounted for 18.4% of all food store sales (20.0% of grocery-store sales) in 1963. National Commission on Food Marketing, *Food from Farmer to Consumer,* Government Printing Office, Washington, D. C., June 1966, p. 72.

ing large but unspecified parts of their sales through department stores, shoe stores, or dress shops.

In other lines of retailing the leaders were generally less important. *All chains together* are 46% of the shoe stores (and they

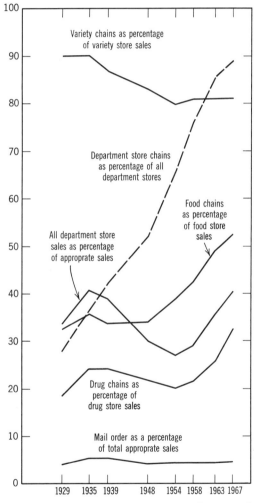

Figure 5-2. Sales of large firms as percentages of certain lines. *Source. Censuses of Business.* 1967 data based on Advanced Report No. BC 67(A)-RS-2 from the 1967 Census.

compete with department stores and haberdasheries), 40% of the tire dealers (and they compete with Sears, Wards, and the gas stations), and less than 30% of most other lines.[4] Except for the dime stores, then, no branch of retailing is any more concentrated on a national scale than the textile industry.

The markets on which retailers compete are local rather than national. Retailing is much more concentrated within local markets. Our best information on concentration in local retail markets is for food distribution. The 4 largest food chains accounted for an average of 50% of grocery sales, or about 46% of food-store sales,[5] in 218 metropolitan areas in 1963. The concentration ratios varied from city to city. Among metropolitan areas with food sales of more than $250 million a year, it ranged from 30 in Los Angeles to 70 in Denver, with an average of 48. Concentration in food marketing seems to be on the increase, partly because of the drop out of small, single-store retailers, and partly because of mergers among the middle-sized chains. The share of the 4 leaders in the same 218 metropolitan areas averaged 45% of grocery sales (about 39% of all food-store sales) in 1954. Industrial markets in which 4 firms control 46% to 50% of sales are commonly thought of as oligopolistic, though the leaders generally have less market power than those in such industries as steel and certainly less than the leading auto companies.

Even in those fields of retailing or localities where sales are fairly concentrated, the big retailers have several checks on their control over the markets in which they sell. The country is full of automobiles, so most customers have large numbers of alternatives. Moreover, many modern retailers are becoming less specialized. The supermarket that sells nylons and the drugstore

---

[4] *Statistical Abstract,* 1968, p. 761.

[5] Sales of all food stores, including meat markets, fish markets, fruit or vegetable stores, candy stores, and retail bakeries, came to $57.1 billion in 1963 as against $52.6 billion for groceries (which include most of the sales of the big chains). The chains compete with most of these food stores. The share of the big chains in food sales was computed by multiplying the ratio 52.6/57.1 times the average concentration of ratio of 50% for groceries. (Based on *Statistical Abstract,* 1969, pp. 754–5. The metropolitan-area concentration ratios are from National Commission on Food Marketing, *Organization and Competition in Food Retailing,* June, 1966, pp. 44–51.)

where you cannot find the drug counter are famous. Any seller who tries to maintain high prices is apt to find the grocers or the gas stations or someone equally far removed trying to take over his profitable lines. At any rate, there seems to be a continuous supply of new shopkeepers, ready to appear whenever prospects are good, and often even when they are not. It takes a good deal more to break into such fields as food retailing than it once did, but the cost of entry is still much lower than in most concentrated segments of manufacturing.

D. *Economies of Scale—Buying*

The large retailers have several advantages over their smaller competitors. Probably the most famous is their ability to buy on preferential terms. Their large orders can sometimes reduce costs of production, handling, and selling for the manufacturer, and they are generally strong enough to insist upon participating in the gains that result. This advantage can be substantial. The tire companies have been able to show enough cost savings on tires sold to 62 large retailers to permit discounts of from 26 to 40% below the prices paid by their smallest distributors.[6]

One of the main advantages of the large retailers when they first appeared was their ability to bypass the wholesaler. He had performed an essential function when retailers were small and scattered, acting as a representative for the manufacturers and buyer for the shopkeepers. He usually provided warehousing, delivery, and credit as well, and charged accordingly. In many localities wholesalers were few in number and quite able to reach and observe agreements among themselves about the prices and services they would insist upon.

The independent wholesaler was decidedly not essential to the large new retailers of the 1910's and 1920's. The buying, handling, and credit functions had still to be performed, but the large retailers could often do it for themselves more cheaply. They were in effect entering the wholesaling business and undermining its oligopolistic structure. In spite of opposition from the wholesalers, the chains were able to gain direct access to the manufacturers.

---

[6] Federal Trade Commission Docket 5677 (1954) in re B. F. Goodrich.

Many old-style wholesalers have disappeared since the 1920's, and their successors have had to change their way of business to survive.[7] Many have switched to a cash and carry basis. Some have organized "voluntary" groups of retailers that make purchase commitments permitting the wholesalers to duplicate the chains' advantages. Some have been replaced by retailer-owned cooperatives. These "voluntary" groups and cooperatives often arrange joint advertising and sell products under their own labels. Some even do part of their own manufacturing. At least in the most favorable of circumstances today, a group of independent stores with their cooperative supplier are reportedly at little or no disadvantage in buying compared with the chains.[8] The shares of these groups in food store sales have grown as fast in the postwar years as the shares of the chains themselves. By 1963, they accounted for 44% of all grocery sales.[9]

E. *Economies of Scale—Operating Efficiency*

In addition to their buying advantages, the large retailers may be able to realize operational gains as a result of centralized planning, promotion, and inventory policies and specialization in buying and management. Sales per worker in organizations of various sizes might be used as a rough indicator of the extent of such gains. Figure 5-3 shows sales per worker in 1963 in the five retail lines discussed in this chapter. In each field except variety stores, the chains show fairly clear operating advantages over the independents.[10] In foods, the advantage is spectacular.

---

[7] This is true mainly in fields like food and dry goods where new methods of retailing have put pressure on the old wholesalers and their clients. There are still plenty of old-style wholesalers in such lines as drugs.

[8] For a good account of the transformation of the wholesaler, see Ralph Cassady, *The Changing Competitive Structure of the Wholesale Grocery Trade,* University of California Press, Berkeley, 1949.

[9] National Commission on Food Marketing, *op. cit.,* p. 30.

[10] The largest gas station chains show low sales per worker, but gas stations are a special case. A few of the major oil companies, particularly Standard of California and Standard of Ohio, operate their own stations. They dominate the "more than 100" group in Figure 5-3. Most of the other *chains* are independent of the major oil companies, but the bulk of the one- and two-station distributors are closely tied to the majors just as the more than 100 group is.

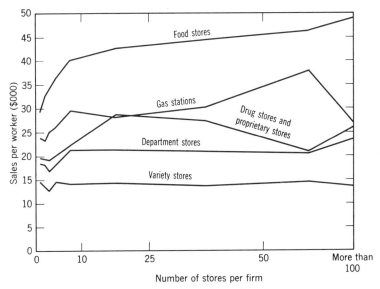

Figure 5-3. Sales per worker by number of stores per organization. ("Workers" includes both employees and proprietors.) *Source. Census of Business,* 1963.

The definite operating advantage of the food chains and the questionable one of the variety chains may help to explain why the food chains should be still expanding at the expense of the independents, as shown in Figure 5-2, while the variety chains have yielded ground to them. With the chains' buying advantage reduced by various forms of cooperative purchasing, the possibility for further growth may depend on operating advantages.

The operating advantages of chains over independents suggested in Figure 5-3 do not necessarily mean that we must look forward to a retail trade of a few dominant firms in the future. While the chains as a group have a clear advantage over the one- to three-store organization, the advantage of the large chains over moderate-sized chains is much less impressive in most lines and does not exist at all in variety stores.[11] The 25- to 50-store

---

[11] The cost figures that are available support this view. The food chains show lower operating expense per dollar of sales the larger the chain, but

food chains are far less vulnerable to the price competition of the A&P than are the corner grocers. A retail world of 25- to 100-store chains would still not be very concentrated.

These economies of scale may mean that the barriers to entry are higher than the annual crop of new retailers might suggest, however. A 50-store chain would require an investment of $25 million in foods today. This is hardly an insurmountable barrier (compare it with the half billion or more required for steel), but it is not insignificant either.

III. COSTS, DEMANDS, AND MARGINS

A. *Retail Costs*

Retailers' costs fall into two broad categories: the *cost of goods sold* and *operating expenses*. The first of these consists mainly of the expense of merchandise purchased for resale and is obviously a variable cost. A retailer would ordinarily drop a line if its price did not even cover what he paid for it. The famous "loss leader" is an apparent exception. A store may sometimes offer merchandise at its wholesale price or even less to attract customers. Such a policy can only apply to part of what the store sells, of course, if it is to survive. The losses it takes on its "leaders" might best be treated as a sort of advertising expense designed to convince consumers that it is a store with exceptionally low prices.

The cost of goods sold per unit of sale certainly does not increase as volume expands. In fact, so long as there are quantity discounts available, it will decrease somewhat as the broken line

---

the medium-sized variety chains have lower operating costs than either the small or large ones. In both cases the cost of goods sold are excluded. Harvard School of Business, Bureau of Business Research, Bulletins, *Operating Results of Food Chains,* and *Operating Results of Variety Chains*—various years, 1956–1960.

The Food Marketing Commission estimated efficient size for a food store to be about 16,000 square feet meaning $430,000 investment per store. Such stores have sales of about $1 million per year. The Commission also estimated that $75 to 100 million in retail sales are required for a minimum cost warehouse unit—implying local chains of 75 to 100 stores. There may be some further economies in purchasing beyond that, but they are exhausted by the time a chain reaches $500 million in sales. National Commission on Food Marketing, *op. cit.,* p. 72.

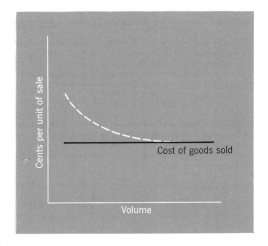

Figure 5-4

in Figure 5-4 does. However, to keep the analysis simple, it will be convenient to assume that the cost of goods sold remains constant over the usual range of volume. The solid line in Figure 5-4 will then represent the cost of goods sold.

Operating expenses are the costs of running the store and providing the retail services. Labor makes up more than half the total for practically all retailers.

Operating expenses have traditionally been treated as fixed costs. Indeed, talk about "spreading overhead" seems to have originated in retailing. Labor is obviously a fixed cost for the old-fashioned family store. Shopkeepers cannot fire their wives any more easily than farmers can. A large part of the labor costs of more modern retailers should probably be classified as fixed also, although sales commissions and part-time sales staff introduce some variable elements. Macy's and the A&P need the services of most of their basic staff just to have their stores open for business. In addition, most of the nonlabor operating expenses, such as real estate and tenancy costs, utilities, insurance, and taxes fall fairly clearly into the fixed cost category, though delivery and some inventory costs are possible exceptions.

With their variable costs constant or declining and with most of their operating costs fixed, retailers should have a fairly con-

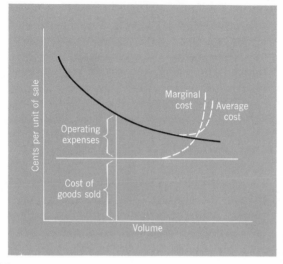

Figure 5-5

tinuously declining cost per unit of sale with expanding volume.
Such a pattern of costs is shown in Figure 5-5. Stores do have
some limits on how much trade they can handle, as you can tell
by visiting a popular supermarket on a Friday evening. The
store's capacity shows up in Figure 5-5 in the rising marginal
and average cost curves after a point. Retailers can and do expand their capacity somewhat by employing part-time help, so
the rise in costs per unit need not be completely abrupt. In general, except for occasional peaks, retailers can lower their unit
costs by increasing volume.[12]

_____

[12] A well-known economist made a statistical study of three departments' expenses at Lord and Taylor, a large New York department store, over a four-
year period. Although he excluded general store overhead and the cost of
goods sold, he got continuously declining costs per unit of sale over the
entire range of sales observed. Even at peak periods costs per unit were still
declining. In one department, operating costs per unit were only half as
much at the peaks as in very slow periods. Joel Dean, "Department Store
Cost Functions" in Lange et al. *Studies in Mathematical Economics and
Econometrics,* University of Chicago Press, Chicago, 1942, pp. 222–254.
Some economists feel that this, and similar studies, exaggerate the declining
cost character of retailing, however. They argue that in peak periods (dur-

B. *Demand at Retail*

A retailer's demand curves depend on the types of goods sold. They fall into two broad categories, *convenience goods* and *shopping goods*. Convenience goods are the sort of things that consumers buy regularly, preferably at the nearest store, such as food, drugs, and gasoline. Shopping goods are the larger, occasional purchases, such as clothing, furniture, or automobiles, for which consumers will shop from store to store trying to find the best buy. Realistically, the distinction between the two is blurred, since shopping habits differ, but it is a useful distinction, nevertheless.

Location is very important in the case of convenience goods. If a buyer's time is worth anything at all, it will not pay to drive halfway across town to save a nickel. Retailers who sell convenience goods try to locate where the density of customers per store is high. As a result, food stores, drugstores, gas stations, and variety stores are usually scattered fairly uniformly across the city.

Stores selling shopping goods are more likely to be bunched together at the heart of the city, or, to an increasing extent, in *large* shopping centers in the suburbs. Since a woman buying a dress will try a half-dozen stores before she decides, clothing stores are more likely to make sales when conveniently surrounded by more clothing stores. Stores selling convenience goods are often bunched together in small shopping centers as well, but for a different reason. They share a parking lot and offer the housewife a drugstore, a hardware store, a gas station, and a supermarket, all at one stop.

The demand curves of sellers of convenience goods may not be very elastic on a day-to-day basis. Most consumers have only a dim notion of the going prices of the hundred small items they buy. On any given morning the demand for a particular grocer's steak may not be much more elastic than the demand for steak in general. Few of his customers will drive to another store if he

---

ing the Christmas rush, say) the customer gets far less service with each purchase than at other times. See comments of George Stigler, summarized in the *American Economic Association Proceedings, 1940,* p. 401.

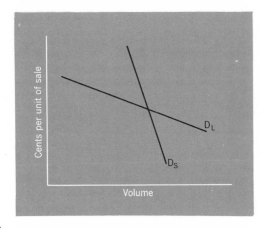

Figure 5-6

charges too much. Most would not even know it. If he tries to
take advantage of what his customers do not know, however, he
will probably be in trouble soon. As time passes, they are bound
to find out about other people's prices and shop elsewhere. A
reputation for high prices, once won, is hard to live down. Any
retailer planning to stay in business must disregard his attractive
but misleading very short-run demand curve (D_S in Figure 5-6)
and set prices according to his more elastic, longer run curve
(D_L in Figure 5-6).

The longer run demand curve is still not perfectly elastic, because each store is more convenient to some customers than any
other. Housewives who live one block off or who like the grocer's
friendly smile or friendly credit will go on buying there even if
they know prices at other stores are lower. At somewhat lower
prices, other customers will find this store attractive. If prices get
low enough this store can draw customers from miles around.

The demand for shopping goods at any given outlet is likely
to be more elastic than that for convenience goods, Most buyers
shop around and have a fairly clear idea of the alternatives when
buying a suit or a washing machine. And since the possible saving is substantial, many buyers are willing to go to considerable
inconvenience to get a good buy. There are differences in price

among sellers of shopping goods, reflecting mainly differences in services offered. The buyer who wants a large selection, a courteous and expert salesman, a guarantee of service or right to return merchandise, and an air of respectability must pay more than another who wants the product without frills. No two stores are exactly alike in reputation and services offered so each is likely to have some regular customers. Most of us can be wooed away to another department store or appliance dealer if we find a bargain, though. Sellers of shopping goods seem to have downward sloping demand curves also, but they are ordinarily very elastic.

C. Margins

Retailers often speak of their selling prices as being made up of the cost of goods sold and their *gross margin.* If the gross margin covers a retailer's operating expenses, whatever is left may be referred to as *net margin.* Since cost of goods sold and gross margin are ordinarily expressed as percentages of selling price, they should add up to 100%. For instance, Figure 5-7 shows margins for five types of stores discussed in this chapter. Out of every dollar spent at food chains, 77.5¢ goes to cover the wholesale cost of the goods purchased, and 22.5¢ is margin. Of this, 21.3¢ goes to cover operating expenses and 1.2¢ appears as profits.[13] Other retailers have higher gross margins. For the most part these reflect more expensive services, but in some instances, margins (and costs) may be pushed up by monopolistic practices. The gross margins in Figure 5-7 are comparable from one line of retailing to another, but the net margins are not. The food chains and department stores are corporations, so the managers' salaries and the corporate taxes are all deducted in finding net margins. The service stations, drug stores, and liquor stores are mostly proprietorships, so no corporate taxes are involved (and

---

[13] These definitions will be used throughout the chapter. They are simplifications of a rather complex terminology made more complicated by differences from trade to trade. The words "markup" or "mark-on" refer to the difference between price and wholesale costs expressed as a percentage of those costs. The gross margin differs from these because it takes cash discounts, inventory shrinkage and "markdowns" into account and it is expressed as a percentage of price rather than cost.

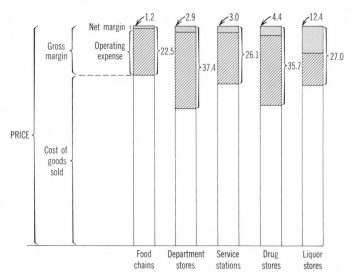

Figure 5-7.   Net and gross margins in five lines of retailing. *Sources.* Food chains: National Commission on Food Marketing, Technical Study No. 7, *Organization and Competition in Food Retailing,* June 1966, pp. 240-241 (data for 1964-5). Department stores: National Cash Register Company, *Expenses in Retail Business* (undated, about 1968) pp. 10-11. Service stations: *National Petroleum News Fact Book,* May 1970, p. 150-153 (data for 1969), based on 8 largest cities plus a random sample of 10 smaller cities. Drug stores: Eli Lilly and Co., *The Lilly Digest,* 1968, p. 51 (data for 1968). Liquor stores: National Cash Register Company, *Expenses in Retail Businesses* (undated, about 1968), p. 28.

personal taxes are ignored). The people who compiled these margins attempted to allow for the proprietors' salaries in the case of drug stores, but the gas-station and liquor-store net margin includes what the proprietors receive for their effort as well as the return on their investment.

Margins are sometimes tricky. High margins do not necessarily mean high profits. Sometimes a store can sell so much more at a lower price that the increased volume more than makes up for the lower profits per unit, leaving it with a higher total profit. In fact, it is sometimes possible to *increase* net margins by *de-*

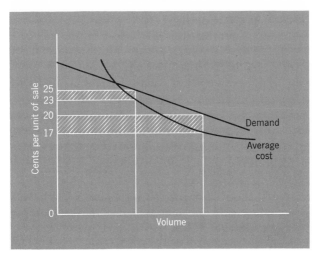

Figure 5-8

creasing price. Figure 5-8 shows how this might happen. With rapidly decreasing costs and a fairly elastic demand curve, the retailer can, by dropping his price from 25¢ to 20¢, actually increase his *net* margin from 2¢ to 3¢. Of course, his total profits rise faster than his net margin. Not only does he make more on each unit sold but he sells more units.

Something like this seems to have happened to the A&P in the late 1930's. In 1937 they intentionally experimented with their prices and were able to increase their sales from $1104 per week per store to $1226. They had to take a drop in their *gross* margins from 18.6% to 18.3% to do this, but the increased volume resulted in a drop in operating expenses from 18.4% to 17.2% at the same time. As a result, their *net* margins rose from 0.18% to 1.22%![14]

---

[14] Morris Adelman, "The A and P Case: A Study in Applied Economic Theory," *Quarterly Journal of Economics*, May 1949, p. 238. For the price cut to be of any significance, the A&P must have accomplished considerable economies in purchasing as well as taking a slight reduction in gross margin, something that seems quite plausible with a 10% increase in volume.

IV. MONOPOLISTIC COMPETITION
IN THEORY AND PRACTICE

A. *Prices and Output in Monopolistic Competition*

The logical next question is just what price and margin will prove most profitable. The firm in Figure 5-8 obviously could not go on increasing profits by cutting price indefinitely. Where should it stop?

The customary analytical solution to this problem is shown in Figure 5-9. With the mild sort of monopoly shown there, a retailer trying to make maximum profits should set price *P*, taking a margin of *PC*, and as a result, sell a volume of *Q*. He would be equating marginal cost and marginal revenue just as the more impressively monopolistic USS did.

Realistically, it seems to be common for stores to take uniform margins on practically all the goods in particular departments. Such a price policy may seem very far removed from the strange-looking diagram in Figure 5-9, but the two are not necessarily inconsistent. It just would not pay to try to work out the most profitable margin on each individual item among the hundreds handled by the typical retailer, especially when he can only guess

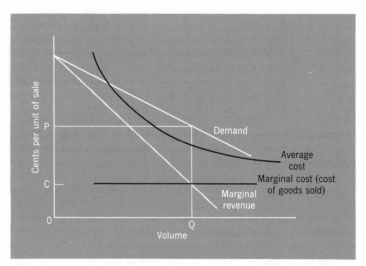

Figure 5-9

about the demands for them. It is hardly surprising that he takes broad categories and adds 10% to wholesale in one group, 15% in a second, etc. It makes life easier.

Life would be easier yet if retailers took the same margin on everything, but they do not. Retailers take low margins on staples where interstore comparisons are easy, such as sugar and milk at food stores. Low margins are also common where the retailer can hope to win large volume by making a special of an already low price, such as a chain's own brand of coffee or a special shipment at exceptional prices at department stores. Both grocers and department stores tend to take high margins on luxury foods or style goods[15] where each store's offerings are somewhat unique and price comparisons are less easy. This is particularly true of some types of clothing, furniture, and sports equipment where the retailers have exclusive dealerships, and often in the case of imports where competing stores are unlikely to carry the same merchandise. What the food and department stores seem to be doing in each of these cases is taking low margins where elasticity of demand is great and high margins when it is not. They are engaging in price discrimination, like good, profit-seeking monopolists.

B. *Long-Run Adjustment—Excess Capacity*

The retailer represented in Figure 5-9 was making a profit in excess of a normal return on his investment. In most lines of retailing, such a situation could not last for long. New stores would appear in the neighborhood to share in this firm's good fortune. As they did, each store would have fewer customers and could sell less at each price. Demand curves would shift downward as shown in Figure 5-10 until there were insufficient profits to attract new firms. Unusual profits completely disappear when the demand curve barely touches the cost curve, as D_2 does in Figure 5-10. When this equilibrium is reached, each store will be forced to take the fullest advantage of its mild monopoly simply to break even.

---

[15] To some extent high margins on style goods simply reflect high marginal costs. Because of the "perishability" of the merchandise, the wholesale price is not the whole marginal cost. The same is true of produce in a food store.

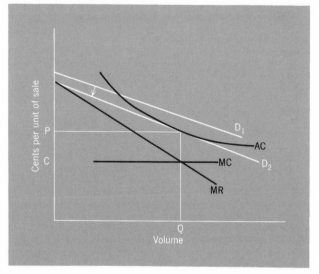

Figure 5-10

As things are set up here, the store would have some excess capacity. It could have more business and operate at lower costs, but only by cutting its price and margin so much that it would be taking a loss. The result of the entry of new stores is 20 supermarkets, each doing half as much business as it could handle. If the same town had only 10, each fully used, there would be a substantial saving in grocers, buildings, parking lots, and neon signs.

C. *Excess Capacity in Perspective*

It is easy to exaggerate the significance of the excess capacity involved in monopolistic competition. The long-run adjustment described here is not the only reason for half-empty stores. There is bound to be off-peak excess capacity. Department stores cannot help being pretty empty in January and groceries on Tuesday if they are to handle the Christmas or Friday rush. There can also be excess capacity because the men who build the stores guess wrong about population trends or public taste. Retailers can make mistakes just as well as farmers and steel producers.

The overcapacity that is the result of monopolistic competition is not all waste either. A town with 20 half-empty supermarkets gets better service than it would with 10 busier ones. Customers need not drive as far to shop, and the saving in transportation costs makes up in part for the loss in unused grocer's services. Consumers differ in tastes as well as in the locations of their homes, and a town's stores can come closer to satisfying everybody's needs if they include stores that offer music while you shop, stores with congenial butchers, and stores with no frills but cheap goods. If everybody's tastes and location are to be provided for, there is bound to be product differentiation, and such excess capacity as may result may be thought of as the price we pay for it.[16]

The excess capacity involved in monopolistic competition would be less severe, the more elastic the demand for the products of individual firms. The elasticity of demand in retailing is normally very high. An economist employed at Macy's estimated the elasticity of demand for seven staple items and four broad categories of goods sold by the store. He found elasticities that ranged from 2.47 to 6.60 and the lower elasticities were explained as being little known brands (elasticity of 3.52) or off-season goods (elasticity of 2.47 in one year and 3.21 in the second).[17]

---

[16] Of course, we can go too far in meeting every need of every buyer. We could keep increasing the variety of services until there was a store for every consumer, but obviously we would then be paying too much for product differentiation. There are reasons to suspect that retailing tends to carry product differentiation too far, but it is extremely difficult to say how much too far. See W. A. Lewis, "Competition in Retail Trade," *Economica,* November 1945.

[17] Roswell H. Whitman, "Demand Functions for Merchandise at Retail," in Lange et al., *op. cit.,* pp. 208–222. In some respects even the high elasticities given here understate the actual elasticities. Prices of related goods at Macy's and prices of the same goods at rival stores were not taken into account in making the estimates. Moreover, the elasticities were all based on a few months' experience and should only show short-run adjustments. When elasticities were recalculated, taking the prices of competing goods at Macy's into account, the estimates were much higher than those given here.

In connection with the A&P price cuts of 1937 mentioned earlier, the discussions of A&P regional presidents at the time have been interpreted to imply an anticipated short-run elasticity of 1.91 to 2.33 and a long-run elasticity of 9.65 to 13.80. Morris Adelman, *A & P: A Study in Price-Cost Behavior and Public Policy,* Harvard University Press, Cambridge, 1959, pp. 472–473.

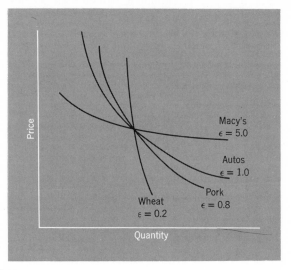

Figure 5-11

The typical elasticity was about 5. This is extremely high compared with the results of other statistical demand analyses. Figure 5-11 compares demand curves with elasticities of 0.2 (wheat), 0.8 (pork), 1.0 (automobiles), and 5.0 (staples at Macy's). If other retailers have elasticities as great as those indicated here, the excess capacity that results automatically from long-run adjustments in retailing would not be very severe.

The demand for goods at individual stores has certainly become more elastic over the last 60 years. At the turn of the century, when few families had their own means of transportation and consumers had little basis for judging the manufacturers, consumer loyalty to merchants who were nearby and "reputable" was likely to be strong. Since then nearly everyone has acquired a car and the manufacturers have conducted a 60-year advertising campaign. The consumer has shifted his loyalty (and the monopoly power that went with it) from the local merchant to the national manufacturer. He will now buy a washing machine or a box of soap from anybody, just so he gets the right brand. Retailers, though not manufacturers, have moved closer to pure competition as a result.

Some economists have argued that very high long-run elasticities are inevitable in cases of monopolistic competition. They contend that severe product differentiation is just not consistent with free entry. If other firms can enter into competition "freely," this automatically means that they can come close to duplicating the existing firms' services. If new firms are unable to produce closely competing products, entry into that segment of the market is not "free."

D. *Nonprice Competition*

Since they are offering somewhat differentiated products, retailers are apt to engage in *nonprice competition*. A retailer can raise his demand curve by having more clerks so that no one need wait, by carrying larger stocks so that customers have greater choice, by providing free parking, escalators, music while you shop, and trading stamps. All of these improvements add to cost as well as to demand, however. Figure 5-12 illustrates such a change. Let us assume that a merchant introduces trading stamps. He succeeds in raising his demand curve from D_1 to D_2, but he increases his unit costs from AC_1 to AC_2 in the process. If the increase in gross revenue is greater than the increase in cost, as is the case here, the new service will be added. As a result the store can make more than a normal profit. It may not even have to raise its

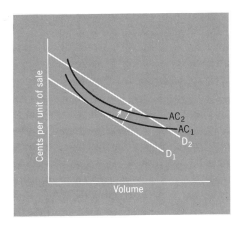

Figure 5-12

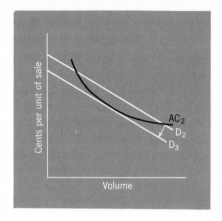

Figure 5-13

price to cover the cost of the stamps, because of the drop in average costs when volume increases.

Other stores can play the same game, however. As other stores introduce competing improvements in product, the demand will shift back down toward D_3, as shown in Figure 5-13. In the long run, profits should disappear again because of entry or imitation; but now costs at each store will be higher with each volume of sales because of the cost of the improved service. If prices are left unchanged, this means that every store must have more volume for its margins to be adequate. In other words, some of the stores have to be squeezed out for the remaining ones to be able to break even selling their new, more costly product at the same price. Alternatively, prices and margins may creep higher, to cover the increased costs, leaving most of the stores still in business.

Many people have criticized the high costs of distribution in the United States. They throw up their hands in horror at a country where every fifth worker is a middleman. The high costs of distribution are often attributed to unwanted services forced upon the public by the process of nonprice competition described here.

The free entry that typifies most of retailing, however, puts a limit on the amounts of such services that can be forced upon us. Every decade since 1900 has seen some group of retailers who had gotten out on a high service, high margin limb dropping gracelessly to the ground as a result of new mail order houses, chain stores, supermarkets, or discount houses. Whenever a substantial number of customers pay for services they do not want, a new retailer seems ready to appear and give them fewer services at a lower price.

E. *Advertising—Pro*

One of the most controversial services associated with differentiated products is advertising. It can do great things for the seller, but what does it do for you or me?

The main economic virtue claimed for it lies in the information it provides. We have an enormous and complex economy and some means of gathering and distributing information is essential for it to work properly. Advertising may improve the allocation of resources in the market place if it gives the buying public a better idea of what is available at what price.

The informative function of advertising can increase competition in some industries. Price cuts and product improvements will only bring in more business if people know about them. And new firms may find it easier to enter a market if they can use ads to build up volume quickly.

Perhaps most important is that advertising can encourage innovation. A firm that has to wait years for the market may be discouraged from developing a better mousetrap, but by advertising it can look forward to reasonable acceptance early. In fact, if increased production means lower operating costs, advertising expenditure may actually lead to lower prices for the consumer during the developmental period.

In addition to its informative function, some people argue that advertising is necessary to sustain a growing economy. Without it consumers would presumably save so much that we would be faced with depression. This argument cuts both ways, however. In years when inflation is a threat, efforts to increase demand make things worse. At any rate, there are other means of maintaining full employment.

F. *Advertising—Con*

The critics of advertising have a number of arguments on their side. To begin with, much of modern advertising offers little or no information value. It is hard to imagine that ads saying simply

"Buy Fords" or even "Buy Fords, They're Beautiful" impart any new information to anyone. This sort of ad simply manipulates our tastes. Advertising is expensive. It cost $18 billion in 1968—more than the federal government spent on space, foreign economic and military aid, agriculture, and Medicare put together in the same year.[18] Part of this went to finance radio, TV, newspapers, and magazines that we would pay for anyway, but a large part was attributable to advertising, pure and simple. Unless advertising provides information or something else of real value, it involves a waste of our resources.

Instead of increasing competition, advertising may actually create or intensify monopoly. The millions of dollars and many years necessary to develop brand loyalties stand as one of the great barriers to entry in such industries as soap and automobiles. Moreover, much advertising is devoted to convincing the public that there is no substitute for particular brands. To the extent that it is successful, it gives the owners of those brands some degree of monopoly power, as witness the premium prices that well-advertised brands of soap, aspirin, or gasoline can command.

The information value of advertising obviously depends on whether the information imparted is correct or not. Outright misrepresentation does occur, although the FTC can issue orders against it today. Misplaced emphasis is a more common sin. Firms spend millions to convince consumers that essentially similar products are different. Great emphasis on unimportant differences or vague implications that some product is "better" or has a special claim to social prestige are typical.

Aside from the economic faults of advertising, many people regret the over-all effect of Madison Avenue on our lives. Ads that say "be a conformist" or "be a snob" or "indulge yourself" are hardly designed to promote the traditional virtues. Ads that say "be a materialist" and "consume more" make it difficult for the United States to raise the taxes necessary to finance adequate social programs because so much goes into personal consumption. In addition, the propensity of many advertisers to support tabloid journalism and TV programs at the fifth grade level are old sub-

---

[18] *Statistical Abstract of the United States,* 1969, p. 775 and *The Budget of the United States Government,* 1969, pp. 53, 96, and 134.

jects of complaint, though these might plausibly be blamed on the readers and viewers, or at least on the readers and viewers who can be swayed. Finally, some object to advertising in general, regardless of its appeal, because it puts Mr. Average Man on a treadmill where he cannot be satisfied no mater how rich he gets.

G. *Retail Advertising*

About a third of the nation's advertising bill is incurred by retailers and wholesalers, and most of this shows up in a good light. It is almost entirely informational. The reader can judge the value of this compared with other advertising by asking himself how much, if anything, he would be willing to pay for it if he had to. It is hard to imagine that many people would pay to see soap or toothpaste commercials, but Sears' and Ward's catalogues would probably sell well at quite respectable prices if they were not given away, and most of us *have* purchased newspapers to see the Thursday grocery ads or to find out what is on at the movies.

Far from restricting competition, as soap or toothpaste ads are likely to do, retail ads seem to enhance it. For one thing, they are usually local in character and are therefore done on a small enough scale that most chains or voluntary groups of efficient size can afford them. Moreover, they clearly make the individual store's demand curve more elastic. Department store sales and supermarket specials only become profitable for the seller if he can advertise them. It would seldom pay to cut price if the only people who knew about it were those who were in the store anyway. And the presence of the Sears' catalogue and the food ads put a severe limit on the ability of local retailers to set high prices. By improving market information, advertising has brought retailing much closer to pure competition.

V. PUBLIC POLICY IN RETAILING

A. *Protecting Little Business*

The new, low-cost retailers and the increasingly competitive pattern of modern retailing have meant trouble for the old-style retailers and wholesalers. These little businessmen have not accepted their fate with quiet stoicism. When faced with new competition that has threatened to destroy them, they have risen in righteous wrath and petitioned Congress or the city assembly for relief. As "pillars of their communities" and members of well-organized groups, the retailers and wholesalers have often been able to get quite a number of legislators to listen.

Most of the protective legislation dates from the 1930's.[19] Most states passed laws at that time putting limits of one sort or another on price competition at retail.[20] Twenty-eight states imposed special taxes on chain store outlets.[21] Much of this legislation is still on the books, though in general it has not prevented the continuing changes in retailing.

B. *The Robinson-Patman Act*

The main federal action was the Robinson-Patman Act of 1936. It was known popularly as the "anti-chain store" bill when under consideration, and many of its provisions were aimed specifically at practices of certain large retailers at the time.[22] Its main purpose was to prohibit "price discrimination," but this phrase has different meanings in law and in economics. A seller "discriminates" under the Act if he charges two customers different prices for "goods of like grade or quality," although he can justify his "discrimination" if he can show that it is no greater than the dif-

---

[19] At the turn of the century, however, the hardware dealers tried to stop the introduction of parcel post because of their fear of the wicked "catalogue houses," and the old-fashioned dry goods dealers tried to get special taxes on the new department stores.

[20] The resale price maintenance ("fair trade") and the unfair practices acts —see pp. 261–270.

[21] Most of these taxes were progressive—the larger the number of stores, the higher the tax, so the chains were encouraged to close small, old-style stores and replace them with much fewer but larger supermarkets. Fourteen of these taxes were still in effect in 1965: Alabama, Colorado, Delaware, Iowa, Louisiana, Maryland, Michigan, Mississippi, Montana, North Carolina, South Carolina, Tennessee, Texas, and West Virginia. CCH, *State Tax Handbook as of September 15, 1965.*

[22] It flatly prohibits brokerage allowance to buying firms, even if the buyer performs functions that brokers are paid for in other transactions, and it permits suppliers to provide advertising allowances or other sales services only if similar services are available on a "proportionately equal basis" to all customers. Both provisions seem to have been directed at practices of large chains, particularly the A&P.

ferences in his costs in supplying the two accounts. Such "cost defenses" have not been easy to establish. At the same time a seller is clearly within the law if he charges the same price to all retailers, regardless of his costs in supplying them. In effect, therefore, the act encourages him, and has sometimes virtually required him[23] to discriminate (in the economic sense) *against* his low cost accounts.

The Act has been widely criticized by economists. By encouraging discrimination against low-cost customers, it tends to protect inefficient distributors and prevents the consumer from benefitting from the lower costs in supplying large buyers. It probably also lessens price competition at the manufacturing level. Openly announced price cuts are seldom the best way for a manufacturer to win more business, since they are easily matched by his rivals. When price competition does break out in concentrated industries, it is more likely to be a matter of secret price cuts on individual large orders, though such under-the-counter competition often turns into open price cutting if it persists. Since secret price concessions are commonly discriminatory, the Robinson-Patman Act can be read as a law prohibiting any but open price competition. The writer has heard a number of businessmen in such industries as aluminum, steel, and machine tools describe the Act as a law against price "chiseling."

The Robinson-Patman Act did not stop the growth of large-scale retailers. Partly this is because there were ways around it. A small carpet mill or canning factory can sell its entire output of a particular good to Macy's or the A&P and not discriminate at all as far as the law is concerned, though its price might be very low. The Act itself provides several further exceptions,[24]

---

[23] Under one provision of the Act, the FTC can directly prohibit quantity discounts beyond some limit, regardless of whether they are justified by costs or not, if it finds those discounts would be "unjustly discriminatory or promotive of monopoly." Its one attempt to set such quantity limits (on tires in 1952) was overruled by the courts on technical grounds. (B. F. Goodrich Co. v. FTC, 134 F. Supp. 39 (1955), 242 F. 2nd 31 (1957).)

[24] Exceptions are allowed for sales to prevent deterioration of perishables or for seasonal goods or for bona fide closeouts. No express exception is made for "functional" discounts (to wholesalers compared with retailers or to retailers compared with consumers), but since a major purpose of the Act was to preserve the existing distributive system, the FTC and the courts

most notably the so called "good faith" defense discussed on page 260.

A major reason why the Act did not stop the revolution in retailing is that the advantage of the new retailers has usually rested on much more than their ability to win discounts from suppliers. The substantial economies of scale in many lines of retailing are barely touched by the Act.

In some cases enforcement of the Act has harrassed independents attempting to compete with the chains by forming cooperative buying groups. The FTC pursued a 20-year campaign against price concessions made by the smaller auto-parts manufacturers to independent parts-dealer buying groups. Many of the parts dealers were forced into mergers with chains as a result. The limits on the buying groups were finally relaxed, though not eliminated, in the mid-1960's.[25]

Enforcement of the Robinson-Patman Act is expensive. It makes discrimination illegal when the effect is "harm to competition," which means when someone gets hurt. Someone is apt to be hurt whenever competition is strong, so the FTC receives many complaints that seem to involve violations. About an eighth of the Commission's investigation work load in the late 1960's arose under the Act.[26] It seems very doubtful whether the resources so used produce nearly as much for consumers as they could in enforcement of the wide range of competitive practice, merger, and misrepresentation laws for which the Commission is also responsible.

Almost all informed observers advocate some changes in the language and enforcement of the Robinson-Patman Act. Many

---

have not questioned such differentials except where wholesalers have also made retail sales.

[25] Steven Nelson, *An Economic Analysis of Antitrust Policy in the Automotive Parts Industry*, unpublished Ph.D. thesis, University of Wisconsin, 1970, *passim*.

[26] *Report of the ABA Commission to Study the Federal Trade Commission*, American Bar Association, Sept. 15, 1969, p. 19. This represents a considerable decline from the mid-1960's. In 1965, 30% of the FTC's investigation work load was devoted to price discrimination. By 1968 and 1969, this was down to 13%.

advocate outright repeal. If we did eliminate the Act we would still have a legal prohibition of price discrimination in Section 2 of the Clayton Act, but it would apply only where there was a reasonable chance that price discrimination would substantially lessen competition or tend to create monopoly.

The field covered by the Robinson-Patman Act is vast and the terms of the transactions involved are often secret. Although the FTC has devoted a large part of its resources to the enforcement of the Act and many attorneys have earned excellent incomes defending Robinson-Patman Act cases, a great number of probable violations must go unchecked. A supplier fighting for a big account is apt to make the necessary price concession as the situation demands and worry in more leisurely moments whether he can provide an adequate cost defense if challenged.

C. *The A & P Case*

The antitrust mainstream, when it touched retailing, sometimes took on a protectionist tinge also. The most famous instance was the conviction of the A&P[27] for "monopolizing," although the firm had only 10% of the national food-store sales and controlled no more than 21% of any area's food trade.[28] The government made several charges, but the main ones were that the firm had systematically sought preferential discounts relative to its rivals and that it had used profits in one area to subsidize losses elsewhere. While isolated acts of this sort might just be good business, the court found that the general pattern reflected an illegal policy.

This decision has been the subject of much controversy. Many economists felt that A&P was being convicted for engaging in competition rather than for destroying it. The case seems to have grown out of the complaints of grocers when the A&P experimented with reduced margins in the late 1930's. The govern-

---

[27] US v. The New York Great Atlantic and Pacific Tea Company, 173 F. 2nd 79 (1949).

[28] Adelman, "The A and P Case," *op. cit.*, p. 243. The 10% figure is based on the A&P annual reports and the 1940 census. The 21% figure refers to "units," which correspond roughly to metropolitan areas. A&P undoubtedly had a larger share of the trade in individual towns in some cases.

ment's brief quoted a statement by John Hartford, the key defendant in the case, that a spectacular increase in meat sales ". . . was accomplished by reducing the gross profit rate until the volume was built up to a point where the expense rate was low enough to permit the store to operate at a profit." The brief then commented, "We know of no more clear and concise words with which to express the government's charge."[29] Actually, the government's charge was nowhere nearly so clear or concise. It covered a large number of other points, but to the extent that it attacked A&P's low margins it was going after what is usually considered a major competitive virtue in retailers.

Some have doubted that the government's charges were plausible, in view of A&P's market position. Why would suppliers offer discriminatory discounts to a firm representing only one tenth of a very competitive market? If it cost them less to supply the A&P than smaller firms, they might offer discounts to win its attractive business, but only if the price concessions exceeded the cost saving would the discounts be discriminatory. Profit-seeking suppliers in competitive industries would not be likely to make such large concessions so long as they have a large number of alternative buyers, which they do in food processing. It was more conceivable that A&P could win discriminatory discounts from firms in the more monopolistic food industries such as cereals, but those discounts were among the few whiffs of price competition ever seen in such markets, and A&P had every incentive to pass them on to consumers. Again, why would a firm in an industry with such easy entry as food distribution in the 1930's pursue a predatory price policy? Local price cuts that eliminate competitors could not offer much prospect of long-run profits, since high subsequent prices would simply mean new competition.[30]

Other economists have questioned whether the A&P case was an unmitigated disaster. A&P won very few of its controversial

---

[29] Quoted in Adelman, "The A and P Case," *op. cit.*, p. 241.

[30] Adelman, *A&P: A Study in Price-Cost Behavior and Public Policy, op. cit., passim,* pp. 404–408. Aside from questioning the rationality of discriminatory discounts or predatory pricing in food distribution, Adelman presents a great deal of evidence seeming to show that neither occurred to any important extent.

discounts from sellers in concentrated industries such as soap, cigarettes, or canned milk. They were able to resist A&P's pressure. And though the government sought to dissolve the firm into seven regional chains, the final award merely imposed a $170,000 fine, which hardly broke A&P's back, and required it to dissolve its brokerage subsidiary. A&P's policies were little altered by the decision. One conclusion was that:

"The great bulk of the good which grocery chains do—with their private labels, their large scale coordinated operations, their low markup and intense competition with established manufacturers and channels of distribution—they can continue to do."[31]

D. *Marketing and the Merger Law*

Until the early 1960's, the competitive character of most of retailing seemed generally to keep the antitrust authorities at bay, but since then the merger law has had an important impact on the large retailers. At the time of the A&P case, food retailing was not very concentrated in most cities, and the barriers to entry were extremely low. By 1963, concentration among food stores was high enough to worry about in many cities and exceeded that in steel in a few. Much of the increase in concentration had resulted from mergers among the chains smaller than A&P. At the same time, the optimal scale of a store and of a food chain had increased. An efficient chain requires capital investments of $20 to $50 million today. Such an entry fee is low compared with those in industries that are commonly described as having serious barriers to entry, but it is no longer insignificant.[32]

In response to the new competitive conditions, both the Justice Department and the FTC began to subject retailing to the sort of surveillance that is given to similarly concentrated fields elsewhere. The most notable case was the government's suit to stop

---

[31] J. B. Dirlam and A. E. Kahn, "Anti-Trust Law and the Large Buyer—Another Look at the A and P Case," *Journal of Political Economy*, April 1952, p. 132.

[32] See text and footnote 11 on pages 225–226. The total investment required for a multi-city chain to make full use of private brands might require an investment as great as $200 million, but many local chains have prospered with much smaller sizes.

the merger of Von's Grocery with Market Basket, the third and sixth largest food retailers in Los Angeles.

Los Angeles was one of the least concentrated cities in food retailing, and had been marked by a rapid turnover of retailers. Yet the court found the merger to be illegal. An important consideration was the trend toward greater concentration. Even if Los Angeles food stores were not very concentrated, they were likely to become more so as the shakeout of inefficient stores continued. Mergers are usually meant to be forever, so the court had to consider what the effect of the merger would be when things settled down. Moreover, a series of mergers no larger than Von's-Market Basket would be hard to stop if that merger were approved.

There has been a good deal of criticism of this decision. Many economists feel that the court strained rather hard to find a reasonable chance that the merger would lessen competition. However, many of the critics would probably approve antimerger suits in other large metropolitan areas in which concentration is substantially higher than in Los Angeles.

After the Von's decision the FTC announced that it would ordinarily challenge mergers among food chains in which combined sales exceeded $500 million and would examine carefully those in which combined sales exceeded $100 million. At the same time it indicated that it would not ordinarily be concerned about mergers whose combined sales came to less than 5% of total sales in the metropolitan area involved. As part of this policy statement, the Commission required all chains with more than $100 million in sales to notify it in advance of any subsequent mergers.[33] Large-scale mergers in the food retailing industry have largely disappeared since then.

VI. GAS STATIONS

A. *Oligopoly in Retailing*

Students with some background in retailing often feel that oligopoly might give a better picture than monopolistic competition

---

[33] FTC, *Enforcement Policies with Respect to Mergers in the Food Distribution Industries,* Jan. 3, 1967.

of the stores in their experience. Retailers are forever "shopping" their competitors. They often price to "meet the competition" and openly charge "customary markups." One might expect to find tacit agreements on price similar to those of the steelmakers.

There are certainly some elements of oligopoly in retailing, but the result is likely to be very different from other cases of oligopoly. Tacit price agreements are unlikely for several reasons:

1. There is no one uniform price to agree upon. Most stores sell thousands of different items and are always having a sale on something. The price of identical chickens on a particular morning can vary from 29¢ to 50¢ a pound at similar supermarkets. Those with high prices for chicken are likely to have low prices on something else. Only the average prices of a whole shopping cart of groceries need to be in line with each other, and even these differ from store to store according to the amounts of service offered.[34]

2. Retailers have strong incentives to cut price. Their main concern is to get us into their stores and keep us coming back, and a reputation for low prices is usually an asset in accomplishing this. Most of the big successes in retailing have started off with aggressive price competition.

3. Even if all the established merchants in town were ready to observe an agreement on margins, it probably would not hold up because of the free entry and high turnover in retailing. New stores, including new branches of substantial chains, are always ready to appear whenever prospects are good, and the rate of business failure is much higher in retailing than in most lines of enterprise. Both those entering and those struggling not to leave are apt to cut prices in their efforts to win new customers or retain old ones. In general, there are too many stores, too complicated a product, and too easy entry for oligopoly pricing to offer a complete explanation for price practices in *most* lines of retailing.

Oligopoly seems more plausible in the case of gas stations than

---

[34] A seller of shopping goods is under more pressure to meet his competition on each item, but he does not have to duplicate every sale price to stay in business, and it is impossible for him to meet the price of other sellers who offer more or less service.

for most retailers. A single standardized product accounts for more than half of their sales, so prices are easily compared. At least the larger and better located sellers of major brands of gasoline must expect the rapid loss of customers if they charge substantially more than their rivals, and retaliation if they charge much less.

B. *The Majors*

Gas stations fall into two broad categories, those dealing in a well-advertised major brand of gasoline such as Texaco or Shell, and those dealing in relatively unadvertised local brands such as Billups, Hancock, Hudson, or Tenneco. We will refer to the first as major brand stations and to the second as independent brand stations. The major brand stations, in turn, can be classified as to ownership and control.

1. A few are actually operated by paid employees of the major oil companies.[35]

2. Some stations are owned by the operators or by third parties and simply deal in a major refiner's product. The refiners typically provide equipment, paving, or at least paint jobs for such stations. In many cases the refiner leases the station from the owner and then leases it back on an advantageous basis. The leases can usually be canceled by either party on short notice.

3. The most important group of major stations is owned by the oil companies but leased to the operators, again with a short-term cancellation clause. The proprietors of such stations are technically independent businessmen. However, the major refiners assist them in promotion, financing, and operations and supervise them to maintain standards. As a result, these proprietors have much in common with the managers of chain store branches.

The major stations usually emphasize service. They attempt to attract motorists by having clean stations, lots of attendants, free road maps, and an air of respectability. They are often fairly small neighborhood enterprises, and do a large business in servicing and in tires, batteries, and accessories.

---

[35] In the 1920's more than one third of the stations were in this category, but practically all major refiners have found it profitable to change their stations to a lease basis.

C. *The Independents*

Some of the independent stations are also operated by single station proprietors but a large proportion are really chains, owned and operated by independent jobbers or by small refiners. Such firms can buy full tanker or tank car lots. Their stations are commonly in locations with high traffic density. A survey of four large midwestern cities showed the modern independent stations selling from 58% to 130% more gasoline per station than the major stations.[36] Like the large retailers in other trades, these firms have been able to bypass the wholesaler or simplify his function and win substantial price concessions in the process.

The independent stations emphasize price in selling. Their antecedents of the 1930's were often unattractive and unadvertised, and price was almost their only appeal. The modern independents continue to make that appeal, but many are as attractive as the major stations and sell products as well known within their local markets as some major brands. Most of the independents' business is in the sale of petroleum products. They do little in the way of servicing as a rule. The independent distributors buy some of their gasoline from independent refineries, but a large part is the unbranded product of major oil companies.[37] The large refiners are willing to do such business because it provides individuals among them with a means of increasing their sales without cutting prices generally. Sales to independents at bargain prices are especially likely when stocks of oil accumulate and must be moved.

D. *Retail Pricing of Gasoline*

The proprietors of major brand gas stations make their own price decisions with more or less guidance from the major oil companies. The major refiners do control prices at stations they

---

[36] S. Morris Livingston and Theodore Levitt, "Competition and Retail Gasoline Prices," *Review of Economics and Statistics*, May 1959, p. 130.

[37] A survey of 30 private branders in 1965 showed them receiving 45% of their gasoline from major refiners. Select Committee on Small Business, House of Representatives, 89th Cong. 1st Sess. *FTC Industry Conference on Marketing Automotive Gasoline,* (hereafter *FTC Gasoline Marketing Conference*), Vol. I, p. 507.

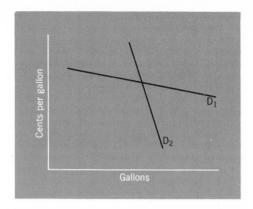

Figure 5-14

operate directly and at some leased stations where proprietors
are on a salary basis, usually during a breaking-in period, but
these are a small part of the total. Major refiners' pressure on the
operators of leased stations could be quite effective, because of
the contract cancellation clauses. In some cases it appears to have
been exerted in favor of stable and uniform prices. In other cases
the dealers have been left on their own or urged or even "subsidized" to price aggressively.[38]

The major gasolines are apparently identical in the eyes of
many buyers, so that each station's individual demand curve is
extremely elastic. At the same time, the elasticity of demand for
gasoline in general is very low. Gasoline is only a small part of
the cost of running a car. Having committed himself to the high
depreciation, interest, insurance, and maintenance expenses involved in owning a car, a driver is unlikely to be swayed by a

---

[38] The best account of local gasoline markets that the writer has seen appeared in the *National Petroleum News*, March, 1969, and contains detailed
analyses of Los Angeles, Kansas City, Milwaukee, and Detroit. These range
from cases of almost continuous price war to cities in which the strongest
majors maintain the price although rivals continuously undercut them. These
reports include cases in which major refiners have kept their stations from
cutting prices in spite of other major brands selling for as much as 3¢ lower;
cases in which major refiners have offered special rental terms to induce
aggressive pricing; and a wide range of policies in between. It does not
seem to be uncommon for different majors to follow such sharply different
policies in the same city market.

tenth of a cent more or less per mile when deciding whether to take the car or the bus.[39]

The position of a major station is represented in Figure 5-14. A price reduction met by other sellers would move him down his very inelastic D_2 curve and leave him poorer. Operators of badly located or unattractive stations may look longingly at their D_1 curves, but they can only hope to pick up business if their price cuts are not met. Some do make price reductions, and many make discounts to truckers, but for the most part these price concessions are not large enough to encroach seriously on sales of other stations.[40] Operators of successful major stations usually emphasize service as a more successful way of winning customers.

Unlike the sellers of major brand gasoline, the independent stations depend on price to attract business. For the most part, their very existence depends on some differential from major brands, and they tend if anything to exaggerate the saving in their advertising. The majors cannot eliminate the differential short of eliminating the independents themselves. It is usually cheaper to live and let live, so long as the differential is not great enough to drain off excessive amounts of business. Just what differential is sufficient and what loss of trade is tolerable are obviously matters where judgment can vary. Most of the time a differential ac-

---

[39] One study by a major oil company indicated an elasticity of demand for gasoline of only 0.13, reported in Cassady and Jones, *op. cit.*, p. 21. The elasticity of demand in a particular market may be considerably greater because of the possibility of buying elsewhere. Lincoln Clark found an elasticity of 0.7 to 1.1 for gasoline in Tennessee when prices in neighboring states were held constant: "The Elasticity of Demand for Tennessee Gasoline," *Journal of Marketing*, April 1951, p. 407.

[40] Whether they actually cut prices and if so, how much, depends on the makeup of the local gasoline market and its recent history. In late 1968 the leading major oil company in Detroit seemed to be purposely ignoring price cutters. The last price wars had been four years earlier. As a result about 40% of the major stations were selling below the "prevailing" price—some as much as 3¢ below. At the same time, Los Angeles had fair price stability, but brief price wars would occur about every six weeks. Some 8% of the major-brand stations were advertising price cuts when surveyed there. In Milwaukee and Kansas City, where price wars had been endemic, the majors seemed to stay more nearly in line during the occasional peaceful interludes.

ceptable to both groups develops. Two cents a gallon for regular is common, but it has been narrowed to 1¢ in some cities and is as wide as 5¢ in others. Unattractive or poorly located independent stations may offer more than others. The independents prospered in many parts of the country in the years after World War II, as they convinced a growing part of the public that their gasoline was just as good as the majors'. The differential was commonly reduced as a result—often in long and bloody price wars in the late 1950's and early 1960's. Many of the more successful independents were acquired by majors from other parts of the country at that time. By the late 1960's, however, the differential had widened once more in many communities, and the independents seemed to be increasing in importance again.

E. Gas Wars

Attempts by independents to increase the differential, or by majors to reduce it, are likely to result in gas wars. Price reductions by one group lead to price reductions by the other, until one of the sides gives in.

If the price war persists for any length of time, the oil companies must come to the assistance of their stations or lose them. Their usual policy is to allow rebates from announced tankwagon (wholesale) prices while the war continues.

It is easier to describe the conditions that lead to price wars than to say who causes them. The immediate move that starts things off may be made by a reckless independent, the operator of a hardpressed major station, or an overzealous salesman from a major refiner.

Some gas wars have been due to attempts of majors to reduce the differential between their own products and those of major refiners marketing through secondary brands that had been selling at the "independent" price. In other cases, major refiners introduced third grades of gasoline that they attempted to sell at the independents' price. Gas wars are most likely to occur in areas where local refineries or easy water transportation offer the independents regular access to cheap gasoline, and in periods when surplus gasoline accumulates so that the independents' costs decline. They are especially common on heavily traveled through routes into the large cities. The demand for gasoline along such routes is much more elastic than the demand for gasoline generally, since low prices there can attract business from a distance. Price cuts by stations on such routes may seem to pay even if they are met by all the immediate neighbors.

The end of a gas was requires some sort of open or tacit agreement. Sometimes a chain of independents will announce a return to the price that held before the gas war, and the other stations happily follow. Sometimes the majors remove their rebates as a signal for operators to call off the war. It seems to be fairly common for local trade associations, local government officials, or even the oil companies at times to arrange agreements ending severe gas wars.

F. *Excess Capacity*

Even if we conclude that they have an unstable form of oligopoly, the gas stations need not have exceptional profits. With free entry, profits can disappear here just as well as in other lines of retailing. For instance, in Figure 5-15 where the tankwagon price plus tax is 26¢, the station can make considerable profit at the accepted

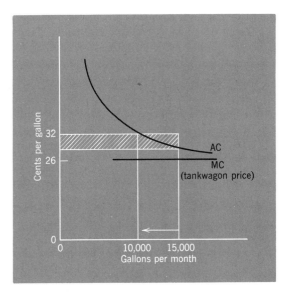

Figure 5-15

margin of 6¢ a gallon so long as it is selling 15,000 gallons. If there are opportunities for such profits, more stations are likely to appear, however. High profits can disappear, even if the 32¢ price is maintained, as the new stations draw off trade.

Entry into the gas station business is especially easy. Perhaps the most important form of rivalry among the major oil companies is their competition for outlets. The way to win a customer for Shell or Standard products is to have a station near his home and others easily available whenever he wants to stop. As a result the large refiners will go to great lengths to blanket the market with stations. They build and equip stations and finance them for the operator on an advantageous basis. Would-be proprietors need very little capital to enter the business and, since the skills involved are widely known and hope springs eternal, there is practically no limit to the number of potential operators as well as stations.

High margins seldom last for long. As new stations appear and excess capacity develops price wars become more common. It takes only a short time for gasoline margins to reach normal levels. In this respect gas stations resemble the competitive industries—where a high supply means low prices and vice versa—and are quite different from automobiles and steel where prices can go up in spite of considerable overcapacity. Oligopoly may give a reasonable picture of the gas stations on a particular day, but it seems less appropriate in accounting for long-term tendencies.[41] This should not be surprising. The tacit agreements of

---

[41] A number of studies of gasoline markets have reached a similar conclusion: that retail margins tend toward competitive levels in the long run. Edward P. Lerned, "The Pricing of Gasoline, A Case Study," *Harvard Business Review,* November 1948, p. 749, felt that margins much in excess of operating "costs" led to price cutting by independents (pp. 742–743, 751) and suggested that the low margins in Ohio in the 1930's compared with other states accounted for the small increase in stations (p. 750). J. S. Bain, *The Pacific Coast Petroleum Industry,* University of California Press, Berkeley, 1945, Pt. II, pp. 227–233, noted a similar role for the independent and found that margins remained at levels that barely covered operating expenses most of the time. See also Dirlam and Kahn, "Leadership and Conflict in the Pricing of Gasoline" *Yale Law Journal,* June, 1952, pp. 838–842. Livingston and Levitt, in their survey of six midwestern cities cited earlier,

the gas stations' oligopoly are far more fragile than those of other oligopolies. Only in the most extreme of circumstances (1921 and 1933) did steel prices change as much as 30% in one year; such fluctuations are almost annual experiences in many local gasoline markets.

G. *The Government and the Gas Stations*

Public policy on gasoline retailing has certainly not been unequivocally on the side of more competition. Many communities have taken price cutting as an unquestioned evil when it comes to gasoline. Several states have laws prohibiting sales of gasoline at less than announced prices, in effect outlawing the "behind the pump" discount. Some cities prohibited self-serve stations when the independents introduced them in the early 1950's. A number of cities have laws preventing gas stations from displaying price signs of more than a square foot in area, thus making price cutting to attract the passing motorist practically useless. Agreements among retailers seem to have been fostered in some localities, especially in small towns or where the unfair practices laws (discussed on p. 270) have been applicable to gas stations. There are instances where operators have met in public and voted on price.[42]

---

found that with one minor exception the higher the margins, the more stations there were pricing at less than the norm.

The reader must be warned that the conclusion reached here applies *only* to the retailing of gasoline. Oil refining has somewhat more in common with steel, while crude oil production is a government-enforced cartel. For discussions of the oil industry in general see Bain or Dirlam and Kahn listed above, or Melvin G. de Chazeau and A. E. Kahn, *Integration and Competition in the Petroleum Industry,* Yale University Press, New Haven, 1959.

[42] For a more complete description of some of these practices see Ralph Cassady, *Price Making and Price Behavior in the Petroleum Industry,* Yale University Press, New Haven, 1954, pp. 246–252.

Most states have active gasoline retailers' associations, many of which are continuously fighting for price controls of various sorts, including resale price maintenance, the enforcement of unfair practices laws, and even direct regulation of retail prices by special state commissions. The oil refiners usually oppose these measures. See Cassady and Jones, cited above, p. 279, or almost any issue of *The Gasoline Retailer.*

H. *Robinson-Patman Once More*

The federal agencies also have an equivocal record on competition in gasoline retailing. Their most important action in this field was a Robinson-Patman Act case in which the FTC found that Standard Oil of Indiana had discriminated illegally when it sold at low prices to four Detroit independent jobbers in the 1930's. As in other communities, these firms were the leaders in price competition. The FTC ordered Standard Oil to stop giving the discounts. Standard Oil appealed, and after years of litigation the Supreme Court ruled against the Commission.[43] It decided that a firm could justify price differentials under the Robinson-Patman Act if such "discrimination" were necessary to meet a competitor's price in good faith. The Detroit jobbers had alternative sources of supply at prices as low as Standard Oil's and the company would undoubtedly have lost their business if it had refused to meet these prices. The Court held that the law did not prohibit bona fide price competition of this sort.

Although the Standard of Indiana case did finally end (after 20 years!), the argument has continued. In the early 1960's it looked almost as if the FTC was conducting a campaign to prevent gas wars or at least limit the majors' participation in them. In one case, the Supreme Court supported the FTC in finding that the Sun Oil Company had discriminated illegally when it gave a rebate to a Jacksonville station that had to compete with a price-cutting private brander because Sun had not extended the rebate to its other customers. Sun was not "meeting competition in good faith"—the private brander was the station's competitor, not Sun's.[44] After that victory the FTC began a large number of actions in the gasoline retailing field. Its 1962 Annual Report mentioned five such cases in process and 14 others under investigation.[45] Most of them had to do with the major oil companies' policies during gas wars—such as local rebates and the sale of gasoline on consignment so that the company instead of the

---

[43] Standard Oil v. Federal Trade Commission, 340 US 231 (1951). The FTC then issued a revised order and it too was appealed. It was finally set aside by a 5 to 4 decision of the Supreme Court, 355 US 396 (1958).

[44] Sun Oil Company v. FTC, 371 US 505 (1963).

[45] FTC, *Annual Report,* 1962, p. 47.

station took any losses due to price cutting. However, after extensive hearings in 1965, the FTC dropped most of these cases and never renewed its enforcement effort in the field. The court had more or less left the question of what gasoline pricing practices fell within the law to the antitrust enforcement agencies. The FTC seems to have decided to keep hands off except where violations are blatant.

Overall, government at all levels has done little to improve the performance of gasoline retailing. If the trade is less efficient than it might be, it is due to excess capacity. The actions of federal, state, and local governments to check price competition intensify this problem, if anything.

VII. CARTELS WITH FREE ENTRY—DRUGSTORES

A. *Resale Price Maintenance Laws*

Agreements among the firms in an industry to limit competition are referred to as *cartels*. Informal cartels have not been very successful in most lines of retailing. Discount houses thrive on such arrangements when observed by *other* stores. There must be some sort of legal enforcement if agreements to restrict competition in retailing are to work.

The most important means of accomplishing this in the United States have been the resale price maintenance or "fair-trade" laws passed at one time or another by every state except Alaska, Missouri, Texas, Vermont, and the District of Columbia.[46] They permit manufacturers to stipulate minimum prices in contracts with their retailers. Then if a contract is violated, the manufacturer can sue the price cutter. In fact, under the "nonsigner" clause included in most fair-trade laws, the manufacturer may sue any retailer selling below list price even if he has not signed an agreement, provided only that some dealer in the state has. In effect, the manufacturer has the power to enforce a price agreement among the sellers of his product if he chooses.

Resale price maintenance is not used in every branch of retailing. It seldom applies to petroleum or food products or to

---

[46] In a number of states, however, court decisions have undermined these laws, and they have been repealed in a few states. See p. 269.

most types of shopping goods.[47] It is common in the sale of non-prescription drugs,[48] cosmetics, liquors, and small appliances.

Fair trade has a long history in the drug field and is more complete there than in most other branches of retailing today.

B. *Fair Trade in Theory*

The effect of fair-trade laws or of any cartel with free entry is analyzed in Figure 5-16. The drugstore represented there might have a demand curve like D_1 in the short run, but since the manufacturer has specified that the price cannot fall below P, only the solid section of the demand curve counts. The profit that results will disappear in this case as in others because of the new stores it attracts into the trade. The new crop of pharmacists cannot drive down the price under the fair-trade laws, but they can spread the volume of trade thinner and thinner until the demand at a prospective new store is down to D_2. After that, the druggist's margin does not seem excessive. It barely "covers costs." The druggist may feel that it does not even do that. If they can convince the manufacturer to specify higher margins, they may be able to increase their earnings for a time. In the long run, of course, the greater the margins, the greater the excess capacity.

Unable to compete in price, druggists may try to expand volume by carrying a greater variety of brands, offering free delivery, or providing some other increased service. An individual

---

[47] Fair trade does not seem to work when the typical sale is large because it is almost impossible to keep sellers from making secret concessions, though some appliance and TV manufacturers still try to specify minimum retail prices. It is clearly inappropriate when brand names are unimportant, as with many food and textile products. Some of the more powerful manufacturers, such as the oil refiners and cigarette manufacturers, have been able to resist pressure on them to fair-trade their products.

[48] There are other limits on price competition in prescription drugs. For instance, 29 states prohibit the advertising of prescription drugs by name or price and ten prohibit such terms as "discount" or "cut rate" in the advertising of prescription-drug departments. Some states require that pharmacies be owned by pharmacists, prohibit self-service for nonprescription drugs, and enforce various other rules designed to keep chains, discount houses, and department stores out of the drug business. All states license pharmacists. See Marion Fletcher, *Market Restraints in the Retail Drug Industry,* University of Pennsylvania Press, 1967.

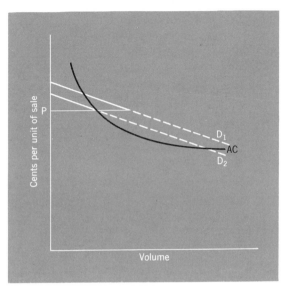

Figure 5-16

store can certainly win customers this way, but drugstores in general will not gain much. The net effect in the long run is simply higher costs at each store (AC_2 in Figure 5-17) but no more profits than before.

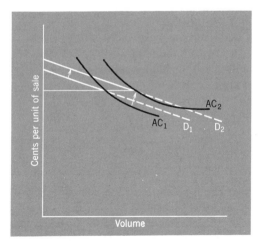

Figure 5-17

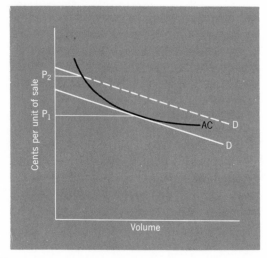

Figure 5-18

C. *Are Fair-Trade Prices Too High?*

Cartels with free entry would cause excess capacity only if the price agreed upon were higher than prevailing otherwise. In Figure 5-18, if the "fair-trade" price were P_1, resale price maintenance would lead to no more excess capacity than we would have anyway, but if it were higher, say P_2, it would mean more drugstores with less business per store.

There has been much debate about whether fair trade actually raises prices or not. A number of surveys have been made by the sponsors of fair trade which seem to show that drug prices actually declined slightly with the coming of fair-trade laws, that they rose less than nonfair-trade prices during the inflation of the 1940's, and that retail drug prices are lower in fair-trade than in nonfair-trade states![49]

---

[49] Some of these studies are suspect since they depend on the reports and often the memories of druggists who have a vested interest in fair trade. For instance, the most ambitious such survey, H. J. Ostlund and C. R. Vickland, *Fair Trade and the Retail Drug Store,* Druggists Research Bureau, 1940, depended on replies to a questionnaire sent to all druggists in fair-trade states inquiring about prices before and after fair-trade laws were passed. The

Other surveys have produced different results. The FTC found that after the introduction of fair-trade laws in the 1930's prices charged by department stores and chains were definitely higher but that prices charged by small independents, especially in small towns, apparently were not.[50] Since then, at least ten academic and government studies of prices for identical products in fair trade and nonfair-trade states, of prices before and after the adoption or abandonment of fair trade here or abroad, and of margins of specialized appliance, record, and liquor dealers with and without fair trade have quite consistently shown fair trade as leading to higher prices.[51] Such a conclusion is easy to believe in view of the retailers' vehement support of the fair-trade laws.

D. *Excess Capacity in Drugstores*

Sales per drugstore in fair-trade and free-trade states should provide some check on the possibility that resale price maintenance would lead to excess capacity. Table 5-3 shows 1963 sales per drugstore in the seven metropolitan areas of more than 500,000 population located in states that had never had fair trade laws. All but one of these has higher sales per store than the average of metropolitan areas over 500,000 in fair-trade states. Drugstores in the seven areas taken together do half again as much business per store as those in other large metropolitan areas. Of course, there are many reasons why some areas should have drugstores with higher volume than others. Table 5-3 does not prove that fair-trade prices have attracted too many stores into the trade, but the high volume of drugstores in the nonfair trade cities certainly supports that hypothesis.[52]

---

same questionnaire appeared in a drugstore magazine with the caption "Cast your vote for fair trade." This and other such studies are criticized in Marvin Frankel, "The Effect of Fair Trade: Fact and Fiction in the Statistical Findings," *Journal of Business,* July 1955, pp. 182–194.

[50] FTC, *Resale Price Maintenance,* 1945, pp. xlvii–vlix. The FTC survey also depended on druggists' memories and probably suffered from some of the deficiencies of those sponsored by advocates of fair trade.

[51] Summarized in S. C. Hollander, "United States of America," in B. S. Yamey, ed., *Resale Price Maintenance,* Aldine, (Chicago, 1966), pp. 96–97. Other sections of Yamey provide similar evidence on the effect of changing the fair trade laws abroad.

[52] A recent, more thorough study compared sales per store in 1963 in 103

Table 5-3.   Sales per Drugstore in Metropolitan Areas of more than 500,000 Population

Metropolitan Area	Sale per Store (Dollars)	Percentage of Stores with more than $500,000 Sales
Dallas	231,200	9.7
Fort Worth	206,500	9.9
Houston	191,400	7.9
Kansas City	229,200	9.6
San Antonio	134,200	1.4
St. Louis	185,800	6.8
Washington, D. C.	368,500	29.4
All seven nonfair trade cities together	221,000	12.7
All other metropolitan areas of over 500,000 population	135,551	5.2

Source. Census of Business, 1963, "Retail Trade: United States."

The slowness of large retailers to develop in drugs is also probably attributable to fair trade at least in part. Figure 5-2 shows that the chains' share of the retail drug trade declined from the passage of the fair trade in the mid-1930's until the late 1950's when fair trade was waning. This occurred in spite of the substantially higher sales per worker in chain than in independent

---

metropolitan areas that were identified by the Census as "major retail centers," after controlling for metropolitan-area size and sales per square mile. On the average, drugstores sold about 40% more per year where there were no fair-trade laws and about 20% more per year where fair trade was weakened by lack of an effective nonsigner clause than in metropolitan areas where full fair trade with the nonsigner clause was in effect in 1963. The difference arose partly because metropolitan areas of a given size and sales density had more drugstores where fair trade was in effect and partly because they had lower total drugstore sales, presumably because of high drugstore prices. The difference between the fair trade and nonfair trade metropolitan areas was greater than would occur by chance as often as one time in twenty. A similar pattern prevailed for general-merchandise stores (department and variety stores), jewelry stores, and sporting goods and bicycle stores, all of which have important fair-trade products. The pattern did not hold up, or it was so weak that it could easily be due to chance, in the case of food stores, apparel stores, furniture stores, and bookstores. Only the last of these was importantly affected by fair trade in 1963 (unpublished paper by Paul Brandon, graduate student at Harvard University).

stores, shown in Figure 5-3. Since the mid-1950's, the decline in fair trade has been accompanied by a very rapid growth of drug chains. Similarly, the nonfair-trade cities in Table 5-3 show consistently larger percentages of their stores in the "more than $500,000 sales" class than do the large metropolitan areas in fair trade states. Fair-trade laws prevent large retailers from passing savings on to the customer and hence, eliminate their most effective means of expanding.

E. *Fair Trade and the Courts*

By the end of the nineteenth century, resale price maintenance was common in Europe, where it met few legal barriers. In the United States the National Wholesale Druggists Association won a resale price maintenance agreement from the manufacturers in 1876, but it was only extended to the retail level in 1900.[53] These agreements were accepted by the courts at first,[54] but in a 1911 decision the Supreme Court concluded that they were "obvious" agreements in restraint of interstate commerce and therefore illegal under the Sherman Act.[55]

Bills were introduced in every Congress from 1914 to 1936 to make such agreements legal once more, but no action was taken until the Depression. The state of California passed the first modern fair-trade law in 1931 and added the first nonsigner clause in 1933. Forty-one other states passed similar laws in the next three years. In 1937 Congress passed the Miller-Tydings Act exempting fair-trade agreements from the antitrust laws wherever state law allowed them.[56]

F. *The Decline and Fall of Fair Trade*

The resale price maintenance agreements were clearly in the interest of many retailers, but what did they do for the manufacturers who had to enforce them? In the first decades of this

---

[53] Ward Bowman, "The Prerequisites and Effects of Resale Price Maintenance," *University of Chicago Law Review*, vol. 22, Summer 1955, pp. 826–827.

[54] Fowle v. Park, 131 US 81 (1889).

[55] Dr. Miles Medical Co. v. Park and Sons Co., 220 US 373 (1911).

[56] It was passed as a rider to the District of Columbia appropriation of that year because of the possibility of a presidential veto.

century, companies with brand names newly established in expensive advertising campaigns seem to have felt that use of their products for "loss leaders" would destroy their prestige. Others, whose products were sold mainly through small outlets in trades with powerful retailers' associations, had to adopt fair trade to keep their dealers' favor.[57] A few manufacturers seem to have used high margins protected by fair trade to get dealers to push their products.[58]

Many manufacturers have soured on fair trade in the last 30 years. If retailers were willing to push the product with low prices, why prevent them? This view was particularly to the point when large retailers had the alternative of selling competing products under their own labels, something they were prone to do when prevented from using their cost advantage in selling national brands.

Fair trade has declined in importance in the years since World War II. The discount houses thrived on the agreements which at once provided a "normal" price from which to offer discounts and kept the prices of "legitimate" stores above theirs. Many manufacturers who were lukewarm toward fair trade did little to enforce their agreements. Producers who did try to get enforcement met increasing difficulties. It was one thing to threaten the large chains and department stores of the 1930's and quite another to police a great number of small discounters in the early 1950's. If an offender was brought into court the judgment was often slight.

Several judicial decisions have weakened the laws further. In 1951 the Supreme Court ruled that the Miller-Tydings Act had not exempted the state nonsigner clauses from the antitrust laws.[59] While the McGuire Act passed in the next session of

---

[57] The Northern California Retail Druggists Association conducted a boycott of Pepsodent until the company agreed to fair-trade it in 1935. The Company made a public apology and contributed $25,000 to a fund of the National Retail Druggists Association to finance the fair trade law campaign in other states. FTC, *Resale Price Maintenance, op. cit.,* p. 143, and TNEC, *Final Report,* 77th Congress, 1st Session, Exhibit 2793, p. 233.

[58] TNEC Hearings, Pt. VI, p. 2564.

[59] Schwegmann Brothers v. Calvert Distillers Corporation, 341 US 384 (1951).

Congress filled this gap, the discount houses got so much momentum during the interlude of poor enforcement that fair trade never really recovered. A lower court concluded that fair-trade laws did not prevent sellers in nonfair-trade states from advertising and delivering through the mails in all parts of the country and the Supreme Court refused to review the case.[60] A number of state courts and legislators have gone farther, 22 throwing out the nonsigner clause, and 9 throwing out the whole fair-trade statute.[61] The increasing difficulty of enforcement drove many manufacturers to abandon fair trade.

A national fair-trade act was introduced regularly in Congress in the 1960's. Such a law would close the mail-order loophole and take fair trade out of the state courts where it has done so badly. The proposal often bore a new euphemism, "the quality-stabilization act," instead of the now less popular phrase, "fair trade." It was supported mainly by retail and wholesale trade associations and had a surprisingly large number of congressional sponsors. The administration, especially the FTC and the Justice Department, consistently opposed it. The 91st Congress (1969–70) was the first in a decade that did not receive such a bill, but it seems very doubtful that we have seen the last of the proposal.

Fair trade has a long history abroad, but in recent years it has been eliminated in many economically advanced countries. It has been completely prohibited in Canada, Sweden, Denmark, France, and Austria and banned, with exceptions for some trades, in Britain and the Netherlands. The United States has generally

---

[60] General Electric v. Masters Mail Order Co. of Washington, D. C., 244 F. 2nd 681 certiorari denied 355 US 824 (1957).

[61] As of July 1970, the fair-trade statutes were unconstitutional in Alabama, Montana, Utah, and Wyoming and had been repealed in Hawaii, Kansas, Mississippi, Nebraska, Nevada and Puerto Rico. The nonsigner clause was unconstitutional in Alabama, Arkansas, Colorado, Florida, Georgia, Idaho, Indiana, Iowa, Kentucky, Louisiana, Michigan, Minnesota, Montana, New Mexico, Oklahoma, Oregon, Pennsylvania, South Carolina, Utah, Washington, West Virginia, and Wyoming. There had never been any fair-trade law in Alaska, Missouri, Texas, Vermont, or the District of Columbia. On the other hand, the laws have been declared constitutional in 16 other states, and Ohio and Virginia had passed new statutes after court decisions had made their original fair-trade laws unenforceable.

been the leading advocate of procompetition policies, but other countries have now gone farther than we have in the area of resale price maintenance. "Fair trade" cartels are still legal and fully enforceable in states accounting for more than half our population.

G. *Unfair Practices Acts*

The "unfair practices" acts are close relatives of the fair-trade laws. They are statutes passed in the 1930's by 32 states under which any dealer in a covered trade is prohibited from selling at prices which are less than his costs. The determination of "cost" is obviously crucial. As spelled out in the acts, it clearly includes operating expenses as well as the costs of goods sold. in 19 states the law specifies minimum markups—typically 6% at retail. In 9 states, cost surveys are permitted which can then be used as prima-facie evidence against price cutters. That is to say, it is up to the defendant to prove that he is not breaking the law if his prices will not cover the costs shown in the surveys.

These surveys have sometimes been very unscientific. Accounting costs are uncertain in the first place, and the businessmen with a vested interest in high prices are not likely to be objective in making estimates. As a result, the surveys have tended to turn into price agreements among association members. Once a minimum margin is agreed upon, price cutters can be threatened with criminal prosecution. The mere threat of litigation may be enough to intimidate a small businessman, especially if the agreement seems to be in his interest anyway.

The unfair practices acts do not have a very impressive enforcement record. State law enforcement agencies seldom devote much time or money to them. Large chains and department stores are unlikely to be deterred by the prospect of lawyers' fees even though little businessmen may be. The acts themselves have been declared unconstitutional in seven states.

VIII. CARTELS WITH RESTRICTED ENTRY—LIQUOR STORES

If it is overcapacity that plagues cartels with free entry, why not restrict the number of firms? This has been done in some lines of retailing. Manufacturers do it when they limit the number of franchised dealers, as with automobiles. State and local governments do it through licensing laws.[62]

A. Restrictions on Competition in Liquors

Probably the most regulated of retailers are the liquor dealers. Every state either licenses or prohibits private liquor stores. Sixteen states sell distilled liquors exclusively through publicly owned retail stores. Each of the remaining states licenses stores in order to control their number and locations and/or to prevent violations of the liquor code.

Fair trade is still alive and well in the liquor business in some states. Of the 35 jurisdictions with private liquor stores in 1969, 7 had no fair trade and 16 applied their ordinary fair-trade laws to liquor, but 12 *required* retail price maintenance in liquors.[63] Some just made fair trade mandatory, but most had separate "price posting laws" that required distillers and wholesalers to specify retail prices and required retailers to observe them.

---

[62] All states and many local governments perform this function for some lines of business. The Council of State Governments recently surveyed the states plus Puerto Rico and the Virgin Islands concerning their occupational licensing legislation in force. It received 48 responses. The numbers of occupations licensed ranged from 25 in Washington to 56 in Michigan. Half the states licensed at least 37. The occupations licensed included architects (all 48 responses), attorneys (48), doctors (48), pharmacists (48), beauticians (47), embalmers (47), barbers (46), engineers (46), real estate agents (46), insurance brokers (45), . . . automobile dealers and salesmen (24), investment advisers (23), private detectives (22), electricians (20), contractors (20), milk weighers (20), boiler inspectors (19), pest controllers (19) . . . and occasionally even tattoo artists, feeder pig dealers, and lightning rod salesmen. Altogether there are 69 occupations in which entry is controlled by one or more states (Council of State Governments, *Occupations and Professions Licensed by the States, Puerto Rico, and the Virgin Islands*, Chicago, December, 1968). While ostensibly the licensing laws are intended to protect the public against incompetents, the demand for such laws usually comes from the trades involved. Once in force, they are commonly administered by representatives of the licensed trades. The number of licensing laws and the entry requirements they impose on particular trades are both on the increase.

[63] Distilled Spirits Institute, *Summary of State Laws and Regulations Related to Distilled Spirits*, June 1969. The 12 states were Arkansas, Califor-

This makes the fair-trade laws much more effective since the violators are threatened with almost certain license suspensions rather than with more problematical lawsuits.

In California, at least, the liquor control laws have also been used to protect the old-style distribution system. Under ordinary circumstances manufacturers must go through independent wholesalers in distributing their products and neither the manufacturer nor the wholesaler may engage in retail operations. The law also contains a number of rules similar to those of the Robinson-Patman Act, apparently aimed at preventing price advantages for large retailers.

The one possibility of price competition in liquor retailing in mandatory fair-trade states has been the private brand. Distributors in some of these states have been able to do very well buying unbranded liquor, often from the better known distillers, and selling it under their own labels. They can meet the fair-trade requirement by filing a minimum price which includes only a nominal margin (6% is a common one, compared with about 20% on national brands). To fill this gap, 6 states have adopted measures specifying minimum margins of 21% to 28%![64]

B. *Monopoly Price and Profits in Liquors*

There can be little doubt that the liquor dealers have exercised a safe monopoly as a result of these controls. In 1952 a study was made of retail prices of 13 nationally known brands of liquor in all states other than those with public liquor monopolies. The lowest prices were in nonfair-trade states in each case (eight in Missouri, four in the District of Columbia, and one in Texas). The median fair-trade state had prices 30% above these minimums.[65]

The most impressive evidence of the exploitation of this state-

---

nia, Connecticut, Delaware, Hawaii, Indiana, Kansas, Kentucky, Massachusetts, Minnesota, New Jersey, and Tennessee.

[64] The states are Arkansas, Connecticut, Indiana, Kansas, Kentucky, and Tennessee. Louisiana, New Mexico and Rhode Island have repealed such laws since 1965.

[65] Charles F. Stewart "Mandatory Resale Price Maintenance of Distilled Spirits in California," *Journal of Marketing,* April 1954, p. 376.

bestowed monopoly is the value of liquor licenses. These are available publicly in California. With one small exception, California did not issue any new license from 1939 to 1961, and since then it has maintained strict limits on the number of new licenses. As a result, the main way to enter the liquor business in California has been to buy someone else's license. As prospective profits increased, so did the license prices. Although they cost less than $1000 when issued in 1939 (the limited number of new licenses cost $6000 when purchased from the state now), the average license changed hands in Los Angeles County at a cost of $14,380 in 1968, and in newly urbanized counties such as Orange or Riverside the average cost was more like $35,000.[66]

The fact that retailers were willing to make such payments to get into the business is a clear indication that substantial profits

---

[66] In 1968 313 old licenses changed hands in Los Angeles County at an average price of $14,380 excluding fixtures, inventory, and premises. Table 5-4 gives the comparable figures of four of the large, rapidly growing counties. By contrast, in San Francisco County (the central city, which has

Table 5-4.

County	Number of Transfers	Average Consideration
Orange	12	$41,667
Riverside	10	35,250
San Bernadino	10	22,480
Santa Clara	10	20,590

barely grown since 1939) the price averaged $7,357 on 75 sales, only slightly more than the price of a new license.

Starting in 1961, the legislature authorized up to one new license per 2500 persons in a county, but with limits on the total number of licenses and the number per county that could be issued in a year. The new licenses were sold by the state at $6000 and could not be resold at a higher price. When the number of applicants exceeded the number of new licenses, they were distributed by public drawing. All but four of the licenses issued since 1962 went to eight rapidly growing counties, including the four listed above (but not Los Angeles). In 1967 the law was changed to permit intercounty transfers of licenses for the first time. Without the new licenses and the intercounty transfers, the difference between Orange County and San Francisco license values would be even greater. (Data are from correspondence with the California State Department of Alcoholic Beverage Control.)

were available over and above what would barely attract dealers. After paying $35,000 for a license, a new liquor dealer might just be able to break even, but those who were present when the restrictions were first imposed were beneficiaries of some substantial windfalls. The monopoly profits of these liquor dealers have been converted into rents.

In spite of ardent support from distillers and liquor dealers, the state-enforced controls over prices and entry in liquor distribution have also weakened in the post-World War II period. Just after World War II, states accounting for approximately half of all liquor stores had mandatory resale price maintenance enforced by liquor control agencies. Several large states have since left the fold. In some, notably Illinois, state courts declared such systems of price control unconstitutional. In others, the legislation was changed. The most spectacular case was New York, where a well-publicized scandal led to a formal investigation and a special session of the legislature to reorganize the whole liquor control system in 1964. State controls over prices were dropped, transfer of licenses between counties was permitted, and 2000 new licenses were issued (the number had been frozen at 4300 for 16 years).

Sixteen of the states have maintained a state monopoly over liquor sales instead of trying to regulate private sales. A recent study of these monopolies concluded that they have *lower* prices than the private distribution states with resale price maintenance but that they earn *more* state revenue net of operating costs than state liquor taxes yield in the private distribution states.[67] The same study shows that liquor consumption is neither encouraged nor discouraged by state-owned monopoly. Such states have generally avoided the extensive liquor industry political activity and influence peddling that have plagued many states with licensed private stores.

Control over liquor sales is certainly not an exclusively economic question. At least ostensibly its purpose is to protect public morals. This purpose may well justify control over the number of stores and who is allowed to buy from them, but it is hard to

---

[67] J. L. Simon, "The Economic Effects of State Monopoly of Packaged-Liquor Retailing," *Journal of Political Economy*, April 1966, pp. 188–194.

see why it requires the control of liquor prices. At any rate, if a state honestly wants to control liquor sales, the state monopoly system certainly offers more effective control than any licensing system can offer.

IX. PERFORMANCE

A. *Retail Profits*

Such information as we have on the number and profitability of retail firms provides fairly good support for the ideas suggested in this chapter. Figure 5-19 shows reported profits after tax as a percentage of owners' equity for incorporated retail firms and compares them with the rate of profits after tax for all manufacturing.[68] Separate profit figures for retailing go back only to 1938, but profits for all trade, wholesale and retail, extend back to 1934. It seems safe to take the total trade figure representing retailing in the earlier years, since retailing is much the largest part of the total and because the combined figures always move with retailing figures in the years since 1938.

Profits appear to have been consistently lower in retailing than in manufacturing except for the years 1944 to 1948 at the end of World War II. This probably reflects the competitive character of retailing. It cannot be due to any less risk. Actually retailing is famous for its bankruptcy rate. While about 25% of all nonagricultural firms are in retailing, just under half of the failures occur there each year.[69]

The exceptional profits right after World War II were fairly clearly associated with inflation and the relative scarcity of retail outlets. Such retailers as there were did very well. However, the profits disappeared very rapidly compared with those in manufacturing. The reason is shown in Figure 5-20. For several years, new firms appeared at a great rate while relatively few disap-

---

[68] The profit rates shown in Figure 5-19 may overstate retail profits because only the larger and more successful retailers are incorporated. On the other hand, profits of small corporations are not reported to the extent that they are paid to the owners of the firms as salaries or expense accounts rather than dividends.

[69] *Statistical Abstract of the United States,* 1969, pp. 472, 488.

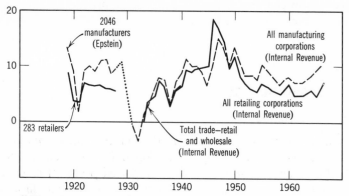

Figure 5-19.   Net income after tax as a percentage of owners' equity. *Source.* 1919 to 1928, R. C. Epstein, *Industrial Profits in the United States,* National Bureau of Economic Research, 1934. 1931 to 1965, Internal Revenue Service, *Statistics of Income.*

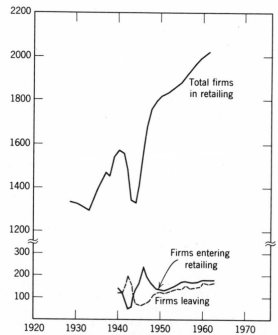

Figure 5-20.   Numbers of firms entering, leaving, and remaining in retailing. *Source. Historical Statistics of the United States,* and *Continuation to 1962.*

peared. Some of the influx can be interpreted as returning service-men setting up shop, but the low rate of disappearance of old firms in those years pretty clearly reflects the high profits being earned. By the time the number of firms had gotten up to roughly the level suggested by prewar rates of growth, profits had been competed away. Thereafter, the number of firms entering was almost balanced by those leaving.

B. *Margins*

Statistics on retail prices show more about the various com-modity-producing industries involved than about retailing. Gross

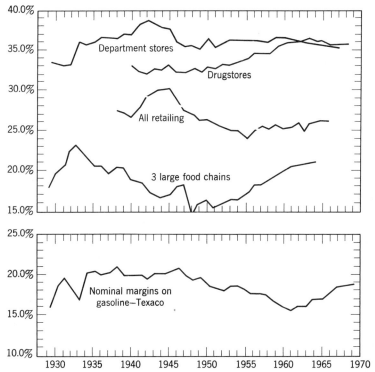

Figure 5-21. Retailers' gross margins. *Sources.* Department stores and va-riety chains: Harvard School of Business, Bureau of Business Research, Bulletins and the Controllers' Congress, National Retail Merchants Associa-tion, Drugstores: *Lilly Digests.* All retailing: *Statistics of Income.* Food chains: FTC, "Report on Food Retailing," *loc. cit.,* Appendix Table 47. Gas Stations: *Petroleum Facts and Figures* and *National Petroleum News Fact Book.*

margins are more appropriate in evaluating the retailers themselves. Figure 5-21 shows the gross margins in all retailing and in four branches of retailing discussed in this chapter. Margins for all retailing were derived from the reported net sales and costs of goods sold in income tax statistics. The other margin figures were reported in regular surveys of firms in the trade.

The gross margins for all retailing declined considerably after World War II. This is a very rough figure, however, since the items sold vary so from year to year. For instance, one reason why wartime margins are so high is that new automobiles and appliances and many of the lower priced items disappeared from the market. Most of these items customarily carry margins of considerably under 30%, the wartime average. When these goods reappeared after 1945, the average margin for all retail transactions dropped as a result.

Even compared with the prewar years of 1938 to 1941, however, overall retail margins were not particularly high in the early postwar years. The main reason for the high profits in the years right after the war was high volume, not high margins.

Margins in particular lines have followed divergent paths. Most of them reached high plateaus with the coming of NRA, fair trade, and similar price-fixing schemes in the mid-1930's. Gasoline margins fell considerably from those levels in the 1950's, when the influence of the independents was growing, and rose again in the 1960's, when the independents were weaker.

Food margins fell in the 1930's and 1940's with the growth of supermarkets and large scale food distributing organizations. The decline ended in the 1950's when supermarkets accounted for more than two thirds of food sales. Since then, food margins have been rising again. The most rapidly rising costs have been promotion expense, particularly trading stamps. The first stores to adopt stamps experienced spectacular increases in volume, so that little increase in margin was necessary, but after 1956 stamps had spread to so many stores that sales volumes were back to normal. Stamps did not induce people to buy much more food —simply to buy it at a different store. With many stores using them, stamps could not increase any seller's business by much, so margins had to rise to cover their costs.[70]

---

[70] FTC, *Report on Food Retailing, op. cit.*, Chapters IX and X.

The rise of discount selling in the 1950's had little effect on the four lines of retailing shown in Figure 5-21, though it may help to account for the slight dip in department store margins. The decline in overall retail margins in the 1950's, when most of the particular margins shown here did not fall, may reflect the spread of discounting in the consumer durable field.

Stable or declining retail margins do not necessarily mean that retailers have lower dollar receipts. If retail prices are rising, retailers may be taking just as much or more margin in dollars while letting their percentage margins decline. On the other hand, the decline in overall retail margins since the 1930's means that the price of retail services has not risen as much as commodity prices generally.

C. *Productivity*

Figure 5-22 compares changes in output per man in distribution (retailing and wholesaling) with those in all manufacturing since 1929. Productivity has grown somewhat more rapidly in manufacturing, though the difference has been slight since World War II.[71]

It is difficult to draw conclusions about the relative progressiveness of distribution and manufacturing from the comparison in Figure 5-22 because the opportunities for progress must differ greatly between two such disparate sectors. Most people would probably have guessed in advance that manufacturing would have greater possibilities for increased productivity. The research and innovations of the manufacturing sector certainly receive much more publicity. Yet distribution has seemed to cut cost about as fast as manufacturing since World War II.[72] It looks

---

[71] The differences between the two sectors had been much greater earlier. Output per man hour quadrupled in the commodity-producing sectors (agriculture, mining, and manufacturing) from the turn of the century to 1947, but it barely doubled in distribution over the same period. See Harold Barger, *Distribution's Place in the American Economy Since 1869,* Princeton University Press, Princeton, 1955, p. 38.

[72] Some would argue that the increase in productivity in distribution is exaggerated, because retailers are offering less service than before. The consumer now waits on himself, provides his own delivery, and, to the extent that he shops less often, has taken over much of the storage function. At the same time, the manufacturers have taken on much of the information

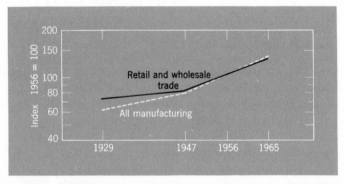

Figure 5-22. Indexes of output per man in manufacturing and distribution, 1929-1965. Derived from V. R. Fuchs, *The Service Economy,* Columbia University Press, 1968, Appendix Table C-3.

almost as though the inventions of the shopping cart and the checkout stand have done as much for us as the computer and the BOF. Certainly it would be difficult to argue on the basis of these statistics that the relatively competitive character of retailing has discouraged progress in recent years. At any rate,

---

function that the shopkeeper once provided as a result of national advertising, prepackaging, and manufacturers' guarantees. (see David Schwartzman, "The Growth in Sales per Man Hour in Retail Trade, 1929–1963" in Victor Fuchs, *Production and Productivity in the Service Industries,* Columbia University Press, 1969, pp. 201–235.) The change to self-service can be interpreted as a natural adjustment to rising labor costs. On the other hand, many consumers will respond that they would prefer self-service even if prices were the same as in a full-service store.

within retailing itself it has not been the fields which are protected from competition that have produced the great innovations. They have come in the wide-open fields where no holds are
barred. The introduction of monopolistic restraints has unquestionably inhibited the innovation process in retailing rather than
the reverse.

X. SUMMARY

In general, retailing is a highly competitive field of enterprise.
Changing forms of retailing in the last half century have mostly
worked toward more competition, especially more price competition. Economies of scale are significant in many lines of retailing
and have resulted in some very large firms, but concentration
ratios are still moderate.

Retailing has been analyzed in terms of monopolistic competition, where each seller has a somewhat differentiated product
but is small enough to act independently of the others. The
differentiated products result in a downward sloping demand
curve for each firm and a mild form of monopolistic pricing. In
the long run, the entry of new firms in such industries results in
overcapacity and the disappearance of profits. The tendency
toward overcapacity can be exaggerated, however, because of
the high elasticity of demand for each firm's services and because
the differences among firms that lead to excess capacity are themselves of value to the consumer. Nonprice competition in retailing
may result in a tendency for margins to creep up as services
increase, but the free entry and price competition that mark retailing put a limit on this tendency. Advertising, the social value
of which is often questioned in the case of heavily promoted
national brands, seems to be clearly of value in retailing where
its information function is obvious and where it increases rather
than restricts price competition.

Oligopoly may provide a more plausible model of retail price
decisions, but the results are similar. Profits disappear because
of free entry, and if prices are greater than the lowest average
cost, overcapacity will result. Price competition is common in
retailing, however, and at least in the case of gas stations, great
overcapacity seems to lead to low margins while near-capacity

operations are associated with high ones. The results resemble competitive industries such as agriculture and textiles more closely than they do oligopolistic industries with few firms and limited entry such as steel and automobiles.

Government policy has for the most part tended to restrict competition in retailing rather than encourage it. The Robinson-Patman Act may have some economic justification, but if enforced it would require discrimination *against* the large buyer, weakening the positions of just those retailers who have proved most likely to innovate and engage in price competition. The A&P case had motivations similar to those of the Robinson-Patman Act, though again it had limited effect.

Resale price maintenance would prevent price competition among retailers altogether. Far from solving the economic problems of monopolistic competition, however, it would probably intensify excess overcapacity. Restricting entry, as with liquor retailing, leads to an undeniably monopolistic position for retailers with questionable benefit to the community.

Retailing has continued to perform in a competitive way. Profits have disappeared, price competition has pushed margins down in many lines, and new low-cost methods of retailing have appeared largely because these restrictions on competition have had limited scope or have been difficult to enforce.

XI.   FURTHER READINGS

There is no single definitive study of retailing. For a review of long-term trends in the industry, not exclusively statistical, see Harold Barger, *Distribution's Place in the American Economy Since 1869*, Princeton University Press, Princeton, 1955. Two good articles attempting to work out an analytical model that will fit retailing are W. A. Lewis, "Competition in Retail Trade," *Economica*, November 1945, pp. 202–234, and Jane Aubert-Krier, "Monopolistic and Imperfect Competition in Retail Trade," in International Economic Association, *Monopoly and Competition and their Regulation*, Macmillan, New York, 1954. Both are by Europeans, but they make extensive reference to American data. A discussion of the same general topic by three American economists, Stanley C. Hollander, Morris Adelman, and Richard B.

Heflebower, appeared under the general title "Price and Competitive Aspects of the Distributive Trades" in *American Economic Association Proceedings*, May 1957, pp. 252–292. L. M. Hall, J. Knapp, and C. Wintson, *Distribution in Great Britain and North America*, Oxford University Press, Oxford, England, 1961, is a thorough statistical study of retailing. Bob Holdren, *The Structure of a Retail Market and the Market Behavior of Retail Units*, Prentice Hall, Englewood Cliffs, N.J., 1960, contains a thorough analysis of retail food competition in a specific case study. A good recent study of food retailing is National Commission on Food Marketing, *Organization and Competition in Food Retailing* (Technical Study No. 7), Government Printing Office, 1966.

An excellent source on all aspects of the petroleum industry, including distribution, is M. DeChazeau and A. E. Kahn, *Integration and Competition in the Petroleum Industry*, Yale University Press, New Haven, 1959. On gasoline retailing itself see Ralph Cassady and Wylie Jones, *The Nature of Competition in Gasoline Distribution at the Retail Level*, University of California Press, Berkeley, 1951, and R. Cassady, *Price Making and Price Behavior in the Petroleum Industry*, Yale University, New Haven, 1954.

On the Robinson-Patman Act and related matters see Corwin Edwards, *The Price Discrimination Law*, The Brookings Institution, 1959. The A&P case was discussed at length in the journals, especially Morris Adelman, "The A and P case: A Study in Applied Economic Theory," *Quarterly Journal of Economics*, May 1949, p. 238, and J. B. Dirlam and A. E. Kahn, "Anti-Trust Law and the Big Buyer: Another Look at the A and P Case," *Journal of Political Economy*, April 1952, p. 118. A more complete discussion of the A&P case appears in Adelman, *A&P: A Study in Price-Cost Behavior and Public Policy*, Harvard University Press, Cambridge, 1959.

The classic on fair trade is Ewald Grether, *Price Control under Fair Trade Legislation*, Oxford University Press, Oxford, England 1939. Two later English discussions of it are B. S. Yamey, *The Economics of Resale Price Maintenance*, Pitman, London, 1954, and P. W. S. Andrews and F. A. Friday, *Fair Trade—Resale Price Maintenance Re-examined*, MacMillan, London, 1960. A review of resale-price-maintenance laws in various countries and the effect of their elimination in some appears in B. S. Yamey, Ed., *Resale Price Maintenance,* Aldine, Chicago, 1966. The whole range of policies controlling competition in drugstores is covered in Marion Fletcher, *Market Restraints in the Retail Drug Industry,* University of Pennsylvania Press, 1966.

On the special treatment of liquor stores, see Charles H. Hession, "The Economics of Mandatory Fair Trade," *Journal of Marketing,* April 1950, p. 707, Charles F. Stewart, "Mandatory Resale Price Maintenance of Distilled Spirits in California," *Journal of Marketing,* April 1954, and J. L. Simon, "The Economic Effect of State Monopoly of Package Liquor Retailing," *Journal of Political Economy,* April 1966.

6

Factor Markets—Steelworkers

So far this book has dealt mainly with the markets for commodities such as milk, steel, or retail services. This chapter is devoted to one of the equally significant set of markets where the resources that go to produce these commodities are traded.

Economists have traditionally classified factors of production into the three broad categories of land, labor, and capital. Labor is the most important of these by most criteria. More than three quarters of all factor earnings originate in labor markets, and these markets seem to attract an even larger proportion of the controversy, if anything.

It is misleading to speak of "the labor market," however. The types of labor employed in the United States today are as varied as the goods and services that are sold on product markets. Farmers, professional football players, economics professors, pretty secretaries, and General Motors executives are all "labor" in the classical sense, but they sell on very distinct markets. A drop in the wage of any one of these will hardly affect the employment of the other four in the short run. In the long run, exceptional pay or working conditions may attract workers from one line to another but, even then, the possibility of someone moving between the jobs just listed (or more realistically, the possibility of young people preparing for one of these instead of another) is pretty limited. The meaningful competition among workers occurs in markets a good deal more narrow than the market for all "labor."

This chapter is devoted to the market for steel labor and, even then, it will be describing a group of related labor markets rather than a single market. Steel workers are chosen for two main reasons. First, they are employed by one of the industries already examined in this book, and performance on product markets cannot be explained thoroughly without some understanding of the factor markets in which the industry trades. Second, no study of modern labor markets would be complete without a great deal of attention to trade unions, and the steelworkers are organized into one of the best known and most debated of American unions. It has at one time or another been involved in a large proportion of the major issues of trade unionism and can, therefore, provide many inferences about unionism generally. The reader should be warned, however, that no one union can possibly represent all unions. What is true of the steelworkers may be quite wrong in the case of the teamsters, or textile workers, or carpenters. Footnotes appear throughout the chapter in the most glaring cases where the experience of the steelworkers may be misleading.

I. STEEL WORKERS

The iron and steel industry, including nonintegrated finishing mills employed about 633,000 persons in 1968—about 3.2% of all manufacturing employment and a little under 1% of all employees in the United States. This is less than the automobile industry (868,000), the aircraft industry (851,000), trucking and storage (1,056,000), or the telephone companies (816,000), but more than any other manufacturing, mining, or utility industry. The steel labor force is far less than the major sectors of retailing, where food stores alone employ 1,640,000.[1]

A. *Types of Steel Labor*

Steel has a mixture of skills that is not very different from that of manufacturing generally. About 20% of its labor force are "nonproduction workers"—executives, office staff, draftsmen, engineers, and salesmen. This growing portion of steel employment usually earns annual salaries and identifies itself with

---

[1] All 1968 employment figures are from the *Statistical Abstract* for 1969.

"management." It has proven largely unorganizable so far. Most of the production workers are male. About a fifth of these workers have unskilled jobs that can be performed with a minimum of training (for example, janitors or materials handlers). About 30% have skilled jobs such as the first helpers who operate open-hearth and blast furnaces, the tandem mill rollers who control continuous hot strip mills, or maintenance machinists and electricians. Their jobs often require long formal apprenticeships and always require much experience. A little more than half of the production workers are semi-skilled workers who drive tractors, band coils at the end of hot strip mills, or operate wire drawing machines. None of these are jobs that you or I could do just off the street, but they do not take years to learn.[2]

B. *Levels of Employment*

Trends in steel employment, in manufacturing employment, and in total civilian employment are compared in Figure 6-1. Steel employment grew faster than all manufacturing, and manufacturing grew faster than total employment until World War II. We were still taking an increasing share of our national income in processed goods, particularly metal goods, and the domestic and foreign substitutes for steel were still minor at the time. Since World War II, however, manufacturing employment has grown more slowly than all employment, and steel employment has actually declined. The decline is most severe in the case of production workers because of the increasing importance of administrative and sales personnel. The shift away from production workers and the shift toward nonmanufacturing employment seem to be permanent changes. With growing mechanization, direct human effort becomes a smaller part of total output and, since comparable mechanization does not appear feasible in distribution and services, a declining proportion of our labor force in goods-producing industries seems almost inevitable.

Steel employment is also less stable than most employments. In the Great Depression, total employment fell by about one

---

[2] Proportions taken from BLS Bulletin 1358, *Industry Wage Survey—Basic Iron and Steel*, March 1962, pp. 8 and 14–34. Job classes 1–4 were counted as unskilled, 5–10 as semiskilled, and 11–32 as skilled.

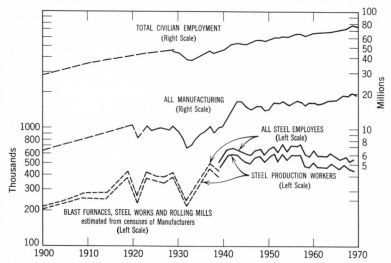

Figure 6-1. Steel and other employments. *Source. Historical Statistics of the United States,* BLS Bulletin 1312, *Employment and Earnings in the United States,* 1909-1964, *Census of Manufactures,* 1947, and *Employment and Earnings,* 1966–1970. Estimated steel employment up to 1939 is based on employment in blast furnaces, steel works, rolling mills, and steel foundries in 1929 and 1937-9. The 1932 steel employment is estimated on the basis of manufacturing employment changes from 1931 to 1932. Total employment for 1900 to 1930 is "gainfully employed."

fifth, manufacturing employment by about one third, and steel employment by almost half. The 1958 recession was only a ripple in total employment, but in the steel industry the drop was almost as sharp, though happily not as long, as those of the 1930's. As we shall see, 1958 marks a sharp break in steel labor market policies and performance.

II. STEEL UNIONS

A. *Craft Unionism in Steel*

Most steelworkers, like the great majority of American laborers, went unorganized until the late 1930's. Yet there have been unions in or around steel since its very beginning. In fact, the union preceded the industry. The first union, known as the Sons of Vulcan, was founded in 1858 to organize the iron puddlers, who had a strenuous, glamorous, and highly skilled craft essential to the old wrought iron industry.[3] The union was small, but the strategic skills of its members made it powerful. It won the country's first nationwide labor contract of any sort in 1865, and it was able to keep itself intact and to maintain wage scales in subsequent depressions—no mean trick for the unions of that day. In addition to the puddlers, some of the rolling mill workers were organized in the 1860's and 1870's. In 1876 these merged with the Sons of Vulcan to form the Amalgamated Association of Iron and Steel Workers. (It later became the Amalgamated Association of Iron, Steel and Tin Workers. We will just call it the A.A.) The merged union ultimately expanded to include most of the skilled trades in the iron mills and was able to organize some of the great new steel mills being built in the 1880's. Between 1876 and 1892 its membership grew very rapidly. By 1892 it could be described by a famous scholar of trade union history writing in 1918 as the "strongest union in the entire history of the American labor movement."[4]

The AA was one of the charter members of the American Federation of Labor (AFL) formed in 1886. Like most of the early unions of that organization, the AA consisted mainly of skilled workmen. These men were much more easily organized than the unskilled workers. Their skills made them hard to replace so strikes could not usually be defeated with outside strikebreakers. They were also relatively few in number so concessions were not too expensive to the employer. Since they were typically the better paid, more established workers with a large stake in their jobs, they were more easily convinced of the advantages of organizing and better able to survive long struggles with management. The unskilled, by contrast, came in great numbers and more were arriving from Europe or the farm every day. Except in periods of extreme labor shortage, they were in a poor bargaining position because they could easily be replaced.

---

[3] This account of iron and steel unions in the nineteenth century is based mainly on John R. Commons and associates *History of Labor in the United States,* Vol. II, Macmillan, New York, 1918, and John A. Fitch, *The Steel Workers,* Charities Publication Committee, 1911.

[4] Commons, *op. cit.,* pp. 495–496.

As one might expect, such craft unions pursued policies in the interests of their constituents. They avoided political activity of the general uplift variety though they would try to influence particular issues that affected them directly. For instance, the AA was a persistent and vigorous advocate of tariffs on iron and steel products. They bargained for wage scales and working conditions for their members rather than for the mass of unskilled workers in the mills. The skilled ironworkers felt they had an interest in long hours since they were paid by the ton. As a result the AA actually opposed a reduction from the 12- to 8-hour day.[5] The steel industry maintained a 12-hour day and a 7-day week until 1924.[6]

The old craft unions of the AFL such as the AA have often been criticized for their limited objectives. The goals of enriching the "aristocracy of labor" and of avoiding general social reform do not inspire many idealists. Yet these unions did succeed in establishing a permanent labor movement for the first time in the United States after almost a century of failure by other types of unions.

B. *The Defeat of the Union*

Until the 1890's the AA maintained cordial relations with the powerful new steel manufacturers such as Jones & Laughlin and Carnegie, though among Carnegie's major mills only Homestead near Pittsburgh had a continuing union organization. Then in the depression year of 1892, Carnegie demanded cuts in Homestead pay scales and threatened to deal directly with the men if his requirements were not met. The result was a momentous strike that began with a pitched battle between strikers and Pinkerton men brought in by the company leaving half a dozen dead on either side. It ended five months later with the men returning to the job without a contract. The most powerful union of the day had been no match for the great corporation that was to typify the twentieth century.

---

[5] Selig Perlman and Philip Taft, *History of Labor in the United States 1896–1932*, Macmillan, New York, 1935, pp. 97–98.
[6] The workers affected had one day off in two weeks—not all steelworkers had such hours.

Most of the other basic steel companies in the Pittsburgh area followed Carnegie in eliminating the union. It survived in the Chicago area and in some iron and finishing mills but its membership was halved.

When USS was formed in 1901 many of the remaining unionized mills were merged with the Carnegie empire.[7] With some mills organized and others not, the Corporation would be able to divert orders to nonunion mills in any dispute. Recognizing this threat, the union demanded that contracts be signed for all the unorganized as well as organized mills in three USS subsidiaries devoted to finishing. The company refused and a strike followed in which the union was again defeated. It had to accept a settlement that left fewer unionized mills than before and forbade any further organizing activity. Thereafter, USS was free to eliminate the union completely whenever the time seemed ripe, something it did in 1909.

These events set the tone for much of large-scale industry. The great corporations that were developing in the first years of this century could apparently follow an openly antiunion policy with impunity. Such mass production industries as automobiles, tires, electrical equipment, petroleum, and chemicals were generally able to keep the union out until the late 1930's.

There was a major effort to reestablish the union in steel at the end of World War I. The war boom had seen a rapid growth in union activity throughout the country. In addition to expanded craft union membership, the semiskilled workers of the apparel industry and parts of the textile and meat-packing industries had been organized before the war ended. The successful leaders of these campaigns then turned to steel. Twenty-four unions claiming jurisdiction within the steel industry joined in a drive for members in 1918. Some of the unions gave only half-hearted support. The largest financial contributions came from the new Amalgamated Clothing Workers and the International Ladies Garment Workers Union. There was much bickering about jurisdiction. In the middle of the drive the leaders of the AA tried to make a separate agreement with USS. Yet in spite of all these

---

[7] Most of this section on the steelworkers in the first three decades of this century is based on Perlman and Taft, *op. cit.*

difficulties the campaign was a big success. More than 100,000 steelworkers had joined by mid-1919.

The Corporation responded with mass firings that precipitated a nationwide strike in September 1919, but the industry refused to bulge. Strikebreakers were brought in and the mills were reopened. Violence was common—some 20 strikers were killed. The company was able to win public sympathy by capitalizing on the antiradical, antialien feeling rife in the country just after World War I. A large part of the press and the public was convinced that the strike was an attempt of Communists or anarchists or someone to take over our basic industry. Gradually the strike petered out. The organizing committee called a halt in January 1920.

This defeat marked an end to the expansion of unionism. Throughout the country, union membership and union power declined during the 1920's. It reached a low in 1933, after four years of depression.

C. *Steel Without Unions*

The success of steel in excluding the union over a period of almost half a century rested on two important policies. (1) USS openly employed its great power to prevent organizing activity, and (2) it undertook to improve its employees' conditions without the union.

Along the first line, the Corporation, like many firms of the day, employed a formidable industrial espionage system with spies throughout the mills and the mill towns. Their main function was to discover union activity and to identify union sympathizers or those who led in disputes. The "troublemakers" faced discharge and blacklisting, which meant that other steelmakers would not hire them. In the smaller communities the steel companies were often able to capture the local governments and the local press. Labor organizers were repeatedly arrested or beaten. Union meetings were virtually prohibited in some towns. The local police often fought the company battles. In some cases, company guards were deputized or the companies supplied arms to the local police.[8]

---

[8] A report of the Interchurch World Movement, *Report on The Steel Strike*

At the same time that it was erecting these obstacles to the union, big steel was introducing a wide range of employee benefits. As we shall see, steel wages were generally good. USS introduced overtime pay for work in excess of eight hours during the 1919 organizing drive, and under great public pressure it went from the two-shift, 12-hour day to the three-shift, 8-hour day in 1924. The corporation had introduced a profit-sharing scheme in 1901. It also provided some company-financed pensions, conducted an effective company-wide safety program, and built a number of well-publicized hospitals, housing projects, recreation facilities, and the like. These policies certainly improved the workers' lot, particularly that of older and better established men, just the ones most likely to lead in any organizing movement. It would be unfair to give the exclusion of the union as the only motive for these improvements. In the 1920's in particular, management was taking a new attitude toward employees. Yet, one of the most common arguments for the new programs was that they protected the companies against the union.

Keeping the union out did not always mean avoiding labor trouble. From 1901, when it virtually defeated the union, until 1937, when it recognized a new one, USS had to fight three major strikes in 1904, 1909, and 1919. There were a half-dozen other such outbreaks in the remaining steel companies.[9] Even when strikes could be avoided, there was a continuing hostility

---

of 1919, Harcourt, Brace, New York, 1920, brought many of these conditions to public attention in the years after the great strike of 1919. In the late 1930's a series of hearings by a Senate Education and Labor Subcommittee (The Lafollette Committee) publicized many similar cases. *Hearings on The Violation of Free Speech and The Rights of Labor,* 75th and 76th Congresses, 1938 to 1940. They found, for instance, that four steel companies (not USS) had spent $178,139 on tear gas in connection with a single strike in 1937. Republic Steel at that time had ten times as much tear gas as the whole city police of Chicago! Report No. 6, Pt. 3, pp. 57, 65.

[9] Some important ones were Pressed Steel Car Co., 1909, Bethlehem, 1910, Colorado Fuel and Iron, 1914, Republic, 1916, Weirton (National), 1933, and Republic, 1935. Some of these involved terrible violence. In the first mentioned, state troopers at one point responded to the killing of one of their comrades by dragging strikers through the streets behind their horses. Perlman and Taft, *op. cit.,* pp. 263–265.

in the mills as witness the men's readiness to join unions when the opportunity arose despite grave penalties.

By suppressing the union, the companies had taken the power to make decisions unilaterally and without recourse. No matter how well this power was handled, there was bound to be complaint. In real life the arbitrary power was often mishandled, especially at the lower levels where favoritism in layoffs and even shakedowns of the workers by their foremen were to be found. The result was an accumulation of uncorrected grievances.

One approach to this problem was to establish some sort of employees' representation under company control. In steel these programs came to be known as Employee Representative Plans. Elsewhere they were called company unions. Bethlehem initiated such a program in 1918 and was copied by most of the major steel companies in 1933 and 1934. Employees elected representatives who could present grievances to management. These representatives had far less bargaining power than independent unions had, but the mere possibility of communication was a real improvement.

D. *The Coming of the Union—Legislation*

The success of the large employers' antiunion policies finally ended in the 1930's. Big business, the hero of the booming 1920's, became the villain of the depressed 1930's. Great numbers of people who had accepted management's view of the unions previously became favorable to them now.

Government policy changed in response. As late as the 1920's the federal courts had been ready to issue injunctions enforceable by arrest and imprisonment against strikes, picketing, or just organizing activities. Now government policy was reversed. The Norris-LaGuardia Act passed in 1932 declared Congress' intention that a worker should have "full freedom of association, self organization, and designation of representatives of his own choosing to negotiate the terms and conditions of his employment . . ." The main practical effect of the act was to eliminate the use of federal injunctions in labor disputes. The National Industrial Recovery Act of the next year required that the "codes of fair competition" adopted under it provide for freedom to

organize and bargain collectively "without coercion from employers."

Later, when the NIRA was declared unconstitutional in 1935,
Congress passed the Wagner Act with much the same labor
provisions. Employees were to be free to organize without interference of any sort from the employer. A National Labor Relations Board (NLRB) was established to conduct shop elections
to determine the will of the majority of workers as to bargaining
representatives. It also had authority to issue orders against "unfair labor practices" by employers such as discrimination against
union members in hiring, firing, and promotions, the establishment of company unions, or the refusal to bargain "in good
faith" with the designated bargaining agent. This legislation was
tested for years in the courts and only became really effective at
the end of the 1930's, but it indicated the direction of public
policy much earlier.

E. *The Coming of the Union—Organization*

The new setting made organization in steel seem practicable
once more. The old and feeble AA experienced an upsurge of
membership in 1933. The union accepted the new dues but did
little more.[10] It turned down an offer of virtual recognition in
negotiations with USS in 1935.[11] When the new members met
separately to plan an active campaign, the established leadership simply expelled them. Meanwhile, the steel companies were
adopting employee representation plans similar to Bethlehem's
as token compliance with the NIRA requirements. Many workers who had found the AA useless switched to these company
unions as safer and more likely to produce something.

Discontent with the older craft unions was widespread at the
time outside the steel industry as well. The cry was for *industrial unions* that would organize all employees in whole plants
of the mass production industries, not just specialized skills. The

---

[10] This section on the organization of the United Steel Workers is based
mainly on R. R. R. Brooks, *As Steel Goes*, Yale University Press, New Haven,
1940.
[11] Department of Labor, *Collective Bargaining in the Basic Steel Industry*,
January 1961, pp. 60–61.

1934 convention of the AFL passed a resolution urging organizing drives in such industries as steel. The next year, when little or nothing had been done, the leaders of the existing industrial unions, particularly the United Mine Workers and the two apparel unions, formed a Committee for Industrial Organizations (CIO) to take matters into their own hands. The craft union leadership of the AFL responded in August 1936 by expelling the CIO unions, and America had two rival labor movements. The AFL and the CIO were united only in 1955 and substantial parts of the CIO (though not the steelworkers) have broken away again since then.

The CIO established a Steel Workers' Organizing Committee (SWOC) in June 1936, to which it (mainly the United Mine Workers) contributed $500,000 and a trained organizing staff. Meanwhile the employee representation plans had shown an increasing degree of independence. Originally set up on a mill-by-mill basis to discuss local grievances, the representatives had by 1936 formed regional councils and were presenting demands involving wages, hours, and vacations. They were coming very close to collective bargaining. Many of the elected employee representatives were won to the support of SWOC after it came into existence. A SWOC sympathizer was even elected chairman of the USS employee representatives.

This put USS in an uncomfortable position. Repudiation of its employee representation program would be difficult, but dealing with it now was little short of dealing with the union. Moreover, SWOC's recruiting drive made a strike likely and, in the current political climate, the Corporation would not have the public support it had in 1919. The permanence of the new climate was demonstrated by the landslide reelection of Roosevelt in 1936, and the likelihood of a successful strike by the victory of the United Auto Workers at GM in February 1937. Late 1936 and early 1937 was a period of rapid economic recovery and after a half decade of losses USS could ill afford a strike. Moreover, the Corporation had a new leadership in the 1930's that was trying to rebuild the ancient edifice. The adamant antiunion stand of Carnegie, Morgan, and Gary was one of many old policies that could plausibly be reconsidered in the changed atmosphere of 1937. On March 2, 1937, USS signed a contract with the SWOC.

It was not the Wagner Act itself that wrought this revolution. The act was generally ignored by steelmen at the time. A circuit court had already declared it unconstitutional in a test case involving the discharge by Jones & Laughlin of ten men for union activity. A month after the USS settlement, however, the Supreme Court reversed the lower court and required Jones & Laughlin[12] to comply with the NLRB's order. After the USS settlement in March, this decision in April, and a brief strike in May, Jones & Laughlin also recognized the union. More than 100 smaller steel firms jumped on the bandwagon.

However, the union was not able to win immediate recognition from the rest of the major independents—Bethlehem, Republic, Youngstown, Inland, National, and Armco. Although the NLRB now had a right to exist, its powers were not clearly defined. Many of its orders in the steel disputes of 1937 were appealed and wandered through the courts for years. In the meanwhile, these "little steel" companies remained adamant. In May 1937, a strike was called against the most unionized of them— Republic, Inland, and Youngstown. One plant of Bethlehem Steel was also drawn in. The strike was reminiscent of 1919 with attempts to reopen struck mills, resulting violence, and intervention by local police. Eighteen strikers were killed. In the worst case, the famous "Memorial Day Massacre," a group of Chicago police charged an unarmed crowd at a meeting near the Republic Steel plant in South Chicago, killing 10 strikers and wounding 90. The little steel strikes failed at the end of the summer, partly because the country was going into another depression.

The organizing fight then shifted to the NLRB and the courts. By the start of World War II most of the NLRB orders had been upheld in court. The union won NLRB elections throughout the Bethlehem mills by 2 and 3 to 1 majorities in 1940 after which that company plus Republic, Inland, and Youngstown signed. During World War II, the union was even able to win shop elections and recognition in the South.

The war and the decade of prosperity that followed it solidified the union's position in steel as in most of manufacturing outside of the South. In the years just after World War II, strong

---

[12] Jones & Laughlin v. NLRB 301 US 1 (1937).

antiunion feeling appeared which found expression in the Taft-Hartley Law of 1947, but though the Law imposed important limits on the unions, it left the essential apparatus of the Wagner Act intact. By the late 1950's it was plain that the union was permanent.

Steel has one of the bloodiest histories in American industrial relations but, in five major industry-wide strikes since World War II, no steel company has attempted to operate a struck mill, and no significant instance of violence has been reported. Steel disputes are no longer wars of survival. Now they are just arguments about the terms of employment.

F. The United Steel Workers Today

SWOC changed its name to the United Steel Workers of America (USW) in 1942. In 1967 it had 1,068,000 members, which makes it larger than any other union except the United Automobile, Aerospace, and Agricultural Implement Workers (1,403,000) and the International Brotherhood of Teamsters, Chauffeurs, Warehousemen and Helpers (1,651,000).[13] It represents almost the entire steel industry as well as aluminum, copper, lead, zinc, and many steel fabricators such as railroad cars and tin cans. Among major steel makers, all but one of National Steel's three mills and five of Armco's are organized by the USW.[14] The USW has never been able to win representation election in these mills, but it has still had an important effect upon them. To keep the national union out, National and Armco have consistently maintained wages as good as or better than those paid in union mills and have provided grievance procedure as reliable as in organized mills. The workers have the advantages of belonging to the USW without having to strike for them.

The USW is made up of 3484 local unions,[15] and it in turn is a member of the AFL-CIO. There is usually a separate local for each plant. The locals are governed by officers elected by the

---

[13] Bureau of Labor Statistics Bulletin 1596, *Directory of National and International Labor Unions in the United States, 1967.*

[14] In addition, the steel facilities of some fabricators are organized by other unions, notably the Ford Motor Company, organized by the United Auto Workers.

[15] B.L.S. Bulletin 1596, *op. cit.*

general membership. Their main function has been the administration of contracts. The international headquarters ("international" because USW has locals in Canada) has taken the lead in contract negotiations and basic union policy.[16]

The international officers are elected in a general referendum among all members of the union every four years. There is also a biannual convention to which locals send delegates in proportion to their memberships. The convention must pass on major policy questions.

Over the first twenty years of its history the USW's international leadership won every election without opposition. Philip Murray, installed as president by John L. Lewis[17] at the establishment of SWOC in 1936, was succeeded at his death by David McDonald, the original secretary-treasurer of SWOC.

Life has been less certain for USW leaders since then. In 1957 a rank-and-file candidate named David Rarick won a third of the vote running against a dues increase and McDonald. At the next convention, McDonald told the delegates to "rip this cancer out of your bowels."[18] They didn't quite, but McDonald survived —not too surprising in view of his control of the central organization and the union press. In 1965 he faced I. W. Abel, the secretary-general of the international, who had the same advantages he did, and this time McDonald lost in a close vote. By 1969, Abel, in turn had an opponent named Emil Narick, a union lawyer who campaigned for more emphasis on wage increases and won 40% of the vote.

This history—except for the rhyming candidates—was typical of national unions in the 1960's. Until then the leaders of most big nationals were about as secure in their positions as the man-

---

[16] This is not true of all unions. In dealing with industries that are local in nature such as printing, construction, and many aspects of trucking, it is the local or some regional division that does the negotiating. As a result, a description of carpenter policy in one part of the country need not apply elsewhere. On the other hand, USW policy to date has been similar throughout the steel industry.

[17] John L. Lewis was president of the United Mine Workers until 1959 and Philip Murray was one of his vice-presidents until he went to SWOC in 1936.

[18] *Monthly Labor Review,* November, 1958, p. 1265.

agements of large corporations. Some even passed the leadership on to their sons! Since then, however, real campaigns have been regular events. The Labor-Management Reporting Act (the Landrum-Griffin Act) helped to effect the change by requiring secret votes, equal access of all candidates to membership lists, and elections at least once every five years.[19] One effect of the shift toward union democracy has been a more militant leadership.

The control of the locals has been another matter. In a large proportion of them, the leadership has been within reach of the membership all along. However, in some cases, neither the membership nor the national union have been able to control the locals. Where this happens, the local leaders sometimes become quite corrupt. They have used union funds for their own purposes, extorted money from workers in assigning jobs or from businessmen by threatening strikes, and accepted bribes from businessmen for not organizing particular plants or not enforcing contracts. Such practices have appeared from time to time in localized industries such as construction or the services. They are rare in lines of business marked by large-scale operations. A small trucker may be quite susceptible to extortion by the agent of a relatively inconspicuous local, but it is almost inconceivable that I. W. Abel would ask for favors from USS or that USS would grant them.

The USW and SWOC before it were a part of the CIO from 1936 until the merger of CIO and AFL in 1955. The USW has been a member of the AFL-CIO ever since. The affiliation puts very few restrictions on the USW, however. The AFL-CIO is a loose confederation of quite independent unions. Its main functions are to lead in political action, to assist in the organization of nonunion segments of the economy, and to serve generally as a forum of the union movement. It can sometimes affect the policies of member unions by admonition of persuasion, but strong

---

[19] Contested campaigns in some other unions have been much less gentlemanly than in the USW. The 1969 election of the United Mine Workers was marked by charges of vote buying, dishonest vote counts, and violence. Shortly after the election the losing challenger and his family were murdered!

unions like the steelworkers may safely go their own ways if they wish.

At this writing an important group of unions are outside the AFL-CIO. The railroad brotherhoods have never belonged. The United Mine Workers withdrew from the CIO in the 1940's and never returned. The Teamsters were expelled from the AFL-CIO in 1957 on charges of corruption. When the United Auto Workers also withdrew in 1968, a new organization entitled the Alliance for Labor Action (ALA) was formed with an Auto-worker and Teamster core. The Chemical Workers and a break-away group from the Retail Workers also joined and were promptly expelled from the AFL-CIO. We seem to be back with two labor organizations once more.

III. COLLECTIVE BARGAINING ISSUES

A. *Steel Negotiations*

There are hundreds of USW contracts, but the pattern for most of them is set in negotiations with the major steel makers. Each company has its own contract. However, since World War II, major contracts have been negotiated simultaneously and their main features have been almost identical.

This virtual industry-wide bargaining is understandable. If the union could strike one company at a time, it could very likely win more than in dealing with the industry as a whole. Both the union and the companies have an interest in standard contract provisions. The union needs uniformity to avoid internal unrest, while each company wants to be sure that its labor costs are no higher than those of its rivals.

Ordinarily, the key contract in the steel industry is that between USW and USS. Table 6-1 presents a chronology of their settlements since World War II. Steel negotiations were regular annual events until 1956.[20] As a rule they resulted in wage increases, but the pay scale was only one of a great number of

---

[20] Steel contracts ran for two years in those days, but they always provided for one reopening on questions of wages and sometimes other issues such as pensions.

Table 6-1. USS Contracts and Wage Settlements since World War II

Date	Strike	Average Hourly Wage Increase (Cents)	Other Major Contract Changes
Feb. 16, 1946	Jan. 14–Feb. 15	18.5	
Feb. 8, 1947		5.2	Job classification
Apr. 1, 1947		15	
July 16, 1948		13	
Nov. 11, 1949	Oct. 1–Nov. 11	—	"Fringe benefits": partially company-financed life and hospital insurance and wholly company-financed pensions to supplement social security
Dec. 1, 1950		16	
July 26, 1952	Apr. 4–Apr. 8, Apr. 29–May 3 and June 2– July 26	16	Modified union shop, six paid holidays
June 12, 1953		8.5	Eliminate North-South wage differential within one year
July 1, 1954		5	
July 1, 1955	July 1 (one day)	15.2	
Aug. 3, 1956	July 1–Aug. 3	10.5	Three-year contract with: (a) automatic raises of about 8.3¢ each July; (b) cost of living escalator; (c) and supplemental unemployment benefits
Jan. 1, 1957		3	⎫
July 1, 1957		12.3	Automatic increases and
Jan. 1, 1958		5	cost of living increases
July 1, 1958		12.3	under 1956 contract
Jan. 1, 1959		1	⎭

Date	Strike	Average Hourly Wage Increase (Cents)	Other Major Contract Changes
Jan. 5, 1960	July 15– Nov. 7, 1959	—	Preserve work rules.
Dec. 1, 1960		9.7	Deferred increase from 1960 agreement
Oct. 1, 1961		10.4	Deferred increase from 1960 agreement
Apr. 6, 1962		—	Contributions to SUB almost doubled. Escalator dropped. Pension plan revised to encourage early retirement.
June 29, 1963		—	13 week "sabbatical" vacations every 5 years for senior employees
Sep. 3, 1965		12.1	Full retirement available to those with 30 years of service regardless of age
Jan. 1, 1966		2.0	Increase under 1965 contract due to upgrading of skilled craftsmen
Aug. 1, 1967		7.6	Deferred increase from 1965 contract
Aug. 1, 1968		23.6	Expand incentive pay, SUB and fringe benefits
Aug. 1, 1969		14.1	Deferred increase from 1968 contract
Aug. 1, 1970		13.4	Deferred increase from 1968 contract

Source. BLS Report No. 186, "Wage Chronology, United States Steel Corporation, 1937–1964," *Monthly Labor Review,* October, 1968, pp. 65–6, and American Iron and Steel Institute, *Annual Statistical Report,* 1968, p. 19.

subjects discussed. The postwar steel negotiations have run the whole gamut of collective bargaining issues.

B. *Job Classification*

One notable accomplishment was the establishment of uniform job classifications in 1947. After two years of negotiations, the union and the companies succeeded in working out systematic evaluation and ranking of the complicated assortment of skilled, semiskilled, and nonskilled jobs to be found in the mills. At USS, jobs were broken down into 31 categories separated at that time by equal steps of 3.5¢ per hour.[21] This classification made it possible for the industry to avoid negotiating each wage separately, something that had previously disrupted the union and collective bargaining regularly. Steel's job classification system has been widely copied.

C. *Fringe Benefits*

The great issue of the 1949 dispute was fringe benefits, particularly pensions. The union conducted a six-week strike and went without a wage increase to win pensions for all workers of more than 15 years' service and partially company-financed hospital and life insurance. Each contract negotiated since then has included some improvements in or additions to the fringe benefits available to steelworkers. By 1968 they included pensions, insurance, paid vacations, paid holidays, severance pay, jury duty pay, and shift differentials. Back in 1949 fringes came to only 5¢ an hour or 6% of straight-time pay. By 1968 they were 73¢ or 21%.[22]

D. *Compulsory Union Membership*

The central issue of the 1952 dispute was the USW demand for a *union shop*, an arrangement by which anyone hired under the

---

[21] The size of the steps has been increased from time to time since then to keep up with the rising basic wage rate. The differential was changed in 1948, 1950, 1952, 1955, in automatic increments from 1956 to 1959, in 1961, and from 1965 to 1970. By 1970 the increments were 9.0¢ per hour. Whenever the differential changed, most workers' wages rose by more than the base rate. The wage increases shown in Table 6-1 are averages which include the effect of these changes in the differential.

[22] American Iron and Steel Institute, *Annual Statistical Report, 1968*, Table 9.

contract must join the union within a specified period. The companies had stubbornly opposed the union shop for many years, but in 1952, after eight months of arguing, two of strike, and much government pressure, they finally agreed to a limited form of it.

Few aspects of collective bargaining have aroused such heated debate as compulsory union membership. Of course, much of management opposes it simply because it strengthens the union, but many people who have no direct vested interest still object that the union shop is an invasion of personal rights. They argue that individuals who oppose the union on principle should not be forced to contribute to it. Defenders of the union shop reply that it is no more of an invasion of personal rights than is the collection of taxes from everyone, even pacifists, to pay for defense.

The main case for the union shop is that it protects the union from "free-riders," nonunion employees who enjoy the benefits won by the union but make no contribution to it. By making the union's existence more secure, the union shop is supposed to encourage more statesmanlike union leadership. Without some sort of compulsory membership, it might be possible for the management to eliminate the unions by hiring nonunion men in some cases.

In the late 1950's and early 1960's there was a campaign to pass state "right to work" laws, which would prohibit all forms of compulsory union membership. Nineteen states had such measures at the end of 1970, but practically all of them were southern, mountain, or plains states where union members are few. Voters in a number of industrial states rejected it by wide margins. On the other hand, a majority of states and the Federal Government prohibit the union shop for public employees such as the postal workers.

The *union shop* should be distinguished from the *closed shop*. Under a closed shop agreement, a worker must be a union member *before* he can be hired, while a union shop simply requires that he join once he is on the job. This distinction is much more than mere hairsplitting. The closed shop gives the union the power to say who gets the job. Some unions such as the building and printing trades have combined it with strict admission and apprenticeship rules to severely restrict entry. This combination of closed shop plus closed union may be very convenient for those who are already electricians or typesetters, but it is hard on those of us on the outside. This criticism does not apply to the union shop where the employer may hire his nephews of blue-eyed blondes or anyone else so long as they join the union on time. The closed shop, but not the union shop, was outlawed in the Taft-Hartley Law, but so far the prohibition has had limited effect. Contracts no longer expressly provide for the closed shop, but in many of the old closed shop trades, union apprenticeship rules and the practice of hiring through union hiring halls effectively exclude nonunion men. These unions still erect strict limits as to who can learn their trades and become members. Various plans to permit members of minority groups access to such trades were given wide publicity in 1970. These have sometimes given some Negroes access to high-paying jobs, but the total number of people admitted was not increased much if at all. The steelworkers, like most industrial unions, have never sought the closed shop. It has been a feature of the older craft unions primarily.

E. *The North-South Differential*

A long-term goal of the USW was the elimination of regional wage differences. Even before 1937 the steel companies paid the same rates in the Pittsburgh, Youngstown, and Chicago areas,[23] but they paid less in other districts such as the East and especially the South. Under union pressure these differentials were gradually reduced until in 1954 even the southern mills were brought up to northern wage rates.

Some economists have raised doubts about the desirability of this policy of nationwide wage uniformity. They point out that by raising southern wages the union eliminated any special incentive for the companies to locate new plants in the South. The higher southern wages would protect the jobs of northern steelworkers and would be very nice for the southerners already in the mills, but there might be fewer southerners hoeing corn

---

[23] George Seltzer, "Pattern Bargaining and the United Steelworkers," *Journal of Political Economy*, August 1951, p. 322–323.

on the hillside and higher wages in other southern industries if the wage differential had persisted.

F. *Escalators and Improvement Factors*

Until 1956 the union negotiated about wages every year, but by then many had come to doubt the usefulness of these annual crises. The auto industry had gotten along quite well under long-term contracts since 1948. In 1956 the companies were able to win a three-year contract from the union.

The contract provided for regular wage adjustments to make up for the raises the union had been able to negotiate each year previously. They were of two sorts. The workers were protected against inflation by an "escalator clause" under which wages were adjusted each January and July for any changes in the Cost of Living Index. In addition, there was an annual "improvement factor," an automatic raise each July over the life of the contract. This amounted to an increase in real wages of about 3% a year, roughly what the steelworkers had been able to win by annual bargaining in the early 1950's but considerably more than many workers were getting.

G. *Supplemental Unemployment Benefits*

The 1956 contract also introduced a provision for unemployment payments. For years the steelworkers had been demanding a "guaranteed annual wage" to protect them against layoffs. The companies were understandably reluctant. In an industry where output could drop by half in a mild recession, an unalterable guarantee of any substantial part of the payroll could be disastrous.

What the USW actually got in 1956 was something called "supplemental unemployment benefits" (SUB), which fell short of a full guarantee. It was quite similar to a provision of the United Auto Workers' contracts of the previous year. The steel companies contributed 3¢ to 5¢ per man-hour to a fund which was used to supplement state unemployment insurance benefits during layoffs. Eligibility for SUB depended on the period of previous service. Maximum total benefit from the state and the company together was 65% of straight time pay after tax for 52 weeks, but many would be eligible for less. If the fund ran low, as it did in the 1958 recession, benefits could be scaled down. In other words, instead of a greater wage increase, the companies agreed to do some of the saving for their workers. One effect of SUB was to redistribute income within the mills. Men with low seniority who suffer most from layoffs benefit from SUB more than older employees. SUB provides an incentive for the steel companies to stabilize employment. Historically steel had been an industry with particularly severe employment instability. During the 1960's, however, the unemployment rate among persons whose last job was in steel fell significantly, despite the declining steel work force. In 1967 and 1969 it was consistently lower than for all manufacturing, and even in the disastrous last part of 1968, the unemployment rate rose to only 4.6%, compared with 3.0% in all manufacturing.[24]

H. *Work Rules and "Featherbedding"*

In the 1959 negotiations, the main issue turned out to be the "work rules," the thousands of local customs governing size of crew, rest periods, and pace and method of work. The steel companies complained that they had inadequate control over these matters and were not able to manage their mills efficiently as a result. They charged the unions with "featherbedding," that is, preserving unnecessary jobs and obstructing the introduction of labor-saving methods.

There are some famous instances of apparent featherbedding to be found in American industry, such as the railroad brotherhoods which preserved the "firemen" for years after the shift to diesel locomotives, and the building trades which have fought hard to maintain many hand methods. The most obvious cases are usually to be found in craft unions whose members have specific skills to protect from mechanization. Industrial unions ordinarily have much less restrictive rules.

In the case of steel, contracts provided that established local work rules should remain in force generally, but that the com-

---

[24] *Employment and Earnings,* Table A-11. The reported unemployment rate is for primary metals, which includes nonferrous metals and foundries as well as steel. Steel accounts for about half of primary-metals employment.

panies might revise them if their "basis" changes. If such revisions were disputed by the union, and if no settlement could be negotiated, the questions went to a neutral arbitrator whose decision was binding on both parties (see p. 312). Arbitrators had ordinarily ruled that the "basis" for a practice has changed if new techniques involving new equipment have been introduced. This meant that there was practically no union obstacle to further mechanization ("automation") in steel, something that was far from true in many other industries.

On the other hand, the arbitrators had not allowed management to reduce crew size simply because management could show that a job could be adequately handled by fewer men. Management could not correct its old mistakes. The adamant stand of the union seems to have been based on a fear that the wholesale change in work rules would put large numbers of its members out of work. When union representatives expressed this fear, they tacitly admitted that the steel mills were overstaffed in many instances.

The final settlement in 1960, after a long strike, left the work rules provisions of the contracts intact, although the union had forgone any wage rate change to accomplish this.

The adamant stand of the USW in the work rules dispute and the far more restrictive policies of some other unions makes some sense from their members' point of view, but it is costly to the general public. Rising productivity is the main reason for our rising standards of living, and while general unemployment is possible, there are much better methods of dealing with it than keeping everyone's income down.

On the other hand, particular trades certainly can be hurt by labor-saving changes, especially if demand for the final product is inelastic and growing only slowly as in the case of steel. Attempts of workers in such circumstances to protect their jobs are understandable even if these attempts are economically undesirable. A much better solution would be to work out means by which the employers and the general public, who certainly gain from the technical changes, can share their benefits with the affected workers, especially in a way that will help them to shift to new employments.

I. *Long-Range Sharing Plans*

In 1963 the USW and Kaiser Steel began an imaginative experiment which may offer an economically more desirable way around the problem of technological displacement.

Under the new plan a worker who is displaced by a technical change or by an "improved work method" is placed in an employment reserve. This protects him against layoff so long as the reserve does not exceed a specified size, offers him first crack at new jobs, and even assures him of his old wage rate for up to 52 weeks of employment at a job with a lower classification. At the same time, the company agreed to pay to participating employees a share of computed reductions in average costs from 1961 levels.[25]

The plan gives the employee a financial interest in cost savings. The payments can be large. They were 33¢ an hour on the average in 1967. The company and the union both seemed pleased with the result. They extended the plan with somewhat more liberal payment and participation provisions in both 1966 and 1968. It has been copied by a few of the smaller steel companies but none of the large ones. Whether the plans will offer enough to workers over the years to make them advocates of technical changes in steel is yet to be seen. At least it offers a new attack on an ancient problem which has more typically been "solved" by a determined fight to keep things as they have been regardless of the cost.

J. *Collective Bargaining in a Weak Market*

Steel negotiations in general were quite different after 1960 than they had been before. There were two main reasons for the change. First, the long strike of 1959 had made another adamant demand unattractive to the rank and file. Second, and probably more fundamental, the depressed market for steel and the declining market for steel labor made generous settlements much less

---

[25] The costs used for this purpose are adjusted for changes in price levels. Moreover, the amount of any given cost saving that is paid out is gradually reduced so that new savings must occur regularly for the payments to continue. The plan is described in *The Monthly Labor Review*, February 1963, pp. 154–160, May 1966, p. 539, and March 1968, p. 117.

likely. No general steel strike was called from 1960 through 1970, the longest strike-free period in the union's history.

The settlements that were reached during this period reflected the new situation. No general wage increase was negotiated until 1965, though two deferred increases from the 1960 agreement occurred in 1960 and 1961. The union gave up the escalator clause in 1962, but the steel companies' contingent obligations to the SUB funds were almost doubled at the same time. Cost of living adjustments were not worth a great deal during these years of stable prices, but an additional assurance of support during layoffs was more valuable than ever. At the same time, the union negotiated a number of measures designed to pass around the jobs such as provisions to encourage early retirement and a unique "sabbatical" leave—a thirteen week vacation every five years for senior employees.

The relatively small wage gains won in the steel negotiations of the 1960's produced enough rank-and-file unrest to jeopardize first McDonald's and then Abel's tenure of office. As a result, wages were revived as a bargaining issue as the decade progressed. By 1968 the wage rate was the union's main concern once more, and a substantial wage increase was negotiated in spite of the severe threat from Japanese steel. One reason was that inflation was resuming. The three-year contract had to allow for all anticipated increases in living costs from 1968 through 1971. As it turned out, inflation accelerated in those years, so the steel workers won less of a real wage increase than they had thought. At this writing the rank-and-file discontent seems to be still increasing. We may soon see a return to large steel wage gains, especially if the "voluntary" quotas on steel imports are continued.

K. *Grievance Procedures*

All this has had to do with the spectacular national negotiations that set the terms of steel contracts, but the union and management are dealing with each other continuously over local day to day issues that arise under the contract. Who gets disciplined or laid off or promoted and why? Before the union, this sort of question was generally left to the foreman who could be completely arbitrary and even corrupt.

From the very first, the USW has insisted on a reliable grievance procedure to handle these questions. Today if a steelworker has a complaint, he may take it up with his foreman and the shop steward—the union representative on the job. If either side is dissatisfied with the decision, the case may be appealed through several steps in the union and company hierarchy, and if the question is still not settled it is arbitrated. USS and the union maintain a permanent board of arbitration made up of union and company representatives with a chairman acceptable to both sides. Smaller companies may have a single umpire or may simply join the union in selecting arbitrators as cases arise. Both parties agree in advance to live by the decision.

This grievance procedure, which is typical of those found in most collective bargaining contracts today, has removed much of the old arbitrariness. The small and continuous disagreements which could be the basis for accumulated resentment or sporadic strikes are settled peaceably.

IV. STRIKES

In winning its impressive list of gains since World War II, the USW has called its members out on five major industry-wide strikes. These have been much the most noticeable aspects of the union. They have usually aroused considerable criticism from the public at large.

They are an essential feature of the union as we know it, however. The whole point to workers bargaining collectively rather than as individuals is their ability to withhold all labor from a mill, that is, to strike. Without the right to strike, the union might be able to gain some of its ends by influence within the corporation or government, but this would convert it into primarily a political pressure group.

The man in the street often tries to assign the blame for strikes. This is an extremely difficult and usually fruitless project. In a certain sense both sides are always to blame since either could stop the strike immediately by giving in. To go any farther the observer would have to decide who was making the unreasonable demand, something that is very hard to determine in view of the complex issues and the habit of both unions and managements of asking for more than they really expect. Most experts do not even try.

A. *The Cost of Strikes*

The time lost from strikes is often exaggerated. To bargain effectively the union needs the threat of the strike, but it can often avoid actually calling one for years at a time. The left-hand portion of Figure 6-2 shows total man-days lost in all labor-management disputes during the years 1927 to 1968 expressed as percentages of total work time available in the economy. Only once, in 1946, did strikes take as much as 1% of the total work time. Usually they did not reach even 0.5%. This does not include losses of suppliers or customers of struck plants. On the other hand, it overstates the actual wages lost by the disputants since much of the time lost during the strike is made up in building inventories in advance and in supplying pent-up demand afterwards.

The strikes that do occur are uncomfortable, but in most of them the discomfort falls upon the disputants. A strike that closes one of the meat packers but leaves the rest operating, or even one that closes every talcum powder plant in the country, is no more than a minor nuisance to the rest of us. We can leave the disputants to wait it out as long as they can stand it.

B. *National Emergency Strikes*

Steel strikes are something else again. They are just too big to be ignored. The shaded portions of the right-hand part of Figure 6-2 show the man-day losses directly attributable to steel disputes. They account by themselves for most of the peaks in strike losses through 1959.[26] In addition to taking a half million men out on strike directly, steel disputes that last long enough can throw another half million out of work in supply industries

---

[26] While the steel industry did not participate in the strikes of 1967–8, the USW did. About a tenth of the man-hours lost in both years were due to the nine-month copper strike by the copper mine and smelter workers who had just become affiliated with the USW and were seeking industry-wide wage uniformity and industrywide bargaining similar to what the USW had in steel. They did not get it.

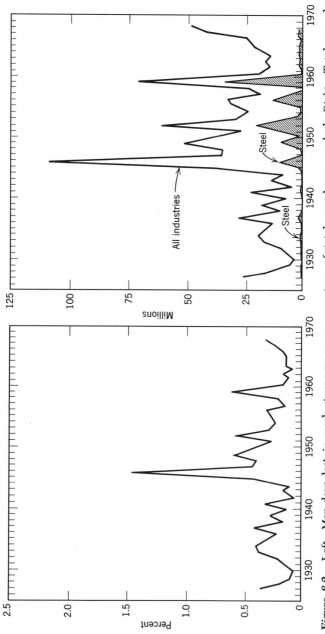

Figure 6-2. Left: Man-days lost in work stoppages as a percentage of total man-hours worked. Right: Total man-days lost in work stoppages (millions). *Sources.* Bureau of Labor Statistics, Report No. 92, "Work Stoppages, Basic Steel Industry," *Historical Statistics of the United States* and *Statistical Abstracts of the United States.*

such as coal and in steel-using industries such as automobiles. By the end of the 1959 strike, every GM assembly line had closed.

C. *Strike Threats and Output Instability*

There were no important steel strikes in the 1960's, but the mere threat of strike during the negotiation of new three-year contracts in 1962, 1965, and 1968 had serious effects. Steel users would stock up on steel for fear of a strike, so that the industry ran near capacity during the last months before each deadline. Then, when the strike was averted, the industry went through a period of excess capacity while its customers worked through their large inventories.

The strike threats played a role in the import problem also. Temporary shortages of some steel products led buyers to turn to foreign sources. Many would place orders abroad for delivery during the expected strike. Even if the strike was avoided these imports still came in, making the postsettlement excess capacity all the more severe. Figure 6-3 shows steel imports as a percentage of total U.S. supply. Contract years are marked with asterisks. The main upsurges in imports occurred in connection with the 1959 strike and the 1965 and 1968 negotiations, but they

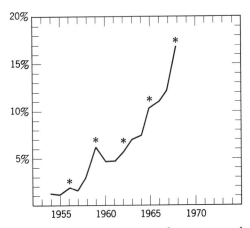

Figure 6-3. Steel imports as a percentage of apparent steel supply. (Apparent supply is shipments plus imports less exports). *Source.* American Iron and Steel Institute, *Annual Statistical Reports.*

never fell back to previous levels afterwards. The excess capacity and imports after the 1968 settlement were the occasion for steel's first postwar period of price cutting, and led to the "voluntary" quotas on steel imports in 1969.

Did the strike threats cause the rising imports? They clearly resulted in the big short-term increases, but the basic reason why imports stayed up after the settlements was that U.S. steel prices were higher than import prices. Steel buyers are hardheaded businessmen, so it seems likely that most of them would have been drawn to the cheaper foreign steel, anyway. On the other hand, the 1968 strike threat surely deserves much of the "credit" for our adopting import quotas.

Neither steel producers, steel workers, nor steel consumers gain from our triannual artificial steel shortages and artificial steel depressions. Both the USW and the steel managements have attempted to eliminate these painful fluctuations by negotiating major issues such as work rules on a continuing basis and trying to agree on new contracts well in advance of strike deadlines. This worked in 1962 when the new contract was achieved with several months to go, but many union members felt they had been cheated by the settlement. Abel's victory over McDonald the winter before the 1965 negotiations owed much to this feeling. Since then the union and the companies have bargained right down to the wire in spite of the instability and imports that resulted.

D. *The Government and Steel Strikes— Seizure and Taft-Hartley Injunctions*

Because of their wide-reaching effects, no administration since the war has been willing to let industrywide steel negotiations go their course unattended. In the 1950's the main concern was to avoid strikes. The government ordered the suspension of two strikes and intervened to affect the outcome of all of them.

To deal with the 1952 strike, President Truman "seized" the steel mills. This had been the main weapon used by the government to deal with the few major strikes of World War II. The courts had repeatedly enjoined strikes against the government, so seizure amounted to a prohibition of strikes. Seizure was just a formality. The management continued to manage, and profits continued to accrue to the owners. The most the government ever did was to change the terms of employment, and even this was uncommon. In the steel case the companies challenged the President's move, and the Supreme Court ruled that, barring an act of Congress, the President had no power to seize struck industries in peacetime.[27] The mills were "returned" to the industry and the strike continued.

Our only formal remedy in national emergency strikes today is the temporary Taft Hartley injunction. It was used to end the $3\frac{1}{2}$-month steel strike of 1959. Under the law the President appointed a "fact-finding board" which held hearings on the strike issues and brought pressure on the companies and the union to settle, but the act prohibited it from making recommendations. After the board reported no settlement, the Attorney General secured an injunction from a federal court prohibiting the strike for 80 days. The steelworkers appealed the order, but the Supreme Court upheld it, ruling that the procedure was constitutional and could properly be applied in this case.[28] Work resumed immediately. The last step in the Taft-Hartley procedure was to be a polling of the membership on the managements' last offer by the NLRB. All indications were that the offer would be rejected by a wide margin and that the strike would resume. Shortly before the date of the vote, the companies were persuaded by informal government pressure to give up their position on the work rules issue, and the dispute was settled.

This procedure has been the subject of much debate. The unions, harking back to the injunctions of the 1920's, see it as a "union-busting" procedure. In fact, it has been used quite sparingly. By 1968, after 22 years of the act, a total of 28 such injunctions had been issued, a little more than one per year.[29] No union has yet come close to being "busted" by one. On the other hand, it offers only a temporary solution to serious disputes. If the union and management have taken rigid and inconsistent

---

27 Youngstown Sheet and Tube v. Sawyer 343 US 582 (1952).

28 United Steelworkers v. U. S. 4 L. Ed 2nd, 12 (1959).

29 B.L.S., *National Emergency Disputes Under the Labor Management Relations Act, 1947–1968*, B.L.S. Bulletin 1633, p. 3.

Two thirds of the injunctions have been in stevedoring and maritime strikes or in such defense industries as aircraft or atomic materials.

positions, as in the 1959 work rules dispute, the procedure by it-self can only postpone the evil day.

E. *Informal Intervention*

The ultimate solution to every major steel strike since the war has involved government intervention to affect the terms of set-tlement. In 1945–46, in 1949, and in 1952, the President or some government agency made public recommendations which the union then adopted as its final position. Although a strike fol-lowed in each case, the final settlements corresponded closely to the recommendations. Price controls were in effect in 1946 and again in 1952, and in both instances settlements were only reached when price control authorities agreed to change ceiling prices for steel. These changes contributed to the breakdown of controls both times. The 1949 dispute occurred during a reces-sion so that the union was in a weak position. Many feel that it would not have won as much without the government's recom-mendation.

The Eisenhower administration professed a policy of preserv-ing "real" collective bargaining free of government control. It avoided making public recommendations of settlement terms, but it was unable to avoid intervention in the steel strikes of 1956 and 1959. In 1956 the press reported that the end of the five-week election year strike was brought about by the intervention with the steel companies of George Humphrey, then Secretary of the Treasury and formerly president of National Steel. In 1959 it was Vice-President Nixon and Secretary of Labor Mitchell who finally convinced the industry representatives to accept the union's posi-tion on work rules rather than let the strike begin again. 1960 was another election year and the steel settlement was obviously important to Republican prospects. A number of economists re-viewing government intervention in steel disputes in the 1950's concluded that, while the government had not succeeded in pre-venting strikes, it had typically resulted in more generous settle-ments than might have been expected without intervention.[30]

---

[30] Frederick Harbison and Robert Spencer, "The Politics of Collective Bar-gaining: The Post War Record in Steel," *American Political Science Re-view,* Sept. 1954, p. 717; Otto Eckstein and Gary Fromm, "Steel and the

F. *"Guideposts"*

The January, 1962 *Economic Report of the President* spelled out a set of "guideposts" designed to assure price stability which, it was hoped, unions and managements would observe on a "voluntary" basis. They were as follows:[31]

1. The general guide for wages is that the percentage increase in total employee compensation per man-hour be equal to the national trend rate of increase in output per man-hour.
2. The general guide for prices calls for stable prices in industries enjoying the same productivity growth as the average for the economy; rising prices in industries with smaller than average productivity gains; and declining prices in industries with greater than average productivity gains.

The same "guideposts" appeared in each of the five subsequent *Economic Reports.* Since the average rate of growth in productivity in the nation as a whole had run at 3.2 to 3.4% per year in this period, the President, in effect, asked for wage increases no greater than that rate.

Steel wage negotiations involved as much government participation under the "guideposts" as before. A great deal of informal pressure was applied to the union by the government in advance of the 1962 negotiations, and the cost of the settlement was well within the guidepost limits. A week later, USS announced a general price increase which the administration was almost bound to oppose in view of its role in the union's moderate policy. Its success in overruling the price increase is described elsewhere (page 179). In 1965 the President made it clear in advance that a general price increase would be unacceptable. A settlement near the guidepost was reached a few days after a postponed strike deadline in spectacular negotiations in Washington with the Secretaries of Commerce and Labor serving as mediators and the chairman of the Council of Economic Advisors, as statistical umpire. In 1968, with the cost of living rising at 3%

Post War Inflation" Study Paper No. 2, Joint Economic Committee, Washington, D.C., 1959.
[31] As paraphrased in Council of Economic Advisors, *Economic Report of the President,* January 1966, pp. 89–90.

a year, the government could hardly expect to keep wage increases within the old guideposts. Instead, it proposed that wage increases stay below the 5½% average that had been negotiated in organized industries the previous year. Again negotiations went down to the wire while imports soared. The steelworkers won more than a 5½% increase for 1968, but the average increase over the three years of the contract was under the proposed standard. The industry tried to raise prices after the settlement, but this time it was stopped by price competition, of all things! The price increase was finally accomplished after import quotas had been imposed.

The administration avoided both steel strikes and seriously inflationary steel settlements in the 1960's, but it is not clear how much of this was due to its policies and how much to the drab market for steel and for steel labor. Whatever effect the government did have was the result of a policy that looked increasingly like public determination of prices and wages in the steel industry.

When President Nixon took office, he announced a policy of returning to free collective bargaining, but by 1970 collective-bargaining settlements were pushing costs and prices up even in the face of substantial unemployment and excess capacity. Some economists advocated another bout of wage and price controls, and many advocated an "incomes policy," that is, a return to guideposts. The administration and another group of economists felt that the inflation could best be controlled by keeping aggregate demand within limits, that an "incomes policy" would not work, and that price and wage controls were just not worth what they cost in distortion and bureaucracy. At this writing, President Nixon has largely stuck to his announced policy, but he has yet to meet a major steel strike.

V. PERFORMANCE

A. *Steel Wages*

What have the steelworkers been able to accomplish with their union? The answer is not as obvious as it may seem. Figure 6-4 compares average hourly earnings in steel and in all manufacturing over the years. Steel wages are certainly higher than average,

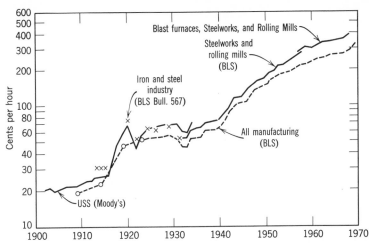

Figure 6-4. Average hourly earnings, steel and all manufacturing. *Sources.* USS data from *Moody's Industrial Mannuals.* Bureau of Labor Statistics data from Historical Statistics of the United States, Bulletin 567, *Wages and Hours of Labor in the Iron and Steel Industry*, 1931, BLS Bulletin 1312-2, AISI, *Annual Statistical Reports,* and *Economic Report of the President,* 1970.

but they always were. Again, steelworkers have been able to make spectacular gains since they were organized in 1937, but so has everybody else.

Figure 6-5 shows steel earnings as a percentage of average hourly earnings in all manufacturing. Steelworkers had generally earned about 20% more than the average worker in manufacturing in the 1920's and the 1930's before the union. When SWOC was formed in 1936, the steelworkers' wage advantage increased sharply, first as the companies tried to head off the union and then as the union made demands to prove its worth. At the peak in 1939 the steelworkers were able to push their average hourly earnings to about one third more than the average of all manufacturing. The union seems to have increased their wage rate advantage by 10 to 12%. Other workers caught up during World War II, however, and it was only in the late 1950's that the steelworkers were able to regain the advantage they had held in 1939. For a short time in 1960 their wage rates were more than 40% above average but the lost markets for steel and, even more,

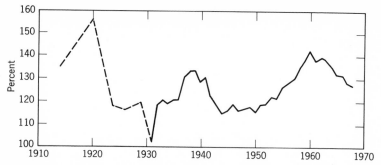

Figure 6-5.   Average hourly earnings in steel as a percentage of all manufacturing. *Note.* The figure for 1920 is appromimate—based on 1920 figure for steel but 1919 figure for all manufacturing. *Sources. Historical Statistics of the United States, Statistical Abstracts,* and *Monthly Labor Reviews.*

for steelworkers were by then a far greater concern than the wage rate. By the mid-1960's they were back to a relative position not very different from that of the late 1930's.

The comparison in Figure 6-5 gives an equivocal picture of the effect of unionism on wages, since steel is compared with "all manufacturing," a large part of which is also organized. Many other studies have attempted to determine the effect of unionism on wages. Some compare wages before and after unionization, some examine wages in industries that serve local markets that are organized in some communities and not in others, and some compare wages in occupations that are organized in some industries and not in others. While the details vary, the general pattern is not far from that found in steel. Unions that organize the entire labor force of industries such as steel, where the majority of workers are unskilled or semiskilled, have usually been able to win wage increases of 5% to 10% for their members relative to other workers. Unions that organize the whole of skilled trades, such as electricians, machinists, or airline pilots, have won wage advantages in the 10% to 20% range. And unions such as the textile workers that do not organize their entire jurisdictions do not improve their members' wage rates much at all.[32] These gains are not insignificant, but they are small

---

[32] A good summary of these studies appears in H. Gregg Lewis, *Unionism and Relative Wages in the United States,* University of Chicago Press, Chicago, 1963, Chapters 3, 4, and 5.

compared with the doubling of real wages since the organization of most of our present unions.

The overall gain of labor in this period is no clearer. The wage and salary share of the national income has crept up from an average of 67% in the 1930's to 71% in the 1960's, and even this small gain can be partly explained by the decline in the proportion of the labor force that is self-employed, particularly the decline in the number of farmers, and by the shift of a portion of profits into depreciation.

The relatively slight effect of organizing a quarter of the workers in the country is understandable. A small group could quite conceivably help itself to a larger proportion of the national income at the expense of the rest of us, but "labor," which already earned two thirds of the total before the union came, can hardly hope to increase its share by much when it organizes. The way to get a bigger slice for the workers generally is to have a bigger pie.

B. *Social and Political Gains*

The noneconomic accomplishments of the USW and of unionism generally are much more impressive. One of USW's clearest gains is the grievance procedure. The worker undoubtedly improved his position when he won a means of appealing arbitrary decisions by the boss. The law of the steel mill is far less capricious than it was 35 years ago.

Many would count the political impact of the union as a gain also. There is little doubt that the big political prizes usually go to the well-organized groups. Some economic groups, including business and the farmers, have had large and politically effective organizations for years, but until the appearance of the union the urban working class was largely unrepresented. Many argue that the development of the unions has brought our government closer to effective democracy by giving real representation to a large, inarticulate group.

This is primarily an accomplishment of the broad-based industrial unions such as the USW. They have been considerably more active than the older craft unions were in endorsing broad reform legislation that benefited the working class generally. Of course, the USW has also been an active supporter of the steel industry's appeal for protection against import competition. American unions are still politically less active and certainly less radical than their European counterparts. There is no American Labor Party like the labor or socialist parties of many European countries.

C. Steelworkers and Inflation

The steel union affects many other people besides the steelworkers. The main concern of critics is that it may contribute to inflation or to the extent of monopoly.

It has seemed obvious to many laymen that the USW's wage demands have led to rising prices. Economists have been much less certain about this. It is true that steel prices usually went up when steel wages did, but it has not always been clear that both would not have risen even without the union.

Table 6-2 compares steel wage rate changes during three inflations with those in a number of industries where unionism has never been strong. All wage rates rose in all these industries during each of the inflations, but the role of the USW was quite different from one inflation to the next.

In the great inflation of 1939–1948 associated with World War II, steel wage increases were relatively modest. A majority of the nonunion industries experienced greater wage increases than steel, and none showed increases that were much less than steel's. This helps to explain the decline in the steelworkers' wage advantage over other industries in the 1940's. The USW helped to damp that inflation, if anything.

The situation was very different during the "creeping" inflation of the 1950's. Few commodities were in short supply then. In fact, excess capacity and unemployment appeared in many industries. Yet the price level rose persistently if slowly, and it practically never declined. This time steel did lead the way. This was distinctly not due to any shortage of steelworkers. Steel employment reached its peak in 1952 and was stable or falling thereafter. Many steel centers had substantial unemployment rates over much of the period.

In the late 1960's the colorful financing of the Vietnam War presented us with another milder run-through of the inflation melodrama. During 1967–1969, when the inflationary pressures were greatest, steel wages again rose only moderately compared

Table 6-2. Wage Increases in Three Inflations in Steel and in Industries Where Unions Are Weak

Industry	Percentage Unionized		Percentage Increase in Average Hourly Earnings		
	1946	1963	1939–1948	1953–1958	1967–1969
Basic steel	80–100	80	99	33	13
Crude petroleum and natural gas	20–39	8	96	22	17
Nonmetallic mining and quarrying	20–39	24	133	22	20
Broad woven fabrics		21		12	
Cotton textiles	20–39		189		14
Silk and synthetic textiles	20–39		181		15
Confectionery	20–39	41	121	23	17
Dairy products		27		17	13
Butter	20–39		123		
Ice cream	20–39		87		
Laundries	20–39	15	99	15	} 16
Cleaning	20–39	15	97	16	} 16
Wholesale trade	1–19	4	93	23	12
Retail trade	1–19	11	103	21	14

Note: Unionization estimates include nonproduction workers.

Source. 1946 unionization and 1939–1948 wage increases from Albert Rees, "Wage Determination in the Steel Industry," *American Economic Review*, June, 1951, p. 309. 1958 unionization figures from Victor Fuchs, *The Service Economy*, Columbia Univ. Press, 1968, Appendix Table I-2. 1953–1958 and 1967–1969 wage increases from *Monthly Labor Review* and *Employment and Earnings*.

with the nonunion industries. The same was true in most other highly unionized industries in manufacturing. One reason for the slow wage increases in unionized lines was that many of them had adopted long-term contracts that committed the parties to previously determined wage increases. So long as inflation was accelerating, these contracts resulted in less wage increase than would have occurred with the annual wage reopenings common in the 1940's or the escalator clauses that had been popular in the 1950's.

In the early 1970's, with inflation largely checked, we may see another creeping inflation like that of the 1950's, with the unionized industries once more in the lead. One reason will be the same long-term contracts, which will carry generous settlements arrived at during the period of open inflation two or three years into the future.

Altogether, many forces contributed to both the galloping inflations associated with our wars and the creeping inflations that occurred even in the presence of excess capacity and unemployment in the 1950's and may be in prospect for the 1970's. The role of the powerful union that negotiated with large employers was mild during the wartime inflations and may even have been negative, in spite of what the public thought at the time. It seems more probable that the union played a role in the creeping inflation of the 1950's and will do so again in the one that may be in prospect for the 1970's.

This conclusion should be put into perspective, however. Everyone is agreed that galloping inflations can be ruinously disruptive. Creeping inflation is clearly far less of a problem.

D. *The Union and Monopoly—Labor Markets*

From time to time the newspapers and congressmen have been exercised about the "labor monopoly" of the USW and of other powerful unions. There is quite a bit of confusion about what this means, but in some respects it may be a legitimate concern.

The USW and other strong unions are certainly monopolistic combinations in labor markets. The workers of the steel industry price their services collectively in hopes of improving the terms on which they sell. If they were selling cheese or toothpicks on this basis, we would call their organization a cartel.

This need not cause great alarm, however. The market for steel labor without the union would hardly be purely competitive. Wages and working conditions were not determined by supply and demand before 1936, they were determined by USS. In 1937 the Corporation had 261,000 employees. In many communities it was the only significant employer. When there were other mills in town they ordinarily hired on the same terms as USS. There was a wage pattern in the industry before the union, with USS leading on wages and working conditions as it did on price.[33]

---

[33] USS led in 11 to 14 wage changes from 1913 to 1932. Seltzer, *op. cit.*, p. 322.

Local markets for steel labor before the union might be called *monopsonistic* (one buyer) or *oligopsonistic* (a few buyers). Installing a monopolistic agreement (the union) on the opposite side of this market was a far cry from installing one in an otherwise competitive situation. If the steel companies had been using their powerful hiring position to depress wages, the union might bring the terms of employment closer to those that would prevail in a perfectly competitive labor market. The increase in wage rates under such circumstances might well be accomplished without any loss in employment if the employer had previously been restricting employment to keep wages down.

It is not clear that the steel companies were forcing wages down by exerting their monopsonistic power before the union came. Other roads to profits were far more socially acceptable than taking them at the expense of the workers, and big steel was famous for its concern about public opinion. At any rate, as we have seen, steel wages were well above those in most manufacturing before the union was organized. If the steel companies can be accused of direct economic exploitation of their employees, it was in the continuation of the 12-hour day well into the twentieth century. The union did not actually bargain this away, but the organizing drive of 1919 was certainly an element in its elimination.

Clearer cases of exploitation are apt to occur where the product market on which the employers sell is competitive. Such employers must take every advantage they can, just to break even in the long run, and those located in isolated labor market may find that one of their "advantages" is the ability to hire and retain labor at substandard wages. This is more likely to be the preunion story of a coal mine in an isolated West Virginia valley than of a steel mill.

E. *The Union and Monopoly—Product Markets*

In addition to exercising monopoly power on labor markets, which is the whole point of the union, the USW may be able to exploit the steel companies' monopolistic position in product markets. This would be true if the steelworkers actually have been able to push prices up more than would have happened in their absence, something which may well have occurred during the 1950's.

It is quite possible that the union might press steel prices up to levels that the steel companies by themselves would not have chosen given nonunion labor costs. The union represents only workers who are already inside. If higher steel wages and prices limit employment opportunities for new men, the present members of the union are not likely to complain. USS is concerned to keep growing, but the USS locals of USW may not be.

The possibility that the union may exploit the companies' monopoly power should again be taken in perspective. Remember that so far the steel union seems to have been able to increase its advantage over the average level of manufacturing wages by 10 to 15% compared with nonunion days, and even this has occurred in only a few years.

The monopolistic effect of unions on product markets differs with the industry. In some fields, such as coal mining and contract construction, the union is in a position to raise wages and hence prices to levels that the producers could not attain by themselves because of their large numbers and free entry. The employers may well benefit from the union in such industries if it can eliminate any cost advantages of small producers in isolated labor markets or in low-wage sections of the country. Management in the larger firms in such industries has sometimes welcomed the union as a "stabilizing" influence.

By contrast, the textile, apparel, and retail clerks' unions have little or no monopoly power because they organize only a segment of extremely competitive industries. Any gains that exceed those that occur without the union are apt to drive the organized employers out of business in the long run.

F. *Unions and Income Distribution*

In the eyes of much of the public, the saving grace of unions is their effect on income distribution. It is widely supposed that unions result in greater equality, mainly because of increased wages.

Again economists are uncertain. If the union made its gains at the expense of profits, increased equality would be likely, because a large proportion of corporate profits do go to the top income groups. It is hard to show much gain for labor at the expense of profits, however. The gains of powerful unions like the USW seem to be mainly at the expense of other workers.

It can be argued that an important group of losers were nonunion laborers. High steel wages tend to reduce opportunities for employment in steel. Those kept out have to find jobs in nonunion lines of work. A large part of the real poverty in America is in these nonunion fields. Table 6-3 shows the percentage of

Table 6-3. Frequency of Low-Income Families by Industry of Longest Job of Family Head, 1968

Industry Classification	Percent of Families
Personal services	33
Agriculture, forestry and fishing	32
Entertainment and recreation services	10
Retail trade	10
Construction	9
Business and repair services	8
Professional and related services	8
Mining	4
Manufacturing	4
Wholesale trade	4
Finance, insurance, and real estate	4
Transportation, communication, and utilities	3
Government	2
All families	8

Source. Bureau of the Census, *Current Population Reports,* Series P-60, No. 66, December, 1969, Table 29.

families that earned less than $3500 in 1968 within the broad industry classes in which their heads worked. A third of the personal-service workers and the farmers were this poor, but only a few of the families connected with the highly unionized mining, manufacturing, transport, utility, and construction industries were. If union members gained by keeping nonunion workers out, they may actually have made the poor poorer!

As we have seen, it is questionable how much unions have gained in high wages. As a result, the adverse distribution effect of the union may be muted.

All this refers to the direct effect of union wage demands. The union may have a greater political effect in the opposite direction. Incomes have become more, rather than less, equally distributed since the coming of the union.[34] This has been widely attributed to the maintenance of full employment, the improved incomes of farmers, the expanded opportunities of Negroes, increased access to education for all social classes, and the progressive income tax. Most of these have been at least partly the result of government action, and the unions have been among the leading groups in society pressing for just these actions.

VI.   SUMMARY

The union only became an important factor in mass production labor markets such as steel in the 1930's. Before that the unions had been largely limited to skilled craftsmen and had been no match for great corporations such as USS. The steel union was finally successful in 1937 after a major change in the political climate and a shift from craft to industrial unions.

Strikes, or at least the threat of strikes, are an essential feature of the union as we know it. Steel strikes are no longer the bloody battles they were so long as the union's existence was at stake. The issues today are the terms of the contract, not whether there should be one. The social cost of strikes in most industries is very slight, but in a few cases, including steel, strikes can become national emergencies, and even the threat of strike can create costly instability. As a result, the government has intervened in all important postwar steel settlements.

Since they have been organized, the steelworkers have been able to win a 600% increase in wages, as well as pensions and other fringe benefits, the union shop, supplemental unemployment benefits, and long-term contracts with automatic wage increases. Many of these gains were highly controversial when introduced but are widely accepted now.

When compared with other industries, however, the gains of the steelworkers seem more modest. The greater part of their

---

[34] The share of the poorest fifth of our families in personal income was 4.1% in 1935–6 and 1941; it rose to 4.7% in 1947, 5% in 1956, and 5.4% in 1966. The share of the richest 5% of U.S. families fell from 26.5% in 1935–6 to 24.0% in 1941, 17.2% in 1947, 16.3% in 1956 and 15.3% in 1966. *Statistical Ab tract*, 1962, p. 329 and *Current Population Survey*, Series P-60, No. 66, p. 22.

improvements are simply the steelworkers participating in the general rise in the national income. This comment is even more true of many other less powerful unions. The clearest accomplishments of the union have been in providing a grievance procedure and in giving the urban working class a political voice. It may be just as well that the union's power to win economic gains is so doubtful. If the union did have a drastic effect on its members' wages, it might contribute more to such problems as inflation, monopoly in product markets, and income inequality than it actually does.

VII. FURTHER READINGS

The economics of labor is another major field within economies. Two good texts in the field are Lloyd Reynolds, *Labor Economics and Labor Relations*, Prentice-Hall, 1969, and A. Cartter and F. R. Marshall, *Labor Economics*, Irwin, 1967. A classic on the theoretical aspects of labor markets is J. R. Hicks, *The Theory of Wages*, Peter Smith, Gloucester, Mass., 1932. A variety of current views appears in *Aspects of Labor Economics*, A National-Bureau-Universities Conference, Princeton University Press, Princeton, 1962.

The classic source on the early history of trade unionism is the four-volume work by John R. Commons and associates, *History of Labor in the United States*, Macmillan, New York, reprinted in 1951. A shorter sketch of the same material is Selig Perlman, *A History of Trade Unionism in the United States*, Macmillan, New York, 1932, reprinted by Augustus Kelly, 1950. The organization of steel is described in R. R. R. Brooks, *As Steel Goes*, Yale University Press, New Haven, 1940. The union's own history is Vincent D. Sweeney's *The United Steel Workers of America—Twenty Years Later, 1936–1956.* Lloyd Ulman, *The Government of the Steel Workers' Union*, Wiley, New York, 1962, deals with the union's internal organization. *Collective Bargaining in the Basic Steel Industry,* a special study by the Department of Labor dated January 1961, gives a fairly complete overview of steel labor as of that date. An interesting analysis of the Abel-McDonald election appears in J. A. Orr, "The Steelworkers' Election of 1965" in *The Labor Law Journal,* 1969, pp. 100–112.

There were a number of studies of various aspects of the steel union's effect in the 1950's. Robert Tilove, *Collective Bargaining in the Steel Industry,* University of Pennsylvania Press, Philadelphia, 1948, and George Seltzer, "Pattern Bargaining and the United Steelworkers," *Journal of Political Economy,* August 1951, p. 319, cover industry-wide bargaining and its effect. Frederick H. Harbison and Robert C. Spencer, "The Politics of Collective Bargaining: The Post-War Record in Steel," *American Political Science Review,* September 1954, p. 705, discusses the government's handling of steel strike emergencies. Albert Rees, "Post War Wage Determination in the Basic Steel Industry," *American Economic Review,* June 1951, p. 389, Lloyd Ulman, "The Union and Wages in Basic Steel: A Comment," and Albert Rees, "Reply," both in *American Economic Review,* June 1958, discuss the possible inflationary effect of the USW. Otto Eckstein and Gary Fromm, "Steel and the Post War Inflation," Joint Economic Committee, 86th Congress, 1st Session, 1959, cover the creeping inflation of the late 1950's. Jack Steiber, *The Steel Industry Wage Structure,* Harvard University Press, Cambridge, 1959, covers such subjects as job classification and grievance procedure in the industry. George McManus, *The Inside Story of Steel Wages and Prices, 1959–1967,* Chilton, 1967, is a lively blow-by-blow account of events in the 1960's.

7

The Performance of American Industries

This book has covered a few important product markets and one major labor market. What is true of these examples need not hold for the thousands of other markets that make up the American economy. Yet some of the conclusions reached in these case studies do apply widely. This chapter attempts to outline the major generalizations that economists seem able to make about realistic product and factor markets.

I. ECONOMIC EFFICIENCY—PROFITS AND WAGES

A. Monopoly Profits

One of the most thoroughly studied aspects of market performance has been the profit rate. Studies have been made for every period from 1936 through 1967, using a wide variety of profit concept and drawing on data from published-corporate reports, income tax returns, or Census reports. The usual indicator of the "degree of monopoly" in these studies has been the concentration ratio. All of the studies with which the writer is familiar[1] have shown higher rates of return in the more concen-

---

[1] At least 31 separate structure-profits studies became public by the end of 1969. They are summarized in L. W. Weiss, "Quantitative Studies of Industrial Organization" in M. D. Intriligator, Ed., *Frontiers in Quantitative Economics,*" North Holland Publishing Company, 1971. Most of the topics taken up in this chapter are covered in more detail in that article.

trated industries during the late 1930's, the 1950's and the early 1960's. In the depression years the oligopolistic industries seemed able to protect their profits against the effects of decreasing demand more successfully than the competitive industries could, and in the periods of stable prosperity they have usually been able to earn a higher return. Other oligopolies have done considerably better than steel did in this respect.

The big exceptions were the inflations of the 1940's and late 1960's when most industries had unsatisfied demand or rising prices or both. The competitive industries did just as well as the oligopolistic ones did then. In the competitive markets, the high demand meant rapidly rising prices and high profits. Prices rose in the oligopolistic markets too, but the sellers often did not charge all that they could. Public opinion seemed to prevent large firms in concentrated markets from taking full advantage of their market situations. It was impersonal market forces that made the price of beef go up, but it was the big companies who were obviously making the decision when the list price of steel rose. Rates of return fell in most industries when the shortages ended. The drop was drastic in competitive industries but only mild in the oligopolies.

Periods of open inflation aside, monopolists do seem to monopolize. The problem is within manageable bounds, however. Around half of corporate profits come from unregulated but highly concentrated industries, but all corporate profits together are only about one eighth of the national income. Moreover, a large part of the profits accruing in oligopolistic industries are "normal returns" on the owners' investments. Depending on what we estimate to be "normal," the sum of monopoly profits might come to 2% or 3% of the national income in years of stable prosperity. Allowing for some noncorporate monopoly profits and some accounting understatement of profits in concentrated industries, the correct number might be 4% or even 5% of the national income, but hardly more. Of course, even 2 to 4% of an $800 billion national income is $16 to $32 billion, which few would consider an insignificant amount.

B. *Unions, Monopoly, and Wages*

The effect of unions on wage rates has been studied as thoroughly as the effect of concentration on profits, and the results are quite similar.[2] Strong unions seemed to win their members some wage advantage in the 1930's and in the 1950's and 1960's, but the advantage almost disappeared during the inflation of the 1940's in many labor markets.

The difference between union and nonunion earnings holds even after personal characteristics such as sex, skill, race, age, education, and location are taken into account. An urban northeastern semiskilled white male of 35 with a high school diploma earned 6 to 8% more in 1959 if he worked in an industry where most production workers were covered by collective bargaining contracts than if he worked in a line where only half were.[3] A skilled worker with similar personal characteristics earned 8 to 15% more where the union was strong than elsewhere. In other words, the union was winning such workers a premium over what they could earn in their best alternative employments, just as high concentration was bringing investors in oligopolistic industries greater returns than they could have received on the same investment elsewhere.

The sum of these "excess wages" is again significant but not huge. Union members are only 24% of the labor force, and the union is too weak to affect wages much for about a quarter of these. The other three quarters may receive wages 10% higher than they would without the union. The "excess wages" might then add up to 1 to 2% of the national income.

Some economists (including the author in a previous book) have suggested that high concentration might result in high wages with or without the union. The author attempted to test this using information from the 1960 Census. It appears that incomes for most occupation groups were higher in the more concentrated industries, but that this could be fully accounted for in most cases by personal characteristics such as age, sex, location, race, and education of the person involved. Concentrated industries employed people with better alternatives and paid more for them, but the wage was apparently no more than

[2] A thorough summary of these appears in H. Gregg Lewis, *Unionism and Relative Wages in the United States,* University of Chicago Press, Chicago, 1963, Chapters 3, 4, and 5.

[3] L. Weiss, "Concentration and Labor Earnings," *American Economic Review,* March 1966, pp. 106–115.

what workers with these characteristics could earn elsewhere.[4] One thing that the concentrated industries seem to get for their high wage rates is low turnover among their workers. This may be because low turnover makes life easier for managers, and firms in the concentrated industries can afford to pay for such luxuries, it may be that such firms pay extra to keep their workers because they give them more training on the job, or it may be merely a by-product of a high wage policy adopted for other reasons.[5] In 1960 the concentrated industries also seemed to employ a disproportionately small number of Negroes even after allowing for differences in location and job mix.[6] Some suspect that firms with monopoly power are apt to take some of their profits in the form of "desirable" employees.[7] The discrimination in employment present in 1960 seems to have been reduced during the 1960's.

C. *Profits, Wages, and the Allocation of Resources*

What difference does it make if some industries yield a higher return to labor or capital than the same resources could earn anywhere else? The traditional answer of economists has been that the economy is less efficient as a result. In a perfectly competitive economy, capital and labor would leave poor employments for better ones until a dollar investment or a man-hour earns the same amount regardless of where it is employed. The prices of the resulting products would just equal the cost of the additional labor and capital employed in producing them, so a dollar's worth of capital or a man-hour of labor would be

---

[4] Weiss, "Concentration and Labor Earnings," *op. cit.,* pp. 106–108.

[5] J. F. Burton Jr. and J. E. Parker, "Inter-Industry Variations in Voluntary Labor Mobility," *Industrial and Labor Relations Review,* Jan., 1969; and L. Telser, "Some Determinants of the Returns to Manufacturing Industries," Report No. 6935, Center for Mathematical Studies in Business and Economics, Univ. of Chicago, Unpublished, 1969.

[6] Robert Strauss, *Discrimination Against Negroes in the Labor Market: The Impact of Market Structure on Negro Employment,* unpublished Ph.D. Thesis, University of Wisconsin, 1969.

[7] Alchian, A. and R. A. Kessel, "Competition, Monopoly, and the Pursuit of Money," in Aspects of Labor Economies (Princeton: Princeton University Press, 1960) pp. 70–81.

adding just as much to the value of output wherever it is used. We could not gain anything by shifting factors from one industry to another.

If oligopolistic markets result in rates of return persistently higher than those in competitive markets or if strong unions win wages above the opportunity cost of the labor, then we will wind up with some of our capital and labor adding less to output than it might. A man-hour in the monopolistic and/or strongly unionized (and hypothetical) light bulb industry might produce $5 worth of light bulbs while in the competitive and weakly organized shoe industry, the man-hour might add only $3 worth of shoes. By moving a man-hour from one industry to the other, we can gain $2 in value of output from the same resources.

In a well operating competitive market, such a shift would happen as a matter of course, though as we saw in agriculture, such adjustments can be slow and painful in practice because of errors in judgment and factor immobility. In industries where sellers are few enough to control price or unions are strong enough to control the wage, the adjustment will not occur at all. The monopolistic light-bulb producers may be very willing to sell more light bulbs, and the United Light Bulb Workers may be eager to see employment increase, but they will not reduce profit margins or wage rates to accomplish these goals. To the extent that capital and labor do earn more than their alternative products, therefore, the economy works inefficiently. We produce too few light bulbs and too many shoes, and receive less total output from our resources than we might.

II. ECONOMIC EFFICIENCY—COSTS

Markets can work inefficiently even if prices are no higher than the opportunity cost of the factors involved. In perfect competition, only the lowest cost methods are used and all excess capacity must disappear in the long run. But costs may be higher than the minimum attainable level in certain markets because of unnecessary excess capacity, persistently inefficient types of plant, or excessive promotional expenditure. To the extent that this occurs, prices will be too high in the affected industries and resources will be misallocated just as they were when high profits or wages were the cause.

A. *Excess Capacity*

Studies of excess capacity are fewer and perhaps less convincing than studies of profits and wages. This is largely because of the problem of distinguishing between excess capacity that results from monopolistic market conditions and the excess capacity that occurs in well working competitive markets because of seasonal or cyclical fluctuations or unexpected drops in demand.

The most probable case of unnecessary excess capacity discussed in this book has been resale price maintenance where the supplier acting through the courts could enforce prices. Most of the other generally accepted cases of avoidable excess capacity are also associated with cartels with free entry. Probably the clearest case has been the American oil industry where prorationing (output quotas) maintained by the major oil producing states with the cooperation of the Federal Bureau of Mines have kept prices high and stable enough to induce the drilling of far more oil wells than are needed. As a result, the rate at which each well is permitted to operate has been gradually cut back until in 1965 an efficient Texas oil well was permitted to produce at only 32% of its (legally determined) maximum efficient rate.[8] In 1965 the United States had 91% of the free world's oil wells but produced only 31% of its oil.[9] Many of these wells were completely unnecessary, having been drilled in fields that had been thoroughly explored and were fully exploited already. They were drilled because another well brought another quota, and they paid off in spite of the excess capacity because of the high price being maintained by the quotas. Some of the new wells did represent new exploration, but the value of even these is open to question in view of the excess capacity already in hand. The situation has improved somewhat since 1965 because the main prorationing states have required wider

---

[8] *Oil and Gas Journal,* April 11, 1966, p. 44. The "allowable" rate was under 30% from 1960 to October 1965.

[9] *Oil and Gas Journal,* December 28, 1965.

spacing of new wells. By 1969 the allowable rate of operation for efficient wells was up to 54%.[10] Some observers expect excess capacity to largely disappear by the late 1970's.[11] Even if this happens, however, prorationing will still maintain many high-cost wells in production, and consumers will still pay too much for oil products. The industry may be more efficient then, but any gain will accrue to the owners of the wells that are permitted to operate closer to capacity.

Excess capacity means high average costs. Much American oil can no longer compete with imports, so under the Eisenhower Administration we introduced import quotas and under the Kennedy Administration we tightened them up. Gulf Coast oil delivered at East Coast refineries now costs almost twice as much as oil imported from the Mediterranean or Venezuela. It has been estimated that in the early 1960's the United States could produce the same oil for $2.5 billion less per year if we had fewer and better-spaced wells, and that with free imports at world prices we could save something like $4 billion a year.[12] By 1969 the estimated loss to consumers was more like $6 billion per year![13]

This would put the cost of excess capacity in oil on the same order of magnitude as the famous excess capacity in agriculture,

---

[10] The overall Texas oil industry was estimated to be operating at about 60% of capacity at the start of 1966 (*Oil and Gas Journal,* April 11, 1966, p. 43) and at about 70% capacity in 1969 (*The Oil Import Question,* op. cit., pp. 218, 242–3). These percentages are higher than the allowable rates of production for efficient wells because of the output from wells exempt from prorationing. "Stripper" wells (that must pump out because natural pressure is not sufficient) and some secondary recovery wells (such as those that bring oil up by forcing water into the well) may produce as much as their owners want. Because of the high prices plus the restriction on output from flush wells, we are getting the largest possible percentage of our oil production from our least efficient oil wells!

[11] *The Import Question,* op. cit., pp. 231–239.

[12] M. Adelman, "Efficiency of Resource Use in Crude Petroleum," *Southern Economic Journal,* October 1964, pp. 116–122. The $2.5 billion efficiency loss has probably been reduced since by better well spacing.

[13] *The Oil Import Question,* op. cit., p. 26. The difference between the consumer loss and the efficiency loss is what oil product consumers pay to oil producers that they wouldn't have to without prorationing and import quotas.

another industry where government has maintained price supports without controlling the number of producers. In fiscal 1969 we spent $4.5 billion for "farm income stabilization" and another billion on "food for feedom" grants. In addition, American consumers paid 75¢ a bushel more than world prices for wheat and similar premiums on a number of other farm products to maintain farm incomes in spite of excess capacity. The entire excess capacity in farming cannot be blamed on the farm program, however. With demand growing slowly and productivity growing rapidly and with mobility from the farm still difficult, some excess capacity was almost inevitable.

Excess capacity in oligopolistic industries is harder to diagnose. Perhaps the pricing policies of firms in these industries do sometimes attract too much capacity or protect it once it is in place. The experience of the steel industry in the 1910's, the 1920's, and again in the late 1950's looked a little as if this were the case, and some economists have felt they could see the same sort of symptoms in such industries as shoes, flour, and cement,[14] although no one has been very positive about it.

B. *Economies of Scale*

Costs can also be high because producing units are too small for efficiency. Competition is supposed to drive out inefficient firms in the long run, but the long-run adjustment may be very long in coming. Monopolistic prices, whether maintained by publicly enforced cartels or private oligopolies, can protect inefficient producers. Yet it may not be possible to attain efficient scale without firms so large that monopoly and oligopoly are inevitable. In most of the public utilities and such transport industries as pipelines and urban transit, local monopoly seems clearly the most efficient form and, in air and rail transport, high concentration seems unavoidable on most routes. Yet large numbers of small firms seem potentially quite efficient in some of the regulated industries, notably in interstate trucking, and there is room for a good deal of competition at a wholesale level in such fields as electric power and communications.

---

[14] J. S. Bain, *Barriers to New Competition*, Harvard University Press, Cambridge, 1956, 189–190.

In most unregulated industries, competition seems to be compatible with efficient scales of plant, at least in those industries that sell on national or large regional markets. The most comprehensive information we have on efficient scale of operation is based on a study of twenty industries made in the early 1950's. The results appear in Table 7-1. Column B shows estimates of the minimum efficient size of plant expressed as a percentage of total national capacity. The survey often yielded a range of estimates of optimum scales so column B necessarily shows a range of percentages of the market in which the optimum plant would fall. Column C shows the minimum concentration ratios apparently required for efficiency in the various industries covered. For instance, if copper production requires a plant with capacity equal to one tenth of the market to have all the economies of scale, the four largest firms must have at least 40% of the market. Column D shows the concentration ratios that actually applied in the indicated industries in 1954.

In the first 5 industries in Table 7-1, plants of efficient size seem to require high degrees of concentration. In the remaining 15, we could apparently have low cost plants *and* national concentration ratios as low as those in such competitive industries as textiles and shoes. Many of the industries in Table 7-1 are several times as concentrated as technical conditions require. There may be some further economies for the firm that operates more than one plant, but the estimates of such multiplant economies in Column E suggest that such gains are generally meager and uncertain. The study summarized in Table 7-1 intentionally emphasized the more concentrated industries. Virtually all of the unconcentrated industries seem capable of low national concentration ratios while still attaining low unit costs. Altogether, while there are some notable exceptions such as automobiles, we have a large enough economy to permit us to enjoy all the economies of scale *and* those of competition simultaneously in most unregulated markets.

The study on which Table 7-1 was based led to the conclusion that most output in each of the industries covered did in fact come from plants of efficient scale and that neither concentrated nor unconcentrated industries had any special tendency toward great amounts of suboptimal capacity. A later international com-

Table 7-1. Optimum Plant Size and Multiplant Economies in 20 Industries

A Industry	B Percentage of National Industrial Capacity Contained in One Plant of Minimum Efficient Scale in about 1951	C Hypothetical Concentration Ratio for Single Plant Firms (Percent)	D Actual Concentration Ratios 1954 (Percent)	E Estimated Cost Advantage of Multiplant Firms
Typewriters	10–30	40–100	78	None
Tractors	10–15	40–60	67	No estimate
Copper	10	40	94	None
Fountain pens	5–10	20–40	55	None
Automobiles	5–10	20–40	98	No estimate
Cigarettes	5–6	20–24	82	Slight
Soap	4–6	16–24	63	$\frac{1}{2}$–1%
Rayon	4–6	16–24	79	No estimate
Gypsum products	2–3	8–12	89	Small
Rubber tires and tubes	$1\frac{3}{8}$–$2\frac{3}{4}$	$5\frac{1}{2}$–11	78	No estimate
Meat—diversified	2–$2\frac{1}{4}$	8–10	39	None
Steel	1–$2\frac{1}{2}$	4–10	54	None to 2–5%
Metal containers	$\frac{1}{3}$–2	$1\frac{1}{3}$–8	80	No estimate
Petroleum refining	$1\frac{3}{4}$	7	32	None
Distilled liquor	$1\frac{1}{4}$–$1\frac{3}{4}$	5–7	63	No estimate
Farm machinery except tractors	1–$1\frac{1}{2}$	4–6	37	No estimate
Cement	$\frac{4}{5}$–1	$3\frac{1}{5}$–4	31	Small or 2–3%
Canned fruits and vegetables	$\frac{1}{4}$–$\frac{1}{2}$	1–2	28	None
Shoes	1/7–$\frac{1}{2}$	4/7–2	43	Small or 2–4%
Flour milling	1/10–$\frac{1}{2}$	4/10–2	43	No estimate

Note: Concentration ratios listed for "copper smelter products," "pens and mechanical pencils," and for an average of five-digit products that go to make up "steel mill products" and steel wire, sheet, and strip products.

Source. Columns B and E from J. S. Bain, *Barriers to New Competition*, Harvard University Press, Cambridge, 1956, pp. 72, 86. Column D, *Concentration in American Industry*, Senate Judiciary, Washington, D.C., 1957.

parison for these and similar industries seemed to show that a somewhat higher percentage of capacity was suboptimal in Britain and a much higher percentage was suboptimal in France, Italy, Japan, India, Sweden, and Canada.[15] The very large American market may be part of the reason for the efficient scale of American plants, but the permissive and even promotive government policies toward cartels in other countries, especially the non-English-speaking countries, is another likely explanation. In the United States the cost of immobility, monopoly, and cartels in the form of inefficiently small plants seems to be minor, but this may be because of our policy of promoting competition.

C. *Advertising*

Another source of waste in market performance may be excessive selling expenses. Of course, selling effort is not wasteful to the extent that advertising or salesmen distribute useful information about prices, availability, or new products. A large proportion of the selling expenses of our country result in little or no useful information, however. They may actually do harm if they lead to irrational choices by consumers. About the same comment applies to salesmen when their main function is to give the consumer a feeling of personal obligation to buy, and to unnecessarily elaborate packaging designed to waylay the housewife on her way through the supermarket.

The only systematic information available on promotional expense is on advertising. Of course, no breakdown of "informative" and "manipulative" advertising is available, but we can do something with the industrial distribution of advertising expense.

Industries that supply businessmen do not advertise very much. Advertising expense is almost always less than 1% of sales for producers of industrial materials such as textiles or steel, or of industrial equipment, or for wholesalers and freight carriers.[16] Advertising expenses in retailing and services account

---

[15] J. S. Bain, *International Differences in Industry Structure*, Yale University Press, 1966.

[16] All the figures on advertising expense in this paragraph are taken from corporate income tax returns for 1966 as tabulated in the *Statistical Abstract of the United States*, 1969, p. 778.

for a third of all corporate advertising—though even here ads average only 1.6% of sales. This is largely informative advertising.

More than one half of all corporate advertising is done by the producers of consumer goods, although the intensity with which consumer goods are advertised also varies greatly. Ads are around 1% of sales for meats, apparel, petroleum products, leather goods, and automobiles, but they come to 15% for toiletries and cosmetics, 10% for drugs, 8% for soap, 7% for beer, and 5 to 6% for cigarettes, cereals, and clocks and watches.[17] Some of this intensive advertising has a certain informative content—as when an auto company announces a new design or an airline tells us that it has just initiated jet service to New Orleans—but a large proportion of it must be classified as largely manipulative in character.

Total payments for advertising time and space were estimated at $18 billion in 1968.[18] Of course, part of this goes to support television and newspaper services that we would pay for anyway, although the allocation of time and space would be quite different without the ads. Suppose that half of the $12 billion spent on radio, TV, newspaper, and magazine ads (but none of the $6 billion spent on direct mail, outdoor, and miscellaneous ads) are unavoidable costs of operating these media. Then the net bill for pure advertising would be something like $12 billion a year. If half of this is worthwhile because of its information content, then we might wind up with a cost of manipulative advertising on the order of $6 billion or another 1% of the national income, more or less.

D. *Competition and Economic Efficiency*

Altogether, the traditional problems of monopoly and competition seem to be significant but not unbearable. Our costs of production are a few percent higher than they might be due to excess or suboptimal capacity and manipulative advertising. In addition, certain groups are permitted to gain a small per-

---

[17] L. G. Telser, "Advertising and Competition," *The Journal of Political Economy*, December 1964, p. 543. These refer to 1957 advertising rates.
[18] *Statistical Abstract*, 1969, p. 776.

centage of the national income at the expense of the rest of us. Both the high costs and the profits and wages in excess of opportunity cost result in further losses because our resources are in the wrong industries. Even allowing for monopoly profits that are not reported and excessive costs that were missed, it is hard to imagine that the national income falls short of what it might be by more than a few percent due to these inefficiencies. Things are much worse in particular industries. Moreover, it is certainly worth solving problems where the costs add up into the tens of billions, even if they are proportionately quite small in our enormous economy. Yet the traditional problems of monopoly and competition just do not look very impressive by comparison with what a good sized depression can do to us or a decade of accelerated economic growth can do for us. It is, therefore, natural to ask what difference market structure makes for depression, for inflation, and for economic growth?

III. STABILITY AND PROGRESS

A. *Price Rigidity and Depression*

During the 1930's many people thought the oligopolistic industries had intensified the Depression by maintaining rigid prices in the face of falling demand. The issue was widely debated by the economists of the day but never really settled. Some felt that they could see the association between oligopoly and price rigidity very clearly. Others doubted that it existed at all. Several who took costs as well as prices into account decided that the net effect of market concentration on price rigidity in 1929 to 1933 was, at most, very mild. It does seem fairly clear that wage rates in the few industries that had powerful unions in the early 1930's held up better than average in those years. The "excess wages" of union workers was at its peak at the bottom of the Depression—if they could find work.[19]

---

[19] The argument about price rigidity in depression is summarized in R. Ruggles, "The Nature of Price Flexibility and the Determinants of Relative Price Changes in the Economy," *Business Concentration and Price Policy*, Princeton University Press, Princeton, 1955. Evidence on wage rigidity is given in H. Gregg Lewis, *op. cit.*, Chapters 5 and 6.

The issue of price and wage rigidity in time of depression has lost much of its punch since the 1930's. Many economists today doubt that price and wage cuts are an appropriate means of solving the problem of general depression.

B. *Administered Inflation*

In the years since World War II, the problem has been more commonly one of inflation. During the open inflations of the 1940's, the unionized and concentrated industries were widely condemned for raising prices and wages but, after the smoke had cleared, it seemed that they had lagged behind the competitive sectors, if anything.

In the 1950's a great deal of concern was expressed about an "administered inflation" that seemed to be in process in which the unionized and concentrated industries were increasing wages and prices, sometimes even in the face of unemployment and excess capacity. The steel industry and union, which we examined in detail, constituted the most famous case. Some economists doubted that "administered inflation" made any sense —even for monopolists there is a most profitable price. Continuously increasing prices would become unprofitable after a while. Wage rates quite definitely did rise faster in concentrated (usually unionized) industries in the 1950's. It is more difficult to establish what happened to prices because they are so much affected by changes in materials prices and in productivity. Once materials and labor costs are controlled for, however, there did seem to be a distinct tendency for concentrated industries to increase prices. And while it might not make sense for monopolists to raise prices year after year, it is quite plausible for them to do so during the half decade after an open inflation in which they had not fully exploited their positions.[20] Even this

---

[20] The administered inflation hypothesis is usually associated with Gardner Means' testimony before the Senate Subcommittee on Antitrust and Monopoly, *Administered Prices*, Parts I (1957) and IX (1959). Criticism appeared in Geo. Stigler, "Administered Prices and Oligolopistic Inflation," *Journal of Business*, January 1962 and H. DePodwin and R. Selden, "Business Pricing Policies and Inflation," *Journal of Political Economy*, April 1963. The analysis taking cost into account and covering later years was L. Weiss, "Business Pricing Policies and Inflation Reconsidered," *Journal of Political Economy*, April 1966.

interpretation makes the "administered inflation" a once-and-for-all event of rather small consequence. The whole inflation of the 1950's raised the wholesale price index by 8% in five years. After 1959, there was no more tendency for prices to rise in concentrated than in unconcentrated industries.

At this writing we seem to be destined to repeat the whole cycle again. During the Vietnam War we had another substantial inflation in which the competitive sectors led. Prices and wages rose more slowly in the concentrated and unionized lines in 1968 and 1969. In 1970 the inflation continued in spite of rising unemployment and excess capacity, but it was increasingly centered in the concentrated lines. We can probably expect to see such price and wage increases continue for a while as the firms and unions involved exert their market power once more.

The dangerous aspect of these price and wage lags is their effect on monetary and fiscal policy. Officials may act too slowly in checking inflation on the way up because much of the effect of excess demand does not appear until later. And on the way down, we may find them fighting inflation even when we have serious unemployment because of the continuing wage and price adjustments in concentrated lines.

C. Progressiveness—Invention

Probably the most important source of economic progress is the development and use of new techniques and products. A great deal of emphasis has been placed on the role of large firms and especially of those in concentrated industries in this process, but the areas of agreement are still limited. The main aspects of the issue are (a) invention—what industry calls research and development, (b) innovation—the application of the new knowledge, and (c) diffusion—the rate at which a successful application spreads through industry.

On research and development, there seems to be general agreement that basic research into the nature of matter, the genetic process, or the origin of the universe, while often profitable to society, is too far removed from any dollar payoff to attract even the largest firms. This is the realm of the nonprofit institution. Business expenditures are primarily devoted to the application of scientific knowledge in the development of new products and techniques.

The formal statistics show a much larger proportion of scientific and engineering personnel in the concentrated industries compared with the competitive sector, and in large firms compared with small ones. This tendency holds, though it is weaker, even when the research and development directly financed by the Defense Department and NASA are eliminated. This still overstates the contribution of size and concentration to R and D effort, however.[21] Within given industries, the bigger firms seldom spend a larger share of their receipts on R and D than do the middle-sized firms, and in a fair number of industries they spend a smaller share. Moreover, though small firms (less than 5000 employees) account for only about 14% of the R and D expenditures, their share of patents is about the same as their share of sales—roughly 40%. In general, patent output per R-and-D input is lower the larger the firm is, in most manufacturing lines. A similar conclusion seems to hold when only "important" patents are considered, though the evidence is shakier. One explanation for the higher patent productivity of small-firm R and D is that many of their inventions result from part-time efforts of their managerial and sales staffs. Another may be that large research organizations, while good at developing improvements in existing techniques, seem to be less well suited to finding major breakthroughs. Bureaucracy is not an impossible obstacle to technical achievement. Much of our fantastic space, nuclear, and missile technology were developed in large organizations. But a majority of our important inventions still originate outside the big labs.[22] Brilliant individuals or small groups in such firms as Polaroid, Control Data, and Xerox have been able to match and sometimes surpass the research achievements of big organizations like Kodak and IBM.

The evidence to date gives some support to the notion that R-and-D effort and patent output is greater in the more concentrated industries. In many cases, however, the research most im-

---

[21] This section is a condensation of material in L. W. Weiss, "Quantitative Studies in Industrial Organization," *op. cit.*, pp. 211–215.

[22] D. Hamberg, *R & D, Essays on the Economics of Research and Development*, Random House, 1966, Chapter 5.

portant to an industry is done by its equipment or materials suppliers. The progress of farmers depends heavily on inventions in the fertilizer, seed, and farm-equipment industries, and that of the power companies derives from R and D in the electrical-equipment industry. Quite unconcentrated industries can be very progressive if they are quick to adopt new processes and materials developed for them by their suppliers.

D. *Progressiveness—Innovation, Diffusion, and Productivity Growth*

Some have argued that large firms in concentrated industries are more likely to innovate than smaller, more competitive firms (see p. 12). Systematic studies of the firms that made the first commercial applications of major new products or processes are still limited to a handful of industries.[23] At least within these, innovation seems to require some threshold size, but once that is reached, the number of major innovations does not necessarily increase as fast as sales. The largest coal companies did do more than their share of the innovating from 1919 to 1958, but the largest steel companies did less. The large but not the largest companies led in petroleum and the railroads. Taking all industries and products together, the top four firms innovated less (relative to their sales) where concentration was high. Apparently the smaller firms and outsiders used innovation to break into these industries. These results depend on too few cases to permit much certainty about the conclusions, but at least they give no support to the notion that high concentration encourages innovation.

Our evidence as to the rate at which new technology is diffused is also based on only a few industries. There is very mild support for the view that it proceeds faster in more competitive industries. Within an industry, the larger firms tend on the average to imitate successful innovations sooner merely because they have more investment decisions to make, but this need not

---

23 This section is also based on L. W. Weiss, "Quantitative Studies in Industrial Organization," pp. 211–219. Most of the underlying innovation and diffusion studies were done by Edwin Mansfield and are reported in his book, *Industrial Research and Technological Innovation*, Norton, 1968.

imply that diffusion is faster where firms are big. That would hold only if the largest firms imitated successful innovations before anyone did in a group of smaller firms with the same total number of investment decisions. Just the opposite seemed to hold in the dieselization of railroads, the only case in which such a comparison has been made to date. When the railroads were ranked by size and then combined into seven groups with about equal total assets, there was a systematic tendency for earlier adoption of diesels by some one in the group, the smaller the size of firms involved.

We have examined productivity growth in connection with each industry studied in this book. It has serious limitations as an indicator of progressiveness, but for what it is worth, output per man-hour and even more, output per unit of labor-plus-capital has been growing at about the same rate in concentrated industries, as a group, as it has in unconcentrated industries in recent years.[24] And the most important determinants of productivity growth seem to lie elsewhere—particularly in the rate of growth of total industry output.

Altogether, it has been difficult to show that either oligopoly or competition have any particular advantage in invention or innovation. With only some of the returns in, it appears that such advantages in progressiveness as competition and monopoly may offer will roughly offset each other.

IV. COMPETITION, EQUITY, AND DEMOCRACY

A. *Monopoly and Income Distribution*

Monopoly on product and factor markets affects the distribution of income as well as its overall level. In the process of producing too little at too high a price, a monopolist increases his own income at the expense of the rest of us. Whether the distribution of income with monopoly is better or worse than the distribution that would hold in a competitive set of markets is a value judgement about which people may differ, but it is clear that a large proportion of the population feels that it is unfair for one person

---

[24] J. Kendrick, *Productivity Trends in the United States*, Princeton University Press, Princeton, 1961, p. 179.

to gain at the expense of another merely because he occupies a strategic position in the economy. This concern for fairness has probably been more important than any concern about economic efficiency in the development of our antitrust laws.

Incomes are probably less equally distributed as a result of monopoly. Most of the very rich in our country can trace their fortunes to an inside position in some concentrated industry.

Of 66 persons identified as having a net wealth of $150 million or more in 1968,[25] 13 derived their wealth from oil (including 7 from the old Standard Oil monopoly). Some 35 others attained their wealth in clearly concentrated industries such as aluminum (5), automobiles (4), drugs (4), photographic equipment (3), steel (2), glass (2), and newspapers (2). Four more fortunes came from highly differentiated goods—the Reader's Digest, Encyclopedia Britannica, Avon Products, and Mars, Inc. Five in addition to oil were associated with publicly sponsored cartels in such lines as shipping, insurance, and airlines. Five more fortunes came from "finance," which usually meant the profits from promoting new firms. Some of these fortunes go back to the big mergers of the turn of the century, and some derive from more recent promotions in such fields as motion pictures in the 1920's, liquor in the 1930's, and drugs in the 1950's and 1960's. Concentrated industries played a large role in all five. Finally, there were five fortunes associated with relatively competitive markets: two from retailing (Woolworth's and Grant's), one in construction, one based on finance companies, plus Bob Hope. Half the national product accrues in competitive markets, but less than a tenth of the great fortunes were won there.

This wealth was generally won by establishing a powerful market position. Sometimes this was via grand mergers or threatened predation, but the rich are not all malefactors of great wealth or their heirs by any means. A number are the heroes of a few pages back who patented processes that the big organizations at Kodak and IBM had been unable to generate. Also included are a successful independent gasoline refiner-distributor, a violator of the international air transport cartel who played a

---

[25] A. M. Lewis, "America's Centimillionaires," *Fortune*, May, 1968, p. 156.

role in keeping trans-Atlantic air fares down, and the publishers of the most respected newspaper in the country. Such wealth is not necessarily won by nefarious means, but it is generally associated with a substantial monopoly of some sort. Competitive industries just do not generate great wealth very often, because the brilliant innovator is imitated before he reaches the hundred-million class.

Once the monopoly position is established, the owners can turn to politics or art collecting. They need not even be connected with the monopoly. They can sell their stock to you and me and invest the proceeds in government bonds—they will still be rich.

At the other end of the scale, the unconcentrated and non-union industries account for more than their share of the low incomes in our country. It is only in such industries as textiles or leather or retailing that actual wage rates are ever low enough to be affected by the minimum wage laws. Of course, agriculture has long had a special place in the United States as one of the country's greatest sinks of poverty.

The connection between monopoly and inequality is quite plausible. If people could move freely from job to job, individuals with equal ability and willingness to work would wind up with about the same wage in the long run no matter what line of work they went into. If one job offered better compensation than another, all things considered, it would attract labor until the advantage disappeared. It takes some limitation on the movement of labor between employments to preserve marked wage differences for equally attractive jobs requiring equal skills.

Something similar can be said about the movement of capital from industry to industry. If there were no restrictions, a dollar would yield its owner about the same amount in the long run no matter where he invested it. With barriers to entry in some industries, however, some people's dollars are apt to prove better than others and to earn permanently better returns.

Monopolistic restraint is only one of many limitations on the movement of labor and capital between employments. Barriers to factor movements have been erected by the government through various licensing laws and by the unions through restrictions on the numbers in particular trades or simply through their establishment of high wages which reduce the number of jobs in certain lines of work. Social prejudice creates some of the most severe limitations on opportunity for some of our poorest groups. And even if all such restrictions on factor movements were eliminated, there would still be poverty due to illness, insanity, and old age. It seems likely that monopoly on product markets intensifies the problem of inequality, but it is only one of many contributing factors.

B. *Bigness and Democracy*

Some observers have seen in the growth of enormous firms and powerful unions a threat to our democracy as well as to the efficient and equitable working of our economy. American democracy grew up in an atomistic environment where no individual outside of the government exercised significant control over the direction that society as a whole took. Could it survive with great firms and unions whose leaders were much more than insignificant atoms in the markets where they traded or in the overall life of the country? Various observers found a number of reasons to fear that it could not.

In the years just before and after World War II, many people worried that monopoly on product and factor markets would lead to regulation and that political freedom would be destroyed along with "economic freedom." Others feared that monopolistic firms would lead to the growth of other powerful organizations to counter them and that the democratic process would be destroyed in the resulting struggle. The fate of democracy in Central Europe in the 1930's made these concerns seem plausible at the time.

Even if we have not seen the demise of democratic forms, some have felt that much of the substance of democracy has disappeared. At the turn of the century, it looked to many as if government had become the agent of the great corporations. In the 1930's and the 1940's the powerful unions that were supposed to be really running the country were a familiar bogey. In the 1950's there were many who feared the effective dominance of the nation's decisions by a small "power elite" consisting of military and big business leaders, and in the 1960's we have heard similar complaints about an "establishment" which certainly includes the same group, although some academic and professional leaders might be included as well.

On a less horrendous level, many regret the great importance of organized pressure groups in modern government. Perhaps the groups are too diverse for anyone to become dominant. The different groups will often offset each other's effect. Yet they unquestionably lead to a great outflow of special interest legislation, and they result in the partial disenfranchisement of the unorganized.

Such pressure groups are a common result of large-scale public intervention in an industry, whether its members are big or not. Of course big business and public intervention often coincide, but the political power of relatively small-scale but highly regulated lines of business such as the farmers, the liquor dealers, the small-town bankers, and the domestic independent crude oil producers can be impressive. It becomes worthwhile for big or little businessmen to devote many resources to political activity once government agencies determine their prices, their output quotas, their effective tax rates, and the competition they must face from new entrants or from foreign producers. As elections became more costly with the rise of TV campaigning many political leaders seem to have become dependent on groups that can raise large campaign funds for them. The resulting diversion of much regulatory policy toward the interests of the regulated and the loss of influence by most of the electorate has alarmed many.

Another common thread in the widespread concern about big business is the fear that it is basically changing the national personality, presumably for the worst. The hard-working, self-reliant individualist is supposed to be disappearing with the small proprietorship to be replaced by a new breed of "organization men" who are good string-pullers and committeemen and who get ahead by conforming.

Finally, some have expressed the fear that the large corporation or union may now exercise so much power over the individual employee or customer that it has, in effect, usurped many of the powers of government. The leaders of these institutions are seldom answerable to the stockholders or members and certainly have no direct responsibility to the general public the way elected officials do. Our recourse from arbitrary decisions may be inadequate.

By and large, these fears are speculations that remain unverified. They are certainly important. They are not obviously false, but they are very difficult to test.

C. *Bigness and Efficiency*

To some extent, these problems are the result of monopoly on product and factor markets. If customers or workers have many good alternatives, the arbitrary power of suppliers, employers, and unions is limited. And widespread regulation of industry can usually be avoided if competitive pressures can be maintained. But much of this is a concern about bigness itself, regardless of the extent of monopoly.

Any general attempt to reduce bigness is bound to be expensive. Firms that sell $250 million a year are not small. They often employ 10,000 workers and sometimes as much as one quarter of a billion dollars in capital. Such well-known firms as Parke-Davis, Pabst Brewing, Fairchild Camera, and Texas-Gulf Sulphur fell into this class in 1969. Such firms are certainly capable of creating organization men, if any such tendency exists, and they have surely influenced public opinion on occasion. Yet a policy of insisting that all firms be as "small" as these would mean breaking General Motors into 100 pieces and even American Motors into 3. Kaiser and Interlake Steel would be too large to pass the $250 million test. We probably could not have firms as large as single plants of optimal scale in such industries as aluminum, automobiles, copper, electrical equipment and oil if we insisted that they all stay under $250 million in sales. And even after such draconian policies, we would still be a long way from an atomistic economy. It would appear that an economy of insignificant firms is just too expensive to be a realistic alternative, given today's technology.

While a policy of restoring the atomistic character of the early nineteenth century economy is hopeless, a policy of maintaining or establishing competition in most markets seems entirely feasible. There is room for a large number of firms of efficient size in the great bulk of our markets. At the same time, it appears that the inventive and innovational advantages of size are consistent with competition in most cases. Perhaps we require firms as large as National or Inland Steel to accomplish the innovations required of the steel industry in the next decades, but it is difficult to imagine that firms the size of USS are needed for this reason. A steel industry made up of Inlands and Nationals would be no more concentrated than shoes and textiles, but no one by any stretch of the imagination could describe it as "little business."

V. WHAT CAN BE DONE

Each economist has his own prescription for the state of affairs described in this book. They range from let-well-enough-alone to nationalization. The particular set of solutions that is chosen depends largely on how serious a problem is envisioned.

A. *Maintaining Competition*

Probably the most widely approved set of policies among economists is one of maintaining competition—that is, preventing the creation of new monopoly. To the extent that this can be accomplished, we can prevent further misallocations of resources, further inequities in the distribution of income, and further centralization of arbitrary power over customers and workers who have limited alternatives.

Formally the maintenance of competition has been a primary objective of American public policy toward business over the whole of this century. Actually there have been serious lapses— through lenient interpretation and weak enforcement of antitrust in the 1920's and through legislation in the 1930's that cartelized most of the economy temporarily (the NRA) and parts of it permanently (oil production, interstate trucking, parts of agriculture, retailing, and labor).

Since World War II, our policy has been more consistent in this respect. We have systematically prohibited collusion including such complex parallel pricing systems as the old basing point system of steel, although we have yet to dismantle many publicly enforced cartels. We have moved to a point where we can now prevent mergers when there is a reasonable chance of their seriously interfering with competition. Certainly the great majority of mergers are harmless and some are socially desirable.

The creation of National Steel is probably a case. But when firms are clearly large enough for efficient operation, a close scrutiny of horizontal and vertical mergers within significantly concentrated industries, would be supported by a majority of economists. The very different policies of the Interstate Commerce Commission and the Civil Aeronautics Board in permitting and even encouraging mergers by some of the largest railroads and airlines in order to keep firms profitable is in great contrast to the main lines of American merger policy today.

B. *Creating Competition*

Somewhat more controversial is the possibility of creating competition where it does not now exist. We could probably attain the greater efficiency of competitive markets with little or no loss in the economies of scale or in progressiveness by a policy of dissolution in a large proportion of our oligopolistic industries. In many cases we would *not* be able to recapture the monopoly profits, however. The Rockefellers have sold their stocks to you and me at prices that reflect the prospective earning power of the firms with the expected degree of monopoly. If we now eliminate the monopoly, we will bring their prices closer to the opportunity cost of the factors involved, but we will not reduce the wealth of the Rockefellers. We will reduce the wealth of the present holders of the stock, but they are very likely earning only normal returns on what *they* paid for the stock. In other words, dissolution can correct misallocation but, where capital resources have changed hands, it cannot do much to make the distribution of income and wealth more equitable. Perhaps for this reason in part—because of the "innocent bystanders" who would be hurt—we have only a handful of dissolutions in the history of our antitrust laws.

A policy of weakening unions would be even more controversial. A large proportion of the population—economists and non-economists alike—clearly feels that the gains in providing workers a means of offsetting arbitrary decisions on the part of employers is worth the economic costs of union control of wages.

Even though dissolution is rare, we have made some moves toward reducing monopoly. From the 1930's through the early 1960's, we consistently reduced import restrictions, thus introducing the competition of foreign suppliers. In such fields as steel, this foreign competition turned out to put a major check on the monopoly power of the domestic industry. In oligopolies like automobiles where the economies of scale make reduced concentration very difficult, imports or the threat of imports are our main realistic hope for enhanced competition. The import quotas imposed or negotiated for such products as oil, steel, and cotton textiles in the 1960's and threatened for many others at this writing work in just the opposite direction. Such quotas, if effective, virtually insulate domestic producers from foreign competition.

The merger policy works in the direction of increasing competition, to some extent. In many markets large firms have not been able to maintain their shares in the past except by additional mergers. They have typically grown but the market has grown faster. Again, where the government has prevented the acquisition of market leaders by the most likely entrants into the markets in question, it has helped to maintain the threat of new competition and has sometimes induced entry. For instance, by preventing Bethlehem from acquiring Youngstown, the government brought about a decrease in concentration in the Chicago steel market (via Bethlehem's new plant) of a sort that would have been unlikely if the merger had gone through. The government's suits against very large conglomerate mergers were less certain in effect, but their prohibition could result in deconcentration if the drive to diversify turned out to be strong enough to make large firms enter concentrated industries by direct investment or by acquiring the smaller "footholds" that the government seemed prepared to permit.

We might be able to do more to increase competition if we were willing to limit heavy promotional advertising expenses, or if we were willing to advance credit to prospective entrants into concentrated markets. We do make such credit available to small firms today. The writer feels that there is a good case for credit to large firms as well—on the scale that Kaiser was able to borrow from the Federal Government when it entered the steel industry in the 1940's.

C. *Improving Competitive Performance*

When it comes to the competitive sectors of the economy, the problem is to improve the adjustment to market changes by reducing instability and increasing mobility. One essential function of the government in both respects is to maintain prosperous conditions. Beyond this, public policy can improve market knowledge by collecting and distributing early and complete information on inventories, output plans, market prospects, and production techniques. Great strides have been made in this area in recent years. Finally, government might intervene in the short run to stabilize the more volatile markets provided that it can limit itself to that goal and avoid shoring up declining industries by permanent supports.

There are many possible policies to improve the flow of labor and capital from depressed industries. Some possibilities are publicly sponsored retraining programs, regional redevelopment for depressed areas, and public purchase of land and capital committed to dying industries. We undertook a number of such programs in the 1960's. The results are not all in as yet but, to the extent that they do what they are expected to do, they assist the depressed industry, solve the basic problem, *and* benefit the general public by directing resources toward more efficient uses. By contrast, import restrictions, price supports, output controls, resale price maintenance, licensing laws, featherbedding, and similar restrictions on competition to bail out such industries are generally harmful. They may save some little-business men and workers from low incomes, but they do so by eliminating the efficiency that competition is supposed to achieve. They inhibit movement of resources, they lead to wasteful excess capacity and they do nothing to solve the underlying problems of excess capacity and/or obsolete capacity.

D. *Regulation*

An alternative policy to increasing competition is regulation. Perhaps we could bring prices closer to marginal costs in some oligopolistic industries and possibly we could even order wage rates that more nearly approximate opportunity costs in some unionized occupations, but the experience of regulation to date does not leave much room for optimism. Even in electric power, where the product is extremely simple and uniform and where demand has grown rapidly, regulation has worked imperfectly. In transportation, where there are more cases of potential competition, more complex products and, in some cases, declining demand, regulation has done about as much harm as good in the view of many economists. And in lines like petroleum production where a fairly competitive market would seem to be the alternative, it has resulted in monopolistic prices, low profits, *and* high unit costs. Most economists would probably vote a strong "no" on regulation of all but a handful of very special industries. Yet when faced with inflation, a fair number of economists and a large part of the public seem ready for general price controls—sometimes specifically limited to the oligopolistic or unionized industries—that would go a long way toward transferring the affected markets to the regulated sector.

The further alternative of nationalization has few adherents today. The writer is convinced, along with a large number of other economists, that the present market system's imperfections are quite capable of sufficient improvements short of conversion to another economic system. The costs of market imperfections are less substantial than those of a mild recession, and the defects of public enterprise are far from insignificant. The problems of monopoly and competition today call for reasonably small adjustments, not revolutions.

Index